Autodesk Official Training Guide

Essentials

Autodesk® 3ds Max®

Design 2010

XBR

Learning Autodesk® 3ds Max® Design 2010

A hands-on introduction to the key tools and techniques that supports the way
designers and visualization experts work. Learn to use the latest technology to
fully explore, validate and communicate your creative ideas.

Autodesk Certification Preparation

Autodesk®

Autodesk®

PUBLISHED BY: AUTODESK, INC.
111 MCLNNIS PARKWAY
SAN RAFAEL, CA 94903, USA

Focal Press is an imprint of Elsevier
30 Corporate Drive, Suite 400, Burlington, MA 01803, USA
Linacre House, Jordan Hill, Oxford OX2 8DP, UK

Library of Congress Cataloging-in-Publication Data
Application submitted

British Library Cataloguing-in-Publication Data
A catalogue record for this book is available from the British Library.

ISBN: 978-0-240-81193-2

For information on all Focal Press publications
visit our website at www.books.elsevier.com

09 10 11 12 13   5 4 3 2 1

Printed in the United States of America

Working together to grow
libraries in developing countries

www.elsevier.com | www.bookaid.org | www.sabre.org

ELSEVIER   BOOK AID International   Sabre Foundation

Acknowledgments

Michiel Schriever
Art Direction

Luke Pauw
Sr. Graphic Designer

Elise O'Keefe & John Hammer
Copy Editor

Andrew Tanousis
Technical Editor

Peter Verboom
Video Producer

Lenni Rodrigues & Linda Sellheim
Project Leads

Lenni Rodrigues
Program Development Manager

Richard Lane
Senior Manager, Customer Learning

Paul Mailhot
Sr. Director, Autodesk Learning

Special thanks go out to:

Laura Lewin, Kathryn Spencer, Rebecca Pease, Carmela Bourassa, Tonya Holder, Mary Ruijs, Amer Yassine, Marc Dahan, Sebastien Primeau, Steven Schain, Luc St-Onge, Paul Verrall, Sarah Blay, Roberto Ziche, Virginia Houts.

Primary Author

Roger Cusson | Training Consultant

Roger Cusson began his career working in Architecture when he caught the AutoCAD bug in 1985. He became a consultant to Architectural firms implementing AutoCAD into their work process and at the same time he began to teach CAD to students and professionals. Roger continued to innovate and began creating 3D renderings of buildings. In 1991 these efforts let to his firm being recognized with an award from *Cadalyst* Magazine.

Roger has worked as a full time professor at Vanier College, and a training manager at Autodesk. His work at Autodesk led to the establishment of the Autodesk Media and Entertainment Press. He managed the production of over 30 Book, DVD and e-learning titles. He was lead author for several Autodesk books on 3ds Max and Viz. His most recent work is *Realistic Architectural Visualization with 3ds Max and mental ray.*

He has been an Autodesk Training Specialists teaching instructors and professionals on 3ds Max, 3ds Max Design, Revit Architecture and AutoCAD. Roger has also been an instructor at Autodesk University and has taught online courses for CG Society. He has managed the establishment of the Discreet Certified Trainer program and organized the 2004 Siggraph 3ds Max Master Classes.

Roger lives and works in Montreal, Quebec, Canada

Table of Contents

Chapter 03 | Lighting

Chapter 04| Materials

How to use this book

How you use *Learning Autodesk 3ds Max Design 2010* will depend on your experience with computer graphics and 3D animation. This book moves at a fast pace and is designed to help you develop your 3D skills. If this is your first experience with 3D software, it is suggested that you read through each lesson, before you begin to work through the tutorial projects. If you are already familiar with 3ds Max Design software or another 3D package, you might choose to look through the book's index to focus on those areas you would like to improve.

Updates to this book

In an effort to ensure your continued success with the lessons in this book, please visit our web site for the latest updates available: *www.autodesk.com/learningtools-updates*

Windows and Macintosh

This book is written to cover Windows and Macintosh platforms. Graphics and text have been modified where applicable. You may notice that your screen varies slightly from the illustrations, depending on the platform you are using.

Things to watch for:

Window focus may differ. For example, if you are on Windows, you have to click on the panel with your middle mouse button to make it active.

To select multiple attributes in Windows, use the **Ctrl** key. On Macintosh, use the **Command** key. To modify pivot position in Windows, use the **Insert** key. On Macintosh, use the **Home** key.

Autodesk packaging

This book can be used with either **Autodesk® 3ds Max® 2010**, **Autodesk® 3ds Max Design® 2010**, or the free 30-day trial version of **Autodesk® 3ds Max®**, as the lessons included here focus on functionality shared among all three software packages.

Learning Autodesk 3ds Max Design 2010 DVD-ROM

The *Learning Autodesk 3ds Max Design 2010* DVD-ROM contains several resources to accelerate your learning experience including:

- Support files

- A link to a trial version of Autodesk 3ds Max software

- Autodesk 3ds Max reference guides

Installing support files

Before beginning the lessons in this book, you will need to install the lesson support files. Copy the project directories found in the *support_files* folder on the DVD disc to the *3ds Max\projects* directory on your computer. Launch 3ds Max software and set the project by going to **File > Project > Set...** and selecting the appropriate project.

Windows: *C:\Documents and Settings\username\My Documents\maya\projects*

Macintosh: *Macintosh HD:Users:username:Documents:maya:projects*

Chapter 01
Getting Started

Introduction

This section designed to get you started with 3ds Max Design. You will be introduced to fundamental concepts and how to maneuvre through the user interface.

Objectives

After completing this section, you will be able to:

- Manipulate the User Interface
- Create and Modify Basic Objects
- Manipulate Scene Files
- Select Objects
- Use Transforms on Objects
- Organize Your Scenes and Objects
- Create Project Folders

Lesson 01 | User Interface

Introduction

In this lesson, you will learn about the 3ds Max Design® user interface. The user interface, or UI for short, is the method by which the user communicates with the software. The UI is split into two main components: the graphical user interface or GUI (what you see on the screen), and input devices, such as keyboard and mouse. You can customize most of the UI.

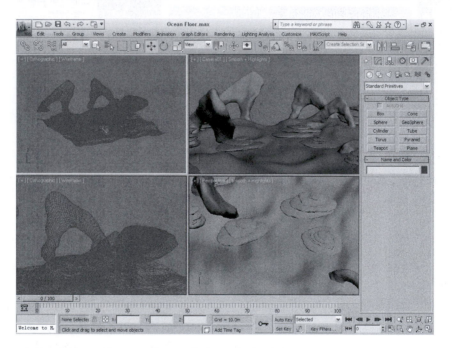

3ds Max Design with a typical scene displaying in the viewports

Objectives

After completing this lesson, you will be able to:

- Use the UI components in the 3ds Max Design interface
- Manipulate a model in the viewport with viewport controls

User Interface Components

The first time you start 3ds Max Design, you will see the following GUI on your screen.

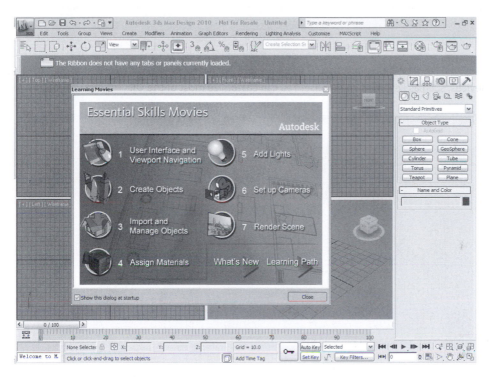

Start-up screen for 3ds Max Design 2010

The UI is logically laid out and easy to use. We'll go through the various elements, so you understand how to work with them and become more familiar with the terminology used. Every time you start the software, a welcome screen gives you the opportunity to review essential skills by playing back short movie clips. Once you are familiar with those, you can then turn off the display of this screen by disabling the check mark in the bottom left corner of the dialog. The welcome screen can be called back by selecting Learning Movies from the Help menu.

Viewports

The viewport area of the UI displays the scene you are working on. 3ds Max Design is quite flexible with how you can arrange the viewports and how your model appears in each viewport.

Adjusting Viewport Size

The size of the viewports can be easily adjusted by clicking the line between the viewports and then dragging it to another point in the viewport area. In the following illustration, the default four equal viewports have been changed to a large perspective viewport by clicking and dragging the center to the upper left.

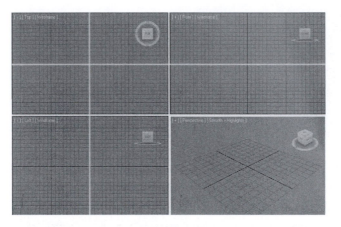

Dragging the viewports to the upper left

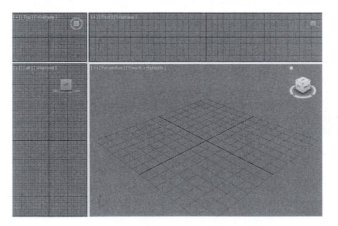

Resized viewports with an enlarged perspective viewport

Viewport Configuration

By default, the software opens with four equal-sized viewports displayed in the UI. You can change this layout with the Viewport Configuration dialog.

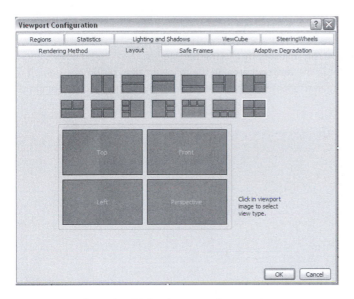

Viewport Configuration Dialog, Layouts tab

The Viewport Configuration dialog shows the variety of viewport layouts available. You simply choose one to make that layout current. You can also click the active layout in the dialog to change what the viewports show before exiting the dialog. Which layout you choose depends largely on your personal preference and the type of scene you are working on. You access the Viewport Configuration dialog by clicking on the **+** icon in the Viewport label to display the following menu; then select Configure.

Menu to access the Viewport Configuration dialog

Home Grid and Default Views

By default, the four viewports that are displayed when you start the software are the Perspective view, Front view, Top view, and Left view. Each one of these viewports has its own home grid, which is the working or construction plane of the view. By default, objects are created on that plane or grid.

When you make a viewport active by clicking it, a yellow border appears. The corresponding home grid also becomes current. The following illustration shows four 3D letters, each created in a different viewport while that viewport was active. **P** is for Perspective, **L** for Left, **T** for Top, and **F** for Front.

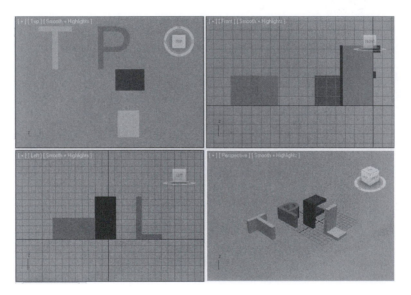

Default four viewports with objects created in each viewport

Tip: *If you don't like the default layout of the viewports, you can create your own layout and save it in a file called maxstart.max in the \scenes folder. The software will look for this file and use it as a base template when you start and reset the software.*

Menu Bar

The menu bar, found at the top of the user interface, contains a series of pull-down menus commonly found in most Windows applications. The File menu is accessed by selecting the 3ds Max icon at the upper left of the application window. The menu bar contains many functions that also appear in other menus. For example, the Create menu duplicates the Create commands on the Command panel.

The Create menu with submenu.

Toolbars

Standard Toolbars

Toolbars play an important role in the software. You can dock toolbars at the edge of the viewports or float them on top of the application window or off to the side, for example, on a second monitor.

Toolbars docked on top and side of the UI. The Layers toolbar is floating.

Toolbars are not always displayed by default. For instance, toolbars such as Layers or Reactor do not display when the program is started for the first time. To display a toolbar, right-click a blank part of the toolbar, such as the area just below a drop-down list.

A list of toolbars currently defined in the UI appears. The check marks indicate which toolbars are currently on screen.

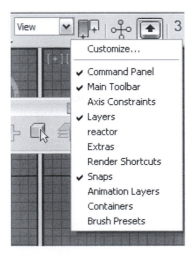

Toolbar right-click menu shows displayed and available toolbars

Chapter 01 | Getting Started

You can dock a toolbar by dragging the toolbar's title bar to the edge of the viewport area. The dragged rectangle changes shape when you can release the mouse and dock the toolbar.

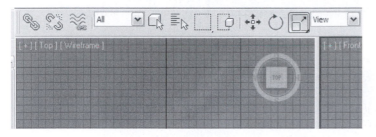

Toolbar being dragged into a docked position

You can undock a docked toolbar by dragging the double lines at the left or top end of the toolbar into an open area of the UI.

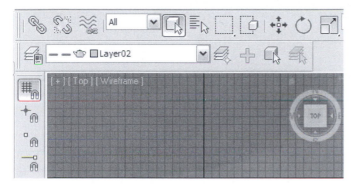

Toolbar being dragged into a docked position

If the software uses a window with a resolution lower than 1280 x 1024, the main toolbar is not fully visible. If you don't see the teapot icons at the right side of the toolbar, this is the case.

You can scroll the toolbar by positioning the mouse cursor over an empty area of the toolbar. The icon then changes to a Pan hand, and you can drag horizontally or vertically, depending on the orientation of the toolbar.

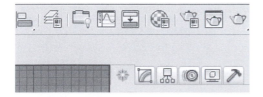

Buttons at the end of the main toolbar

Quick Access Toolbar

The Quick Access toolbar is located in the Application Title Bar above the menu bar. The Quick Access toolbar contains functions that are very commonly used in a typical session for the software.

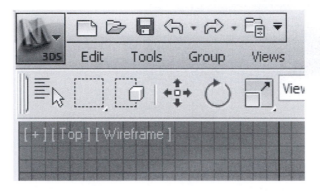

Quick Access toolbar

Graphite Modeling Tools

The Graphite Modeling Tools, also known as the modeling ribbon, is a new element of the user interface. It contains many new tools to model polygon geometry. It is located directly under the Main toolbar and is by default in a docked and partially hidden state.

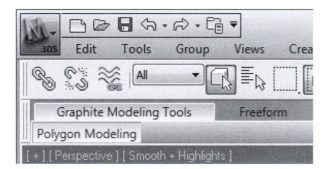

Graphite Modeling Tools partially hidden

A single click on the down arrow will hide the tools in the ribbon completely.

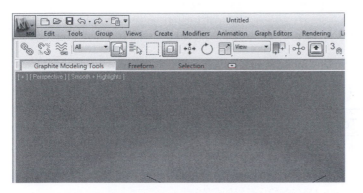

Graphite Modeling Tools completely hidden

Clicking a second time will reveal the tools in their entirety.

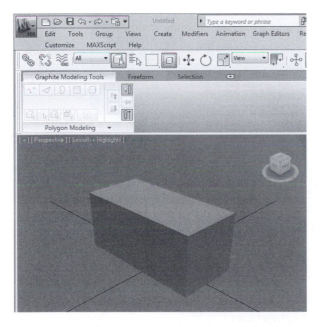

Graphite Modeling Tools panel opened

The Graphite Modeling Tools are context sensitive and will expose different tools as they are required. One operation that would be commonly done would be to convert a primitive to an Editable Poly.

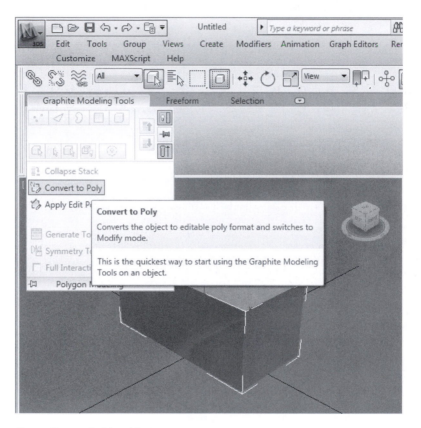

Converting a primitive object

Once you have an Editable Poly object selected, the ribbon changes, exposing a vast array of modeling tools.

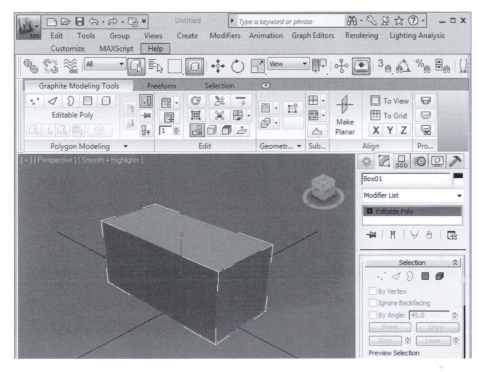

Entire Graphite Modeling Tools

Command panel

The Command panel is the most frequently used element of the user interface. The Command panel is organized in a hierarchical fashion, with six rollout panels, activated by clicking tabs at the top of the rollout panel.

Some of the rollout panels contain buttons and drop-down lists that further organize the panel. For example, the Create panel includes a row of buttons. Depending on which button is active, there may be a drop-down list.

The Create tab of the Command panel

As with toolbars, you can float or dock the Command panel. If necessary, you can place the Command panel on a second monitor.

The Command panel can also be arranged into multiple columns by dragging the left side of the panel toward the viewports.

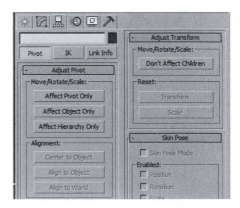

The Command panel floating over the viewports

The Command panel arranged in a two-column format

Create Panel

The first Command panel rollout is the Create panel. It contains different levels of creation parameters that allow you to build different types of geometries. By default the **Create →Geometry → Standard Primitives** area of the panel is displayed.

Briefly, some areas of the Create panel are described below.

Geometry

In the geometry area, you find commands to create 3D geometric objects.

The Create panel, Geometry selection

Lights

Lights are used to illuminate the 3D scene. Two types of lights are available: standard and photometric.

The Create panel, Lights selection

Shapes

Shapes are divided into two basic types: splines and NURBS curves. Shapes are typically 2D but can be created in 3D as well.

The Create panel, Shapes selection

Cameras

Cameras enable you to frame your compositions in a way that captures the attention when an action is taking place. There are two types of cameras, both of which can be animated.

The Create panel, Camera selection

Space Warps and Systems

The last two buttons on the Create panel represent the Space Warps and Systems areas. These areas contain more advanced features.

Helpers

There are a number of helper types. A helper is a non-renderable object whose purpose is to help you model and/or animate objects in the scene.

The Create panel, Space Warps selection

The Create panel, Systems selection

The Create panel, Helpers selection

Hierarchy Panel

The Hierarchy panel is used when manipulating objects that are linked to one another. In such a situation the objects are in a parent/child relationship. This panel controls some of the relationships between these objects. The panel is also used to control the location and orientation of an object's pivot point.

Modify Panel

The Modify panel controls let you modify the base parameters of objects or change them using Modifiers.

The Modify panel

The Hierarchy panel

Motion Panel

The Motion panel is used to control the animation of objects. Animation controllers can be assigned to objects in this panel.

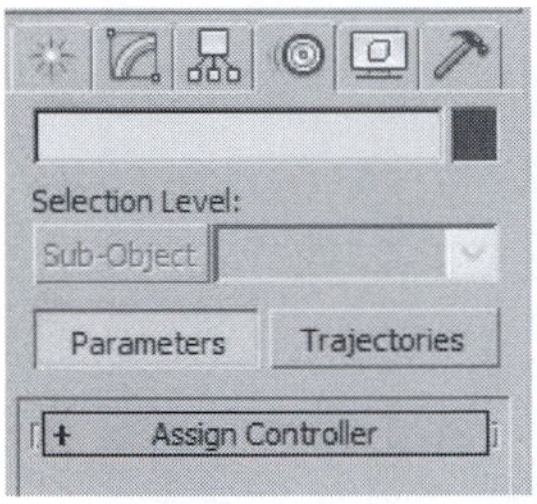

The Motion panel

Display Panel

The Display panel is used to control an object's color, visibility, freeze/thaw status, and other display properties.

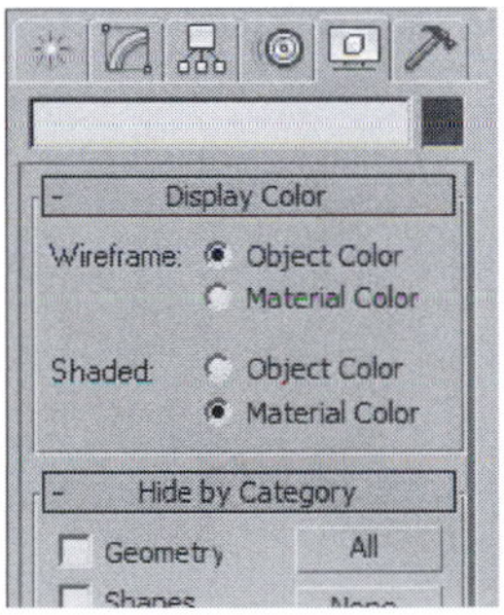

The Display panel

Utility Panel

The Utility panel contains a variety of commands generally not found elsewhere in the user interface.

The Utility panel

Quad Menu

The quad menu is a floating menu that adapts to the context, whenever the menu is activated. In order to access the menu, right-click in the active viewport.

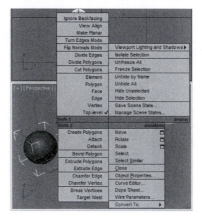

Quad menu when no object is selected

Quad menu when a 3D Editable Mesh object is selected

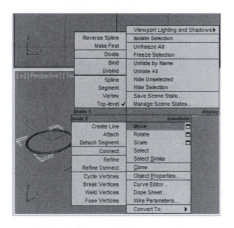

Quad menu when a 2D Editable Spline object is selected

Time Slider, Track Bar, and Timeline

The area just below the viewports is where the time slider, track bar, and timeline are found. You can scrub the animation backward and forward by dragging the time slider. Alternatively, the arrows on the time slider allow you to move one frame at a time.

Timeline

The track bar shows you the keys of a selected, animated object along a timeline. In this example, the timeline is displaying in frames and showing that the selected object has keyframes at frames 0, 20, 30, and 50.

Status and Prompt Lines

The status line shows information pertaining to the object selected and the scene itself. In the example, the status line indicates a single object selected. The prompt line prompts you to perform an action. The XYZ coordinates show the location of the selected object's pivot point.

| 1 Object Sel 🔒 | ⊕ | X: -45.208 ⬍ | Y: -22.01 ⬍ | Z: 0.0 ⬍ | Grid = 10.0 |
| Click and drag to select and move objects | | | | 🗖 | Add Time Tag |

The Status and Prompt lines

Animation Controls

There are two approaches to enable animate mode in the main UI. They are both identified in the animation controls area. These two modes are called Auto Key and Set Key. When Auto Key is active, the frame around the active viewport turns red, as does as the time slider background. When this mode is on, most changes that you apply are recorded and can be played back later.

When Auto Key is on, you move the time slider to the desired frame, and then make a change to the scene, in this case, moving the sphere between two points in space. At frames 70 and 80, keys that retain the state of an object are automatically created for the ball's motion.

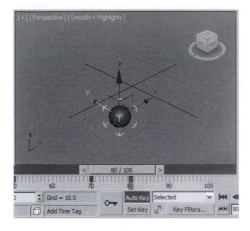

Auto Key animation mode

The upper part of the playback controls area works much like the buttons on a VCR or DVD player. The current frame is listed in the numeric field. When you change the number, you go to that frame.

Time Configuration

The Time Configuration button at the extreme lower right of the playback control area brings you to the Time Configuration dialog. One of the things you will frequently do in this dialog is change the length of the animation.

Set Key is the other animation approach that favors pose-to-pose animation. Set Key mode is usually used for animating characters but can also be used in animating other hierarchy linked objects. In Set Key mode, changes are not recorded unless you click the Set Key button.

Set Key animation mode

You should always turn off animation mode when you have completed a given animation sequence.

Playback Controls

The playback controls let you play your animations live in the viewports. Also found here are tools that allow you to adjust the animation.

Time Configuration dialog

Playback Controls area

Viewport Controls

You can break down the controls of the viewports into two general areas. The viewport navigation controls allow you to change the orientation and positioning of the views in the viewports. The viewport menus allow you to control the configuration, rendering mode, and type of view in the viewport.

Viewport Navigation Controls

The viewport navigation controls are found in the viewports and at the lower right of the UI. These buttons let you control the positioning of the vantage point of the viewer of the 3D scene. The icons are context sensitive and can change depending on the type of view currently active.

Here is the most common layout of the viewport control icons found at the lower right of the UI. This layout appears when an orthogonal viewport is active, such as Top, Front, or Orthographic viewport.

Viewport Control Icons

Some of the buttons in this area contain flyouts with additional options. After you choose a different flyout button, it becomes current, making it easier to choose a second time.

Flyout in the Viewport Control Icons

The ViewCube is a graphical representation of several standard views and controls available for changing the view in the viewport.

ViewCube

SteeringWheels are a pop-up icon that appears in the active viewport. It combines many of the common view controls into a single interface.

SteeringWheels

Viewport Label Menus

At the upper left of each viewport there are three labels that identify specific menus related to viewport functions: General, Point-of-View, and Shading.

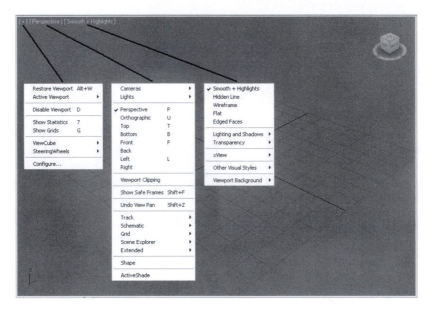

Viewport with three viewport menus displayed

General Viewport Label Menu

The General Viewport label menu provides options for overall viewport display or activation. Some of the more important operations in this menu include:

- Show Grids from the menu toggles the grid status on or off.

- Show Statistics gives you information about the geometry displayed in the viewport.

- Configure gives you access to the Viewport Configuration dialog.

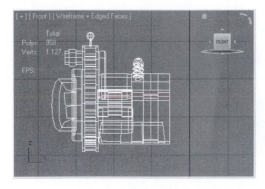

Viewport with Grids and Show Statistics on

Point-of-View Viewport Label Menu

The Point of View Viewport Label menu incorporates viewpoint-related functions:

- You can change the view in the current viewport by selecting one of the preset views like Front, Top, Orthographic, Perspective, etc.

- Undo View Change undoes the last view operation, be it a Zoom, Pan, Arc Rotate, etc.

- Several options like Track and Scene Explorer will replace the view in the current viewport with dialog that normally floats on top of the application window.

Rendering Levels

The viewport right-click menu offers a number of different rendering modes. You'll probably use these most often:

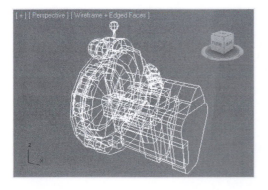

Viewport displaying in Wireframe mode

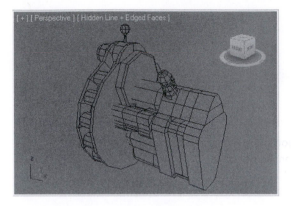

Viewport displaying in Hidden Line mode

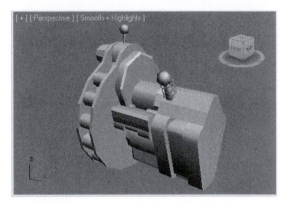

Viewport displaying in Smooth + Highlights mode

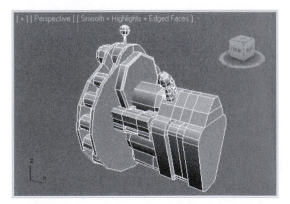

Viewport displaying in Smooth + Highlights mode with edged faces on

Since most 3D artists switch among these rendering modes frequently, the software includes predefined keyboard shortcuts to speed access to these modes.

- The **F3** function key toggles between Wireframe display and Smooth + Highlights.

- The **F4** function key toggles Edged Faces display.

Adaptive Degradation

Adaptive degradation can improve viewport performance when you transform geometry, change the view, or play back an animation. It does this by changing the display settings of objects temporarily so that the computer's graphics system can handle the changes in the screen display without slowing down animation playback or responsiveness of the software. Adaptive degradation is on by default.

Adaptive degradation toggle in the status area of the UI

Viewport Backgrounds

You can display an image as a background image in the active viewport. Each viewport can display a different background. This can be very helpful when you are modeling 3D objects, using the reference background image to keep the proportions in check. You can also use animated sequences (including .avi and .mov files) when you are trying to match animated 3D elements with digitized camera footage. Viewport Background can be configured by in the Views menu and the Viewport Background sub menu.

Dialog Boxes

Dialogs are used to present the user with information that doesn't fit easily into other areas of the UI. These may contain a large amount of information, graphs, thumbnails, schematic representations, and so on. Some typical dialogs include the following:

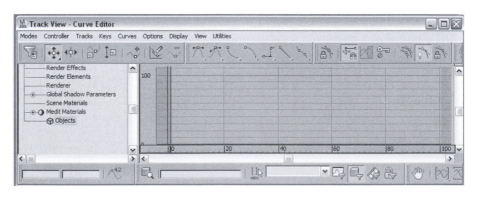

Scene Explorer dialog box

Track View—Curve Editor dialog box

Chapter 01 | Getting Started

Keyboard Shortcuts

3ds Max Design uses keyboard shortcuts to invoke commands. In many cases, experienced users can do much of their work faster using the keyboard. Note that many keyboard shortcuts are indicated in the pull-down menus, and many are commonly used. A few shortcuts have been indicated throughout this lesson. A list of the standard keyboard shortcuts is available on the Quick Reference Cube. Keyboard shortcuts can also be customized in the Customize User Interface dialog.

Help

The software contains a complete Help system. The Help menu gives you access to the User Reference, Learning Movies, Tutorials, and Additional Help, among others.

Exercise | Working with the User Interface

In this exercise, you will be manipulating a model in one or more orthographic viewports.

1. Open the file *Gas Station Blockout.max*. This is a rough block-out of a gas station scene.

2. Right-click in the **Orthographic** view to make it active.

3. Press **Alt** + **W** to enlarge the viewport to full screen.

4. In the **Views Menu** select **ViewCube** → **Configure**...

5. In the Dialog that appears, set the **ViewCube** Size to **Normal**. Click **OK** to exit the dialog.

6. Click the upper left corner of the **ViewCube** icon in the **Orthographic viewport**. The view rotates **90** degrees.

7. Press **Shift** + **Z** to undo the view change.

8. Click on one of the compass direction letters in the **ViewCube** icon and drag the cursor left and right. The view will rotate freely.

9. Click on the **Front** selection in the **ViewCube icon**.

10. Roll the mouse wheel to zoom out of the view until you see the gas station building.

11 Hold down the mouse wheel and pan the building to the center of the viewport until your view looks something like the following:

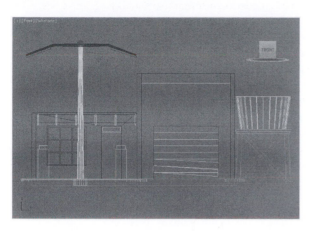

12 Press **Alt + W** to return to a **4 viewport** configuration.

13 In the active front viewport click the **General Viewport Label Menu** (Plus Sign). Select **ViewCube** → **Show the ViewCube selection** to toggle off the **ViewCube** in all viewports.

14 **Right-click** the **Top** viewport to make it active.

15 Click the **Zoom** button in the viewport controls area.

16   Zoom in with the cursor approximately centered on the building. The building scrolls out of the viewport. You can adjust the zoom control, so that it zooms about the mouse button.

17   Press **Shift** + **Z** to undo the zoom operation in the **Top** viewport.

18   From the Customize pull-down menu, choose **Preferences**.

19   On the dialog that appears, click the **Viewports** tab.

20   Turn on **Zoom About Mouse Poin**t for both **Orthographic** and **Perspective** views, and click **OK**.

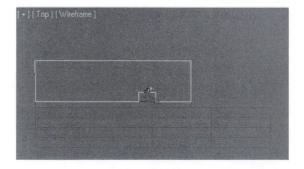

21   Repeat the operation of zooming into the model with the cursor centered on the building. Depending how close you placed the cursor to the center of the building, the building will stay visible in the viewport much longer.

22   Undo the view change by pressing **Shift** + **Z**.

23   With the **Top** viewport still active, click the **Zoom Extents** button.

24   All visible objects in the scene are now displayed in the **Top** viewport. The building is only a small area in the center.

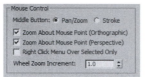

25 Click the **Zoom Extents All** button.

All the viewports zoom out in a similar fashion. If you want to return to your previous views in each viewport, you'll have to perform an Undo Viewport operation in each viewport individually. If you'd like to isolate a few objects, you can use Zoom Extents Selected.

26 Press the **H** key to open the **Select From Scene** dialog.

27 Highlight the object *Bldg_High*, and click the **OK** button on the dialog.

Name	Revit ...	Revit ...	Revit T...
Awning			
Circle01			
Building Sketch			
Curbs			
cactus			
Bldg_High			
Bldg_Low			
Camera01			
Camera01.Target			

28 Click the **Zoom Extents All** button and hold until the flyout appears.

29 On the flyout, choose the button with the filled white square. All four viewports zoom about the selected object.

Exercise | Perspective View Manipulation

In the following exercise you'll learn how to manipulate a model in a Perspective viewport.

1   Open the file *Gas Station Blockout_01.max*.

2   Make the **Orthographic** viewport active and press the **P** key. The orthographic view changes to a perspective view.

3   Click the **Field-of-View** button, which may be located in a flyout of the **Zoom Region** button.

4   Click and drag in the **Perspective** viewport and the view will move in and out along the perspective view line.

> **Note**:   *Use care with the Field-of-View tool. Extreme distortion of the perspective can occur if the field of view is made too large. Use Undo View Change (**Shift** + **Z**) to return to the previous view.*

5   In the **Views Menu** select **SteeringWheels** → **Toggle SteeringWheels** (**Shift** + **W**).

6   The **SteeringWheel** icon appears in the **Perspective** viewport.

7   Place the **SteeringWheel** close to the center of the building and place the cursor in the **Zoom Control** of the **Wheel**.

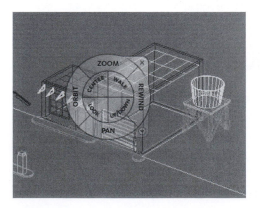

8 Click and Drag the cursor in the **Zoom Control** and the view zooms about the marker in the view.

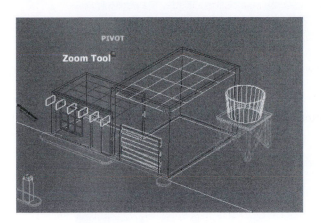

9 With the **SteeringWheel** in the center of the building, place the cursor in the **Orbit Control** area of the **Wheel**.

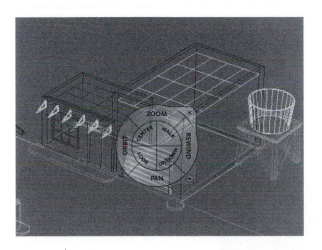

10 Click and drag the cursor to orbit the **Perspective** view.

11 Place the cursor in the **Pan Control** area of the **SteeringWheel**.

12 Click and drag the cursor to pan the view in the desired direction.

13 Place the cursor in the **Rewind Control** area of the **SteeringWheel** icon.

14   Click and Hold the cursor. Previous views are displayed along a strip.

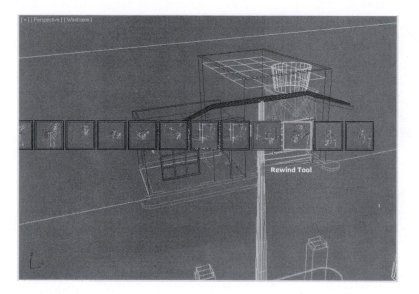

15   You can move your cursor to scroll back to a desired view or click on the **Rewind Control** to step back one view at a time.

16   Type the letter **C** and the **Perspective** view will change to the view of a camera present in the scene. If there was more than one camera, the software would prompt you for which camera you wanted to use.

17   Click on the **Dolly Camera** button.

18   **Click** and **drag** your cursor up and down in the view. The camera will approach the target location.

19   Press the **F3** function button to switch the viewport into **Shaded mode**.

20 Press the **F4** function button to switch the viewport into **Edged Faces mode**.

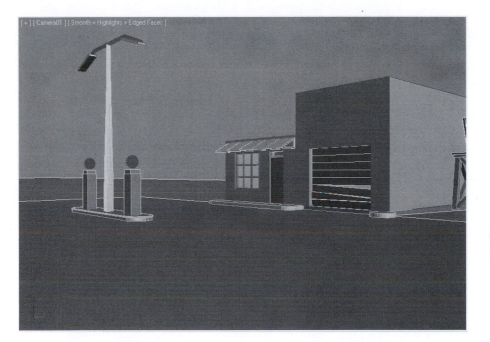

Lesson 02 | Creating and Modifying Basic Objects

Introduction

In this lesson you will create and modify basic objects in 3ds Max Design®. Overall you will be able to describe some guiding principles of object creation in the software. In addition, you will see how to modify some of the basic properties of an object and to access information about an object in a scene.

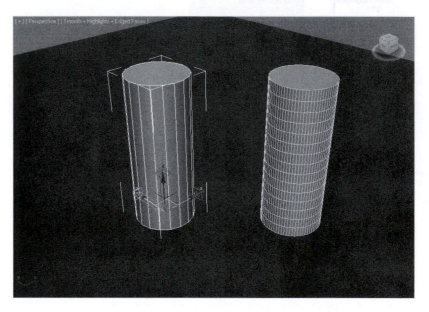

Two similar cylinders with different parameters

Objectives

After completing this lesson, you will be able to:

- Create a basic object in 3ds Max Design
- Modify parameters of your basic objects
- Identify the object orientation
- Identify and manipulate an object's pivot point
- Access object properties

Basic Geometry Creation and Modification

Geometry creation is generally begun by accessing tools found in either the Create Menu or in the Create tab of the Command panel.

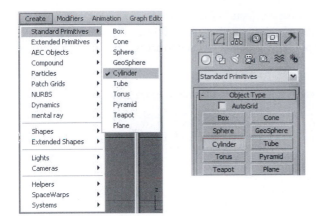

Creation Tools can be accessed through the Create Menu or the Create tab of the Command panel

When you create an object, a standard practice is to switch from the Create panel to the Modify panel before making changes to the object's parameters. Often you'll create an object "by eye" in the viewports, and then change its dimensions to round numbers.

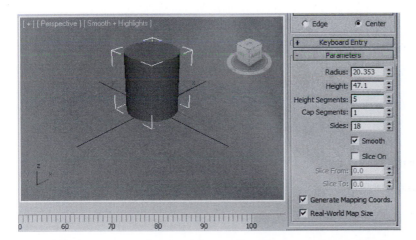

The cylinder has fractional Radius and Height values after creating it by clicking and dragging in a viewport.

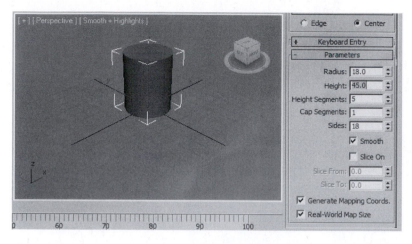

The Radius and Height values have been changed to round numbers in the Modify panel.

On the Modify panel and other command panel rollouts, you can animate numeric values, such as the radius and height of a cylinder. Parameters represented by check boxes or radio buttons usually cannot be animated.

Construction Planes and Object Orientation

When you create an object, its initial orientation is determined by the viewport where it was created.

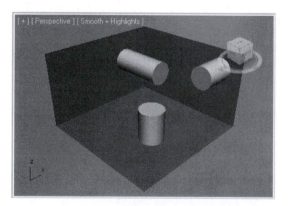

Cylinders created in the Top, Front, and Left viewports

Each viewport has a base plane acting as an origin; this is where the objects are created. Creating cylinders in the Top, Front, and Left viewports is like creating these objects on the floor, front, and side walls of a room.

Pivot Point Location and Orientation

When you create an object, the location of its pivot point is usually chosen by default, but you can always move the pivot point if needed. When an object is created the object has a local coordinate system, which is oriented toward the view in which the object was created. The orientation of the pivot point shows the object's local coordinate system.

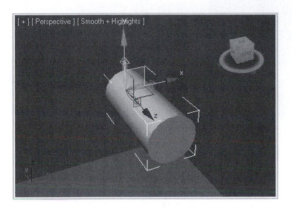

Location of an object's pivot point is determined by default. Orientation is dependent on the view in which the object was created.

Changing the Object's Pivot Point

The Hierarchy panel contains the tools required to relocate and reorient an object's pivot point.

Affect Pivot tool in the Hierarchy tab of the Command panel

Typically you would need to reorient or reposition an object's pivot point when an object needs to transform about a specific point. For example, if a box-shaped object needs to rotate around its corner rather than the center of the base, you may wish to relocate the pivot point to the corner of the box to accomplish this.

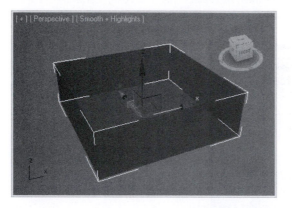

Pivot point in its default position; box will rotate about the center.

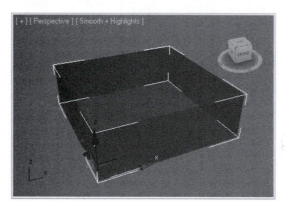

Pivot point moved to a corner of the box. The box will now rotate about the corner.

Once you select a tool in the Hierarchy panel such as Affect Pivot Only you can use transform tools like Move and Rotate to reposition and reorient the pivot point of the selected object. You must then turn off the Affect Pivot Only tool so you can then use transforms at the object level.

Object Properties

Each object in 3ds Max Design has a series of object properties associated with it. Typically, you may need to access these properties for reference or to change them. When an object is selected, the right-click menu will contain an Object Properties selection. Selecting this option will bring you to a tabbed dialog box containing a series of grouped properties.

Object properties dialog in 3ds Max Design

In the general tab of the dialog, some basic object information is presented. This information includes Object Name, Material Name, Layer, and Faces. Most of the remainder of the general tab includes areas for rendering control and display properties. In 3ds Max Design the rendering control and display properties are assigned on a layer- \by-layer basis. The layer will control the properties of the object unless otherwise changed at the object level. The most obvious result of this will be that initially, objects created in 3ds Max Design will all have the same color if they are on the same layer.

Naming Objects

One object property that is used extensively is the object name. When creating objects you have the ability to change the object name. Best practice is to create the object and then change its name in either the Modify tab of the Command panel or in the Object Properties dialog box.

Object Naming Convention

Typically, the naming of objects follows the established naming conventions in a particular workplace. Most naming conventions are based on the object and possibly how they are used. You may see names such as:

- *Car Body*
- *Car Tire DF*
- *Car Tire PR*

If you had multiple objects with the same function in a scene, you might number them or give them distinctive names, for example:

- *Gas Tank 01*
- *Gas Tank 02*
- *Gas Tank 03*

The objects named below suggest something about the role of objects in a scene.

- *Gas Tank Rusted*
- *Gas Tank New*
- *Gas Tank Explode*

A few other rules to keep in mind:

- If you use concatenated names, such as *gastanknew*, use uppercase letters to make the names more legible: *GasTankNew*.
- Be careful not to mix up the order or class by which you are describing the object. Work from bigger to smaller. For example, *Car Body*, *Shoe Left*, *Shelf Top*, and so on.

Faces

When you are creating objects and require a low polygon model you will be particularly interested in the number of faces that are being generated. The Object Properties dialog offers this information, but even more interesting is an interactive face counter that can be toggled in the viewport. This information can also be configured to show total and selected object information.

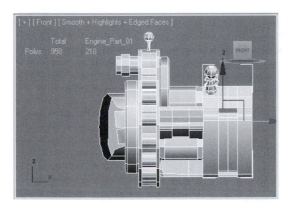

Viewport Statistics showing the number of faces for the selected object and for the entire scene.

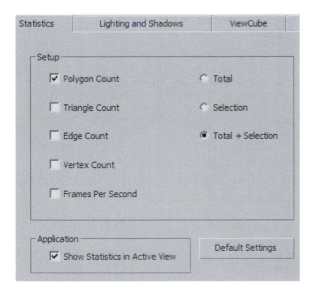

Viewport Configuration Dialog, Statistics tab showing configuration of the statistics display in the viewport.

Exercise | Creating and Manipulating a Simple 3D Object

In this exercise, you will be creating simple objects and then making some basic changes to these objects.

1   Start or reset 3ds Max Design.

2   In the **Create** tab of the **Command panel**, click the **Cylinder** tool.

3   **Click** and **drag** to create two cylinders in the perspective viewport that are approximately the same size. Don't worry about exact dimensions at this point.

4   Press **Esc** to exit creation mode.

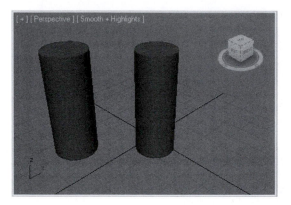

5   Select the cylinder on the left and click on the **Modify** tab of the **Command panel**.

6   Click in the **Edit Box** at the top of the panel and rename the object *Cylinder Low Poly*.

7   Select the color swatch to the right of the name of the object.

8   Choose a new color for the object in the **Object Color** dialog.

9   In the **Parameters** rollout, change the **Radius** and **Height** of the cylinder to whole values.

10   Change the **Height Segments** to **1**.

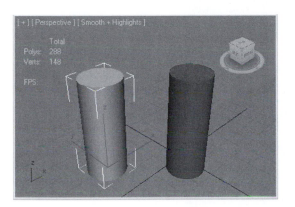

11   Press the **7** key to display the statistics of the objects in your scene. Pan if necessary to see the objects and statistics display more clearly.

12   Click on the **General Viewport Label Menu** (**+** symbol in upper left of the viewport) and select **Configure**.

13   Select the **Statistics** tab.

14   In the **Statistics** tab remove the check in the **Vertex Count** and **Frames Per Second** selection.

15 Change the **Setup** to **Total + Selection**.

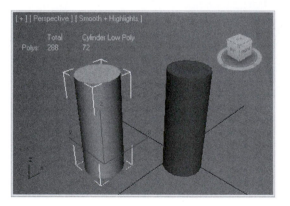

16 Click **OK** to exit the dialog. Note how the **Statistics** display has changed to display only the polygon count and shows the count for both the selected object and the entire scene.

17 Select the cylinder on the right. Note the difference in polys used by each cylinder. Even though the two cylinders appear identical, the one on the left uses fewer polygons since you reduced the number of height segments.

18 Rename the object *Cylinder High Poly*.

19 **Right-click** to display the **quad** menu.

Chapter 01 | Getting Started

20 In the **Display Properties**, click on the **By Layer** button. This will switch the **Display Properties** to **By Object**.

21 Click on the **See-Through** property to activate it. And click **OK** to exit the dialog.

22 In the **Command panel**, select the **Hierarchy** tab.

23 Click on the **Affect Pivot Only** tool.

24 The Pivot point will display at the default location at the base of the cylinder.

Lesson 03 | Scene File Manipulation

Introduction

In this lesson, you will learn about starting up a new scene file, setting your units and grid, and manipulating 3ds Max Design scene files.

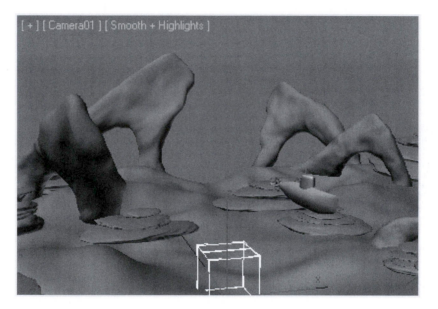

Scene Assembled in 3ds Max Design

Objectives

After completing this lesson, you will be able to:

- Use the different options when creating a new scene
- Establish units for a new scene
- Access scenes already created
- Save your scenes in a variety of different methods
- Import and export files
- Describe the different references used in 3ds Max Design

Starting a Scene File

When you launch 3ds Max Design, you can decide to start a new scene file or work on an existing one. The Application menu appears when you click on the Application button at the upper left of the 3ds Max Design Window. In the Application menu, you will find familiar options such as New, Open, Save, Save As, and other options like Reset, Import, Export, etc. In addition, on the right side of the menu you will see a list of files that were recently opened. Selecting these file names will open the file.

The 3ds Max Design Application menu

New

When you start working on a new scene, you can choose New from the Application menu like you do in most Windows applications. However, you have a few additional options to choose from in 3ds Max Design.

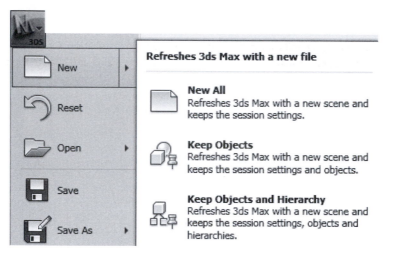

The 3ds Max Design Application menu

When you start a new file, you can choose the following options:

- **New All**: removes all existing geometry
- **Keep Objects**: keeps geometry in your current scene to use in your new scene
- **Keep Objects and Hierarchies**: keeps geometry in your current scene plus any dependencies between objects

Keep in mind that even if you choose to start afresh (New All), some aspects like viewport display, units setup, and material definitions remain unchanged in your new project. This may work for your benefit in some cases. If you'd rather start anew by resetting everything to their default assignment, using Reset is a better option than using New.

Reset

When you plan to start working on a new scene and want to discard everything in your current one, it is often better to use Reset instead of New. Using Reset resets everything as if you have just fired up the application. It releases any memory lagging from your old files and resets everything to its original default, including viewports, materials, and units. It is often the safest way to start a new scene.

Establishing the Units of Your Scene

The Customize menu contains the selection Units Setup for establishing the units of the scene. When you access the dialog you will note that there are settings for a System, Display, and Lighting units. For the time being we will only talk about units of distance measure.

System Units

The System Units are the underlying units setup for your 3ds Max Design installation. Once you set up the System Units, these units remain active until you return to this dialog and change them. System Units are not affected by the Reset option in the Application menu. When you click on the System Units button the System Unit Setup Dialog appears with standard units of measure to choose from.

System Units dialog

System Units are stored in the scene file and facilitate the use of multiple units of measure either amongst .*max* files or when importing files from other applications.

Display Units

The Display Units affect how units are entered and displayed in the 3ds Max Design interface.

Display Unit Scale area of the Unit Setup dialog

Units displayed in Parameters rollout

Accessing Existing Scenes

Open

Open is a straight forward feature to understand. It enables you to open existing files that are natively compatible with the application, in this case files with the extension .max. In addition to using Open, which accesses a dialog box that enables you to browse for files, you can use the Recent Documents list that lists up to 50 files you have recently worked on. By default, the Recent Documents list has 10 entries but you can change that number in the Preferences dialog. Also, a Pin icon is available to prevent a document from scrolling off the Recent Documents list.

Files in the Recent Documents list

Saving Scene Files

When you are working on a scene, there are several functions available to you to save your data to disk. The Save commands are found in the Application menu.

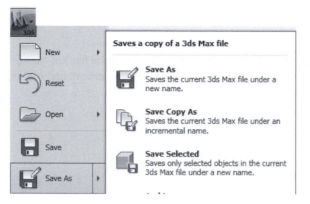

Save commands in the Application menu

Save

When you choose Save from the Application menu, the program prompts you to name your file. If, for example, you call you file Dog, the software creates a file named *Dog.max*. Once you've named your file, the Save command doesn't prompt you for a file name. It automatically saves your file under its current name.

Save As

The Save As command lets you rename and save an existing file. Using the previous example, if you originally saved the file as Dog and then use the Save As command, you are prompted to enter a name. If you enter *My Dog*, the new file would be called *My Dog.max*. In addition, the file that is now current for editing is *My Dog.max*. The file *Dog.max* remains in the state it was in when you last saved it.

As a convenience, the Save As dialog include a Plus button. Clicking this button saves the file with an automatic sequence number appended to its name.

For example:

- *My Dog.max*
- *My Dog01.max*
- *My Dog02.max*
- *My Dog03.max*

In some work situations, it's convenient to save several versions of a given scene file. For example, one file might contain geometry only; another would contain the material treatment; and another would save the lighting of the scene. Sequential saved files can also be used to store several different options for a character or different poses of a character in an animation.

Save Copy As

If you want to save a file under a different name but keep on working on your current file, use the Save Copy As command. Save Copy As works the same way as Save As but the newly saved file on disk does not become the current scene.

Save Selected

Save Selected is a tool you use when you need to extract models from a project and save them to a separate file. Save Selected works like Save Copy As, in that it saves the file to disk without making it current, leaving you to continue working on your original scene.

Several big rocks selected in an underwater scene

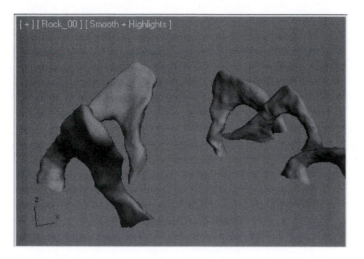

Resulting file when Save Selected is used

Archive

Archive is a tool that you can use to save your file into a compressed zip file. When 3ds Max Design saves the compressed file it also saves any support files required by the scene. The advantage to using Archive is you will not need to worry about missing map files in bitmapped materials or missing web distribution files for photometric lights, etc. Once the file is uncompressed it will be ready to open as a standard 3ds Max Design scene file.

Hold/Fetch

The Hold and Fetch commands, found on the Edit menu, are used together. When you use the Hold command, it saves a temporary file with the contents of your scene, bookmarking its present state. Then, when you use Fetch, the software loads the contents of the Hold file, restoring the scene to the state it was in when you used Hold.

 Note: *Neither Hold nor Fetch affects the state of your saved .max scene file.*

Importing and Exporting Files

The Import and Export selections in the Application menu contain options to bring files of various formats into and out of scene file in 3ds Max Design.

Import

The Import option in the Application menu brings in files from external programs, and merges or replaces objects from native 3ds Max Design files. Files can be imported from applications such as 3D Studio DOS, AutoCAD®, Adobe® Illustrator, MotionBuilder®, and Inventor among others.

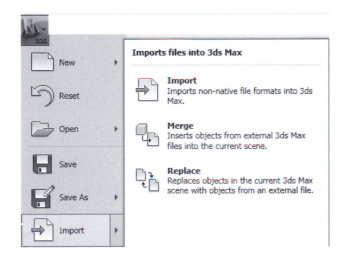

Import Options in the Application menu

Merging

Merging files is a method of combining all or part of one .max file into another. While you are in the application, using the Merge function prompts you to pick another scene file. After you specify a .max file, you can choose to merge some or all of the elements in the scene.

When you merge a file, you take objects from one file (e.g., *My Dog.max*) and place it in another (e.g., *DogHouse.max*). The *My Dog* file is unaffected by this operation, but the *DogHouse* file has new objects in it.

Import FBX Files

FBX file import has been an option to import files from the MotionBuilder animation software product. Recently the FBX file format has been employed in transferring data from Revit® to 3ds Max Design.

The FBX file format is a self-contained file that includes all supporting files like bitmaps and photometric web files. Once this file is imported, the file will be expanded and the supporting files will be placed in a folder bearing the same name.

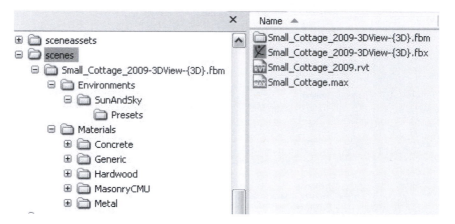

Folder Structure Created by Expanding an FBX File

Export

The Export options in the Application menu command saves 3ds Max Design scene files into most of the same file formats that Import supports. It also exports to 3D DWF™ file format supported on the web.

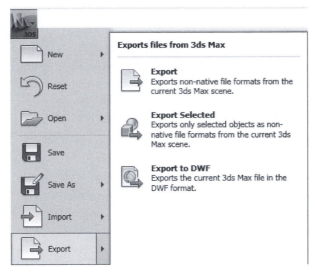

Export Options in the Application menu

References

References are links to files that are external to the current 3ds Max Design scene. Using references is different from importing because a reference is a live link to an external file. 3ds Max Design can reference .max, .dwg, and .dxf file formats. The Reference Selection in the Application menu shows the different options you have to reference external files.

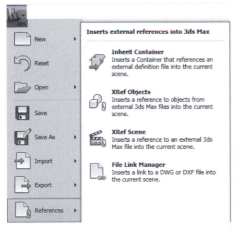

Reference Options in the Application menu

Containers

The Inherit Containers option places a container object in your current scene. Containers are created in the Tools menu, under the Containers selection. Essentially, a container is created by selecting objects in a scene and saving them in specialized 3ds Max Design files with the .maxc extension. Once a Container file is created, it can be brought into any 3ds Max Design scene file. If the content of the container is updated, it will update scene files that reference the container.

Xref Objects

This option gives you the ability to reference objects in an external 3ds Max Design file into the current scene. These objects can then be further modified in the current scene. Updates to the original objects will update the objects in the current scene.

Xref Scene

This option allows you to reference an entire 3ds Max Design scene into your current scene. The referenced scene is not editable in the current scene. Changes to the referenced scene will be reflected in the current scene. This is a good approach when you need to have background 3D geometry that does not need to change from scene to scene.

File Linking

The File Link Manager option gives you the ability to Attach a link to external .dwg and .dxf files, which are native to AutoCAD. Many other CAD applications have the ability to create files of this type, including the Revit family of products. Once the contents of the .dwg or .dxf file is linked into 3ds Max Design, you can add materials and modifiers to the geometry. Typically, File Linking is used by designers who prefer the geometry creation toolsets inherent in CAD applications yet wish to make use of 3ds Max Design's superior rendering capabilities.

Once a .dwg or .dxf file is resaved by the application that created it, you have the ability to reload it in 3ds Max Design. Generally, if the design modifications are not substantial, you can render your view, without having to make changes in 3ds Max Design.

Exercise | Creating a Scene File

In this exercise, you will create a new underwater scene and populate it with geometry from other files already created.

1   Go to the **Application** menu and select **Reset**.

2   Depending on whether you have have unsaved changes in your current file, the following dialog may appear.

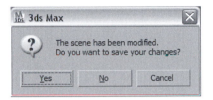

3   Click **No** to discard the changes in your current file.

4   Click **Yes** in the 3ds Max dialog.

5   In the **Customize** menu select **Units Setup**.

6   In the **Units Setup** dialog select the **System Unit Setup** button.

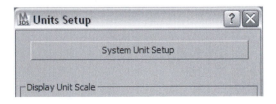

7   In the **System Unit Setup** dialog select **Meters** from the **System Unit** list.

8   Click **OK** to close the dialog.

9   In the **Units Setup** dialog change the **Display Unit** to **Metric**, and select **Meters** from the list below the **Metric** selection.

10   The underlying file units and the display units are now set to meters.

11 In the **Quick Access** toolbar select the **Save** button.

12 Name the file *Sub Approaching* and click **Save**.

13 In the next few steps you will bring in geometry from 3ds Max Design files in a variety of methods.

14 In the **Application** menu select **Import** → **Merge**.

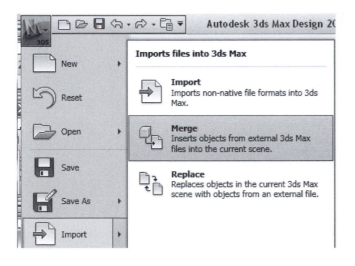

15   Navigate to the folder that contains your files and select the file *Rocks.max*. Then click **Open**.

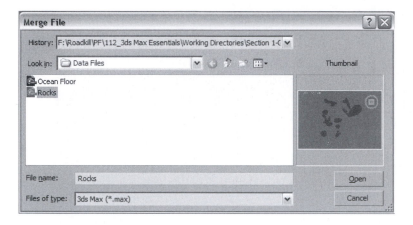

16   In the **Merge** dialog select the **All** button, and click **OK**.

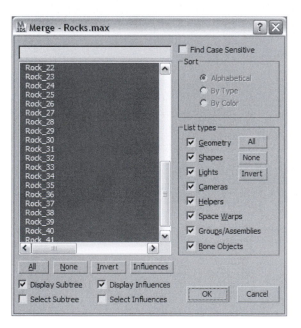

Chapter 01 | Getting Started

17 A series of objects are imported into the empty scene. These objects can be easily manipulated in the new scene.

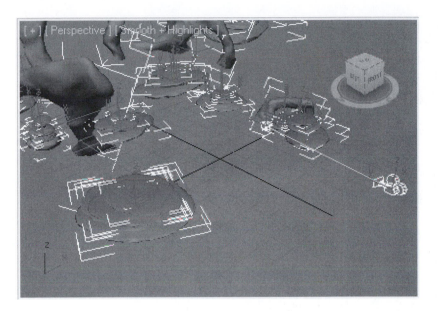

18 Make the **Perspective** viewport current and type **C** at the keyboard to display the **Camera** view.

19 In the **Application** menu select **References** → **Xref Scene**.

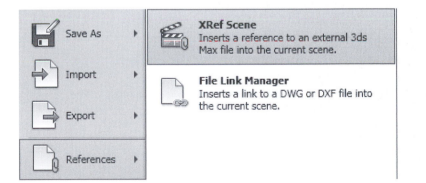

20 In the **Xref Scenes** dialog click on the **Add** button.

21 Navigate to the folder that contains your files and select the file *Ocean Floor.max*. Then click **Open**.

22 Close the **Xref Scenes** dialog.

23 Click away from any object in the scene to deselect all objects.

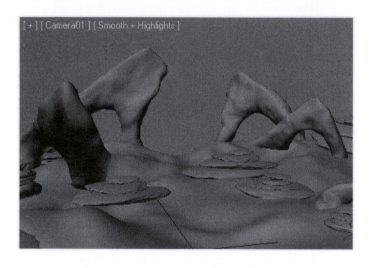

The Ocean Floor scene is referenced into the current scene and displays the surface of the ocean floor. The geometry from the Ocean Floor scene cannot be modified in the current scene.

24 In the **Application** menu select **References** → **Inherit Container**.

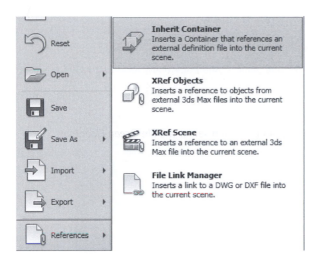

25 In the **Inherit Container** dialog navigate to the folder that contains your files and select the file *Sub-Container01.maxc*. Click **Open.**

26 A Submarine appears in the current scene.

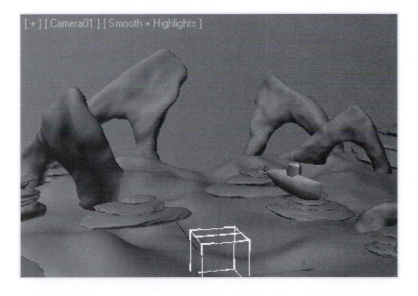

A container object will allow some additional flexibility for the referenced object.

Lesson 04 | Selecting Objects

Introduction

In this lesson, you will learn about selecting objects. There are many tools and options available to you when selecting objects.

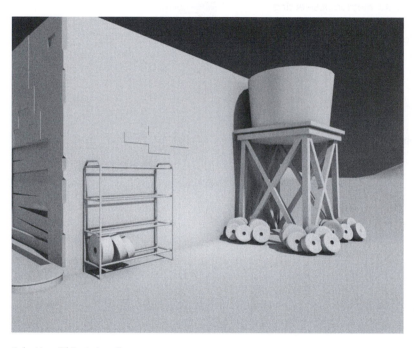

Selecting Objects in a Scene

Objectives

After completing this lesson, you will be able to:

- Select objects in a scene
- Use the Scene Explorer to select objects
- Select Similar Objects
- Rename Objects
- Use the Selection Filter

Chapter 01 | Getting Started

Selecting Objects

3ds Max Design gives you numerous ways to select objects. This section covers the most important selection methods.

Selection Tool

The most fundamental method of selecting objects is by using the Select tool on the main toolbar. When you start 3ds Max Design the Select tool is normally active and is indicated as such by the icon being highlighted in blue. When the select tool is not active the icon is gray and you must click on the button to activate it.

The Selection tool on the main toolbar active and ready to select objects.

- When the Select tool is active and you click an object, you select that object. Any prior selection is canceled.

- If you click in an empty area and then drag across a viewport, by default you'll select whichever objects are crossed by the selection region you create.

- If you hold the **Ctrl** key down while you click objects individually, the objects will be added or removed from the selection set. The **Ctrl** key acts as a toggle.

- Holding down the **Ctrl** key while you drag a selection region adds all objects in the selection region to the selection.

- Holding down the **Alt** key while you click objects or drag a selection region removes those objects from the selection.

Selection Lock Toggle

Near the bottom of the 3ds Max Design window is the Selection Lock Toggle icon. When you turn it on, the icon turns blue to indicate that the selection is locked. No changes can be made to the current selection until you turn off the icon to unlock the selection. The Selection Lock Toggle is useful when you have numerous operations to do with a selection, especially when the scene is crowded and it would be easy to select other objects by accident.

The Selection Lock Toggle activated.

Select Objects from Scene

In a scene, you'll often remember an object's name, or you might need to select numerous objects with similar names. If these objects are difficult to select by clicking in a viewport, using the Select From Scene dialog can help.

The Select From Scene dialog.

To access the Select From Scene dialog, click its icon on the main toolbar or press **H** on the keyboard.

Icon to access the Select from Scene dialog.

If you have hierarchical structures in your scene (as is the case in the above example), then you can select the whole hierarchy by selecting the top parent (in this case, *Car*). In order for this to work, you need to enable the Select Children option in the Select menu. You can also toggle this mode on and off using **Ctrl + C**.

Option to Select Child Objects.

Scene Explorer

Another dialog that provides much the same functionality as the Select From Scene dialog is the Scene Explorer. The Scene Explorer is accessed through selecting the New Scene Explorer selection in the Tools menu. An added advantage to the Scene Explorer is that it will synchronize the selection in the dialog with the selection in the scene.

Option to Select Child Objects.

Select Similar

The Select Similar tool is a useful tool to select objects that have similar properties. You can access it in the Edit menu or by selecting an object and right-clicking.

The Select Similar tool selects objects that are of the same base object type and are on the same layer. If materials or modifiers have been added to an object, it will prevent an object from being considered similar.

Using Select Similar can be particularly useful when importing or referencing geometry from CAD software. Often, geometry will be imported as a series of faces on a layer. By selecting one face and then using Select Similar, all faces on the layer with the same material will be selected.

Rename Objects Tool

It's not easy to perform proper scene management while in the midst of creating a scene. You'll often find yourself having to rename objects that you created a long time ago. Fortunately, 3ds Max Design provides a flexible tool to rename objects, called Rename Objects. You can find it in the Tools pull-down menu.

Selection Filter

As your 3ds Max Design scene becomes more and more filled with objects of different types, the Selection Filter list can become useful.

When you choose one of the items in the list (e.g. Lights), all other object types are unavailable for selection and you can select only lights. Don't forget to set the list back to All when you are done.

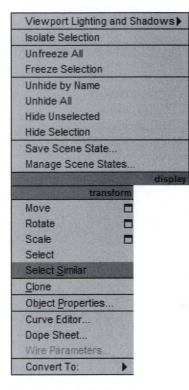

Select Similar in the Quad menu.

Selection Filter List.

Selection Window/Crossing

When you use region selection in 3ds Max Design, you can toggle the selection mode to be either a crossing region or a window region. The crossing region selects everything that touches the region as well as what is completely contained within the region.

The window region selects only objects completely inside the selection window. To switch the region mode, click the Window/Crossing Toggle button on the main toolbar.

Window/Crossing toggle in Crossing Mode.

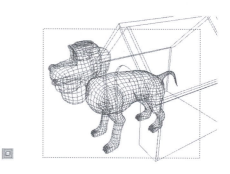

Insert Figure4-11.png

Insert Figure4-12.png

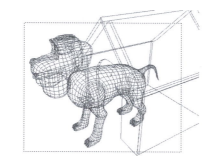

When Crossing mode is active (the default), making a selection region, as shown, selects both the dog and the doghouse.

When Window mode is active, making a selection rectangle as illustrated selects the dog only. Window mode selects only objects completely contained within the selection rectangle.

Selection Region Type

Five different selection region methods are available in 3ds Max Design: the default Rectangular selection region and four other types. You choose the mode by using the Selection Region flyout on the main toolbar.

Selection Region Flyout.

The following illustration shows the five kinds of selection regions. Clockwise from the upper-left corner: Rectangular, Circular, Fence, Paint, and Lasso selection regions.

Selection Region Types.

Exercise | Selecting and Renaming Objects in a Scene

1   Open the file *Tires.max*. In this scene are several objects representing tires.

2   Unfortunately, through the current naming convention, you cannot tell which object is which.

3   Click on the **Window/Crossing** toggle so that **Window** mode is **enabled**.

4   Make a region selection around the tires on the tire rack.

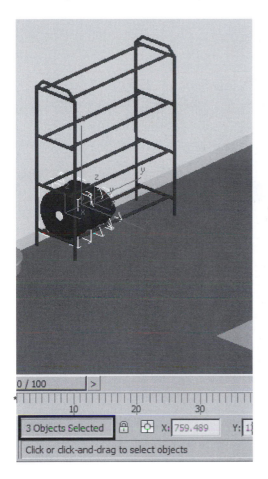

5   The status line will tell you that there are three objects selected. The selected objects will
have a bounding box surrounding them.

6   In the **Tools** menu, select **New Scene Explorer**.

7   Scroll down if you need to see the selected objects in the **Scene Explorer**.

8   Note that the objects have names that do not identify them well.

9   In the **Tools** pull-down menu, choose **Rename Objects**.

10 Make sure the radio button at the top of the dialog is set to **Selected**.

11 Enter the **Base Name**: *TireOnRack*.

12   Select the **Numbered** checkbox and leave **Base Number** at **0** and **Step** at **1**.

13   Click the **Rename** button.

14   Move the **Rename Objects** dialog if necessary so you can see the changes in the **Scene Explorer**.

15 Exit both the **Scene Explorer** and the **Rename Objects** dialog.

16 Select one of the tire objects on the ground at the base of the water tower.

17 Right-click and choose **Select Similar** from the **quad** menu.

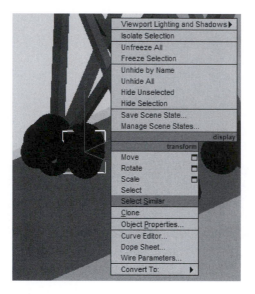

18 All the tires are selected including the tires on the rack that we had renamed previously.

19 Hold the **Alt** key down and create a region around the tires on the rack to remove them from the selection.

20 Select **Rename Objects** from the **Tools** menu.

21 In the **Rename Objects** dialog, change the base name to *TireOnGround*.

22 Make Sure the **Numbered** checkbox is selected, the **Base Number** is **0**, and the **Step** value is **1**.

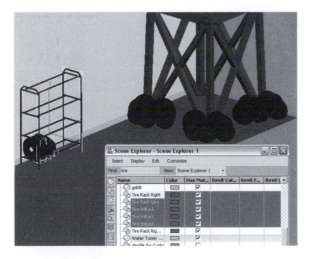

23 Click **Rename** and close the dialog.

24 Click anywhere in the scene to deselect the tires.

25 Press **Alt** + **Ctrl** + **O** to display the **Scene Explorer**.

26 Type the word *Tire* in the **Find** value in the **Scene Explorer**, and press **Enter**.

27 Scroll down the list of objects. Note that all objects in the list that start with the word *Tire* are selected. The **Scene Explorer** selects all these objects in the scene.

Lesson 05 | Transforms

Introduction

In this lesson, you will learn about transforming objects. There are three basic transforms: move, rotate, and scale. In addition, there are more advanced transforms that are essentially derived from the basic transforms but can make certain operations easier to accomplish.

Move, Rotate, and Scale being used to change an object's position, orientation, or size

Objectives

After completing this lesson, you will be able to:

- Use Basic Transforms
- Use different Coordinate Systems
- Apply Snaps and Grids
- Use Other Essential Transforms

Basic Transforms

You use basic transform tools in 3ds Max Design to move, rotate, and scale objects. Other tools you'll see a little further on in this lesson essentially do the same thing, but with a different user interface that can automate several operations into one command. You'll start with the basic transform tools.

Move

Move lets you position an object anywhere in a scene. You can move objects freely or along a specific axis or plane. Move is useful when modeling and animating. You can move objects in the viewport using the Transform gizmo or the Transform Type-In.

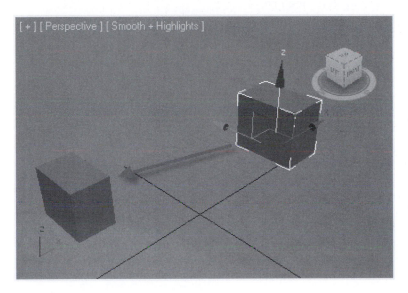

Moving an object freely lets you displace the object anywhere in 3D space

Move Transform Gizmo

The Move Transform gizmo appears at the pivot point location of an object. The gizmo allows you to restrict movement of the object by dragging an axis or a plane in the gizmo.

When using the Move tool, if you drag one of the three axes in the gizmo, movement is constrained to that direction. In this example, movement is restricted to the X-axis.

If you drag one of the rectangles in the gizmo, you restrict motion to a plane. In this example, the XY-plane was chosen, so the object cannot move in the Z-direction.

Move Transform Type-In

In addition to the gizmo, the Move tool has a Transform Type-In dialog box that lets you enter the displacement numerically. When you right-click the Select and Move button, the Transform Type-In dialog appears.

The Transform Type-In shows you the XYZ coordinates of the pivot point in the Absolute World group of the dialog and allows you to adjust the position in this absolute format. The Offset group is for displacement relative to the object's current position.

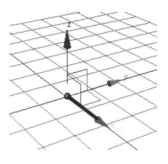

The Move Gizmo with the X-axis selected for movement

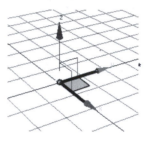

The Move Gizmo with the XY-plane selected for movement

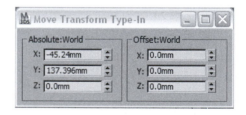

The Move Transform Type-In dialog

Rotation

Rotating objects is another type of transform used frequently when working with 3ds Max Design. The results you obtain depend greatly on the location of the point you rotate about and the axis of rotation. By default, the pivot point is used as the rotation center.

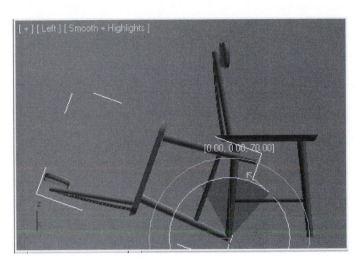

[+] [Left] [Smooth + Highlights]

[0.00, 0.00,-20.00]

The wooden chair is rotated with the pivot point the bottom of the rear legs

Rotate Transform Gizmo

The Rotate Transform gizmo appears at the pivot point location of an object. The gizmo comprises five circles. The following illustrations describe the functions of these five circles.

The XYZ-axis rotation restrictions are represented by the red, green, and blue circles. For example, if you click the red circle and drag, the object rotates about the X-axis.

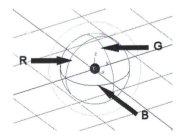

The XYZ rotation axes are represented by the RGB circles

You can rotate the object freely by dragging the outer circle defined by the profile of the sphere. Or you can place the cursor anywhere inside the gizmo but not on one of the concentric circles.

To restrict the rotation about a line perpendicular to the view plane (line of sight), drag the outer circle that is offset from the sphere.

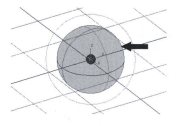

The sphere profile allows free rotation

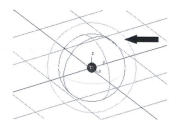

The outer circle allows rotation about a line perpendicular to the view plane

Rotation Transform Type-In

In addition to the gizmo, the Rotate tool has a Transform Type-In dialog for entering rotation values numerically. As with the Move Transform Type-In, the Rotate Transform Type-In has absolute and offset (relative) methods of numerical entry.

The Rotate Transform Type-In dialog

Chapter 01 | Getting Started

Scale

3ds Max Design provides three commands for scaling objects: Select and Uniform scale, Select and Non-uniform scale, and Scale and Squash. You'll find all three operations on the Scale tool flyout on the main toolbar.

With Uniform scale, the first tool on the Scale flyout, all three dimensions of the object are scaled equally.

The Scale Tool Flyout on the Main toolbar

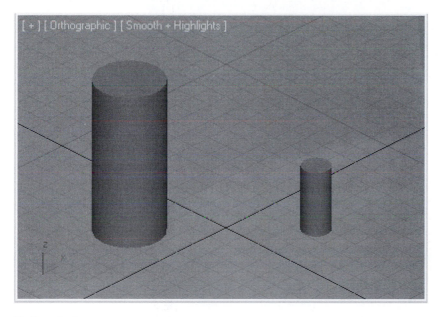

[+] [Orthographic] [Smooth + Highlights]

Uniform Scale

With Non-uniform Scale, the second tool in the scale flyout, you can scale one or two dimensions while the other remains constant. In the illustration, the Z-dimension of the cylinder has been scaled while X and Y have not changed.

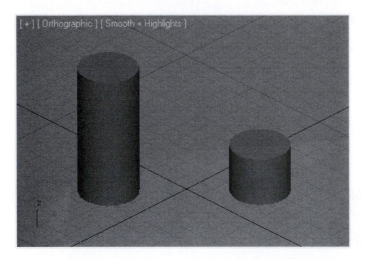

Scale along one axis

Scale and Squash, the third tool on the Scale tool flyout, lets you change one or two dimensions while the other axis or axes automatically adjust in the opposite direction. In the illustration, the Z-axis has been scaled down while Scale and Squash increases the X and Y directions to compensate, with the result that the object's original volume is maintained.

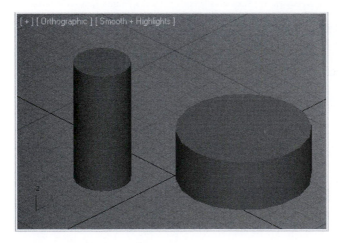

Scale and Squash along one axis

Scale Transform Gizmo

The Scale Transform gizmo appears at the pivot location of an object. You can use the gizmo to scale along one axis, on two axes, and uniformly. When you drag one axis of the gizmo, the object is scaled along that axis.

When you drag the plane between two axes, the object is scaled in that plane. In the illustration, the XZ-plane was clicked with the result that scaling occurs on the X and Z axes.

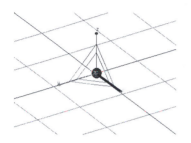

Using the Gizmo to Scale along one Axis

Using the Gizmo to Scale in a Plane

When you drag the inner triangle, you scale on all three axes simultaneously.

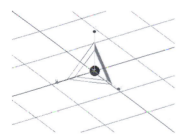

Using the Gizmo to Scale in all three dimensions

Scale Transform Type-In

In addition to the gizmo, the Scale tool has a Transform Type-In dialog for entering Scale values numerically.

Scale Transform Type-In

Absolute:Local
X: 100.0
Y: 100.0
Z: 100.0

Offset:World
%: 100.0

Using the Gizmo to Scale in all three dimensions

Transform Base Point

When you transform objects, you have a choice of the base point. By default, scaling uses the pivot point of the object. Alternatively, you can use the selection center and the transform coordinate center. You can set the mode with the Transform Center flyout.

Transform Center flyout.   *Rotating multiple objects using the pivot point center.*

Coordinate Systems

Nine coordinate systems are available in 3ds Max Design. In this section, you'll see some of the more common and useful systems. You can change the current coordinate system using the Reference Coordinate System list on the main toolbar.

The Reference Coordinate System list.

World

The World Coordinate System is based on the XYZ axes in the 3D workspace. The XY plane is the ground plane and the Z axis is perpendicular to this plane. The World Coordinate System does not change, and is practical in that respect since you always know the orientation of the space around you.

In the illustrations, the Move Transform gizmo shows the orientation of the coordinate system. Note that the orientation does not change if a different view is made active.

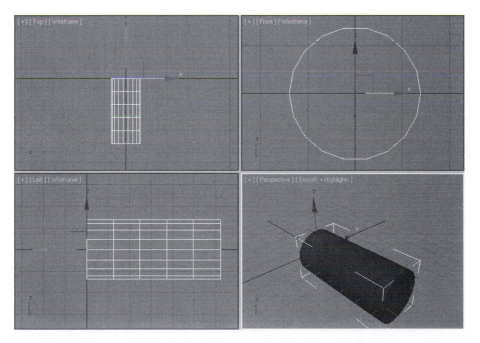

World Coordinate System in use, Perspective view active.

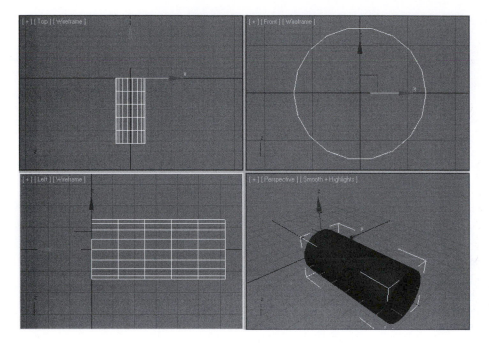

World Coordinate System in use, Left View Active.

View

The View coordinate system is the default coordinate system used in the 3D scene. This coordinate system adapts to the active viewport to keep the XY plane perpendicular to that viewport. This applies to isometric (2D) views only. If a 3D view, such as the Perspective viewport, is active the View coordinate system behaves like the World coordinate system, where the XY plane lies flat on the ground and the Z-axis is vertical. Note the orientation of the Move transform gizmo in the illustrations. The orientation of the gizmo changes when switching between the Perspective and Left viewports.

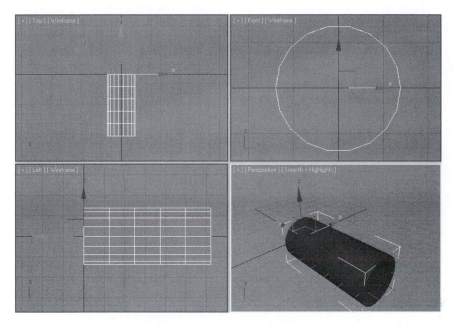

View coordinate system with the Perspective viewport active

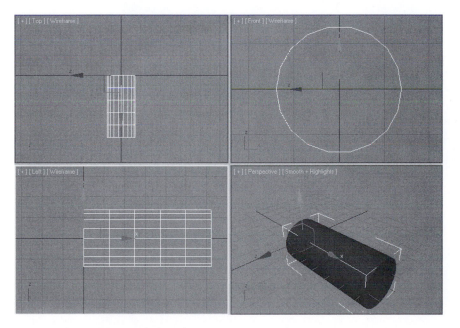

View coordinate system with the Left viewport active

Local

The Local coordinate system is based on the coordinate system of the object being transformed. An object's local coordinate system follows the rotation of the object. The Local coordinate system orients itself to the object. In this case, the Z-axis of the coordinate system points along the height of the cylinder while the XY plane lies on the base.

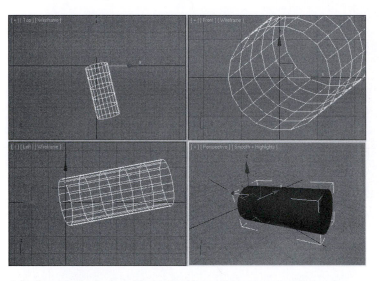

A freely rotated cylinder with the World coordinate system active

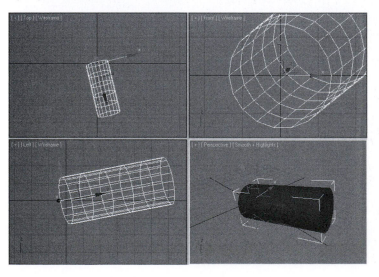

A freely rotated cylinder with the Local coordinate system active

Pick

The Pick Coordinate System is so called because it allows you to pick another object to use as a transform center. Once you choose Pick and then pick the object, the selection center must be set to Use Transform Coordinate Center.

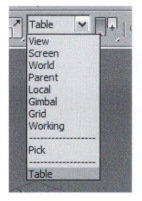

Once you use the Pick reference system, the selected object will appear in the reference list

In the illustration, the pivot point of the Table object is used as the center of rotation when clones of the chair are created with the rotation transform tool.

Chairs rotated and cloned using the table pivot point as a reference

Working

The Working coordinate system is based on a Working Pivot available in the software. The Working Pivot can be moved and rotated to an appropriate position and orientation and then used to transform other objects.

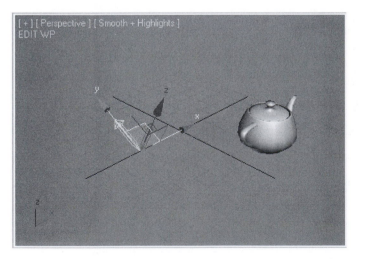

Tools to edit the Working Pivot are located in the Hierarchy panel.

The Working Pivot moved away from its default location (0,0,0) and rotated.

Chapter 01 | Getting Started

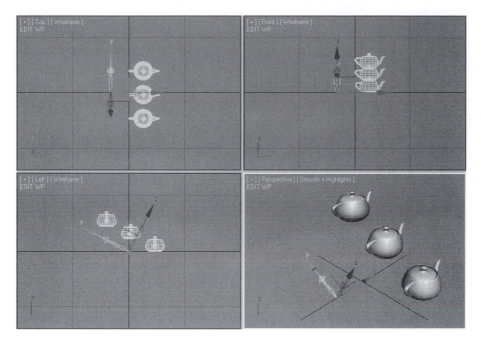

The Working Pivot used to copy an object.

Snaps

Four different snapping types are available in 3ds Max Design. Each type of snap has a toggle on the Main toolbar. A left-click enables or disables the snap; a right-click brings you to a dialog where you can establish the settings for the snap. The four snaps are listed in order from left to right.

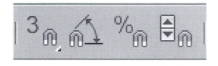

Snap toggles on the main toolbar

- **Grid and Snaps**: For snapping to grids and parts of objects, such as vertices and midpoints of edges.

- **Angle Snap**: Limits rotation increments to a fixed number of degrees.

- **Percent Snap**: Used with the Scale tool to control the percentage of scaling of objects.

- **Spinner Snap**: Sets the single-click increment/decrement value for all spinners.

Grid and Snaps

When you right-click the Snaps Toggle button on the main toolbar, the Grid and Snap Settings dialog appears.

This dialog provides access to Grid settings and Snap settings. The Grid Points option is enabled by default. Object Snaps can be useful when you're laying objects out along a grid or tracing an existing object and want to snap to the object's vertices. Grid and Snap can also be toggled with the **S** keyboard shortcut.

If Grid Points snapping is on when you create a box, each point of the base lands on a grid intersection, and the height is restricted to the grid spacing.

Grid and Snap Setting Dialog

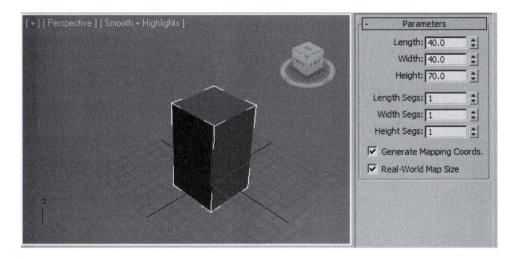

Creating a box with Grid Points Snap on

If you turn on Vertex snapping, you can position new geometry accurately using the vertices of existing geometry in the scene. In this case, the vertices defined by the bottle object are used as a guide to draw a shape.

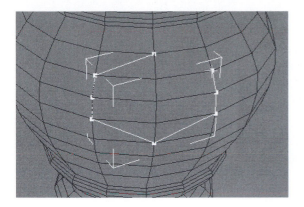

Vertex Snap used to help draw shape

Angle Snap

When you want to rotate an object precisely without the use of the Rotate Type-in, Angle Snap is quite useful. Angle Snap restricts the rotation of an object to a predetermined angle increment. Right-clicking the Angle Snap Toggle opens the Grid and Snaps Settings dialog with the Options panel active.

The Angle value controls the Angle Snap mode

The Angle Snap value is controlled by the Angle value in the General group. The default setting of 5.0 is useful for most situations. To turn on Angle Snap, click the Angle Snap Toggle and the button turns yellow, indicating the mode is active. You can also use the **A** keyboard shortcut.

The Angle Snap restriction of rotation is made clear with XYZ rotation values appearing outside the Rotation gizmo.

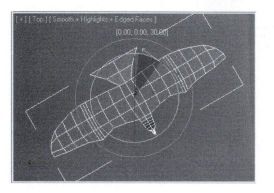

Rotation Angle appears above the Rotation Gizmo

Scale Percent Snap

Percent Snap controls the Scale value. Percent Snap is less commonly used and works in much the same fashion as Angle Snap. The Percent Snap Toggle activates the mode and right-clicking the button brings you to the same dialog as Angle Snap.

The Percent value controls the Percent Snap mode

Other Essential Transforms

Align

The Align Tool lets you line up a selected object, called the source object, with the position of a target object. You can also use Align to match a source object's orientation to that of a target object. You can access the Align tool from the Align button on the main toolbar.

The Align button on the main toolbar and the Align Selection dialog

Align XYZ Position

When you use Align to reposition an object in XYZ, you can use one of four different alignment options: Minimum, Center, Pivot Point, and Maximum. You can apply this setting separately to the current and target objects on any combination of axes. For example, take the two objects shown below:

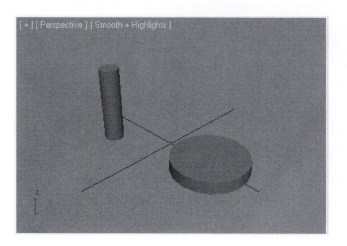

Two arbitrary cylinders in space

Using Align on these objects can yield a variety of results. A simple application of Align is where the pivot points are aligned.

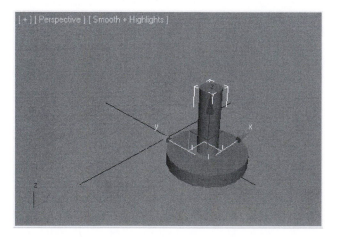

Aligning Pivot Points

Chapter 01 | Getting Started

Another more complex application of Align can separate alignments on different axes into separate operations. Simply perform one operation at a time and select Apply. In this example, on the X axis, the pivot points are aligned; on the Y axis the maximum positions of the objects are aligned, and on the Z axis, the minimum of the source object is aligned with the maximum of the target object.

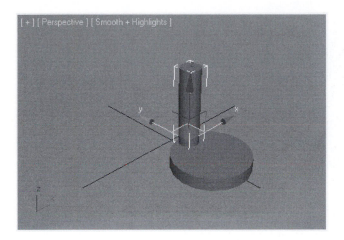

Complex use of the Align tool

Align Orientation

If two objects are not properly aligned with respect to one or more axes, the Align Orientation group of the Align dialog lets you adjust the source's object orientation to match the targets.

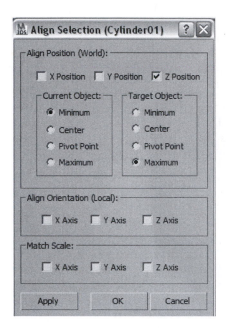

The Align Orientation group on the Align dialog

In the example, two cylinders are oriented in different directions; the Z axes of the object are not aligned.

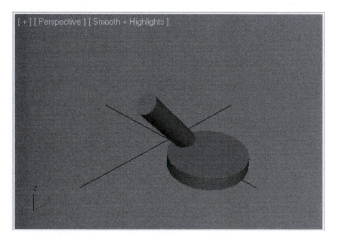

Two cylinders with different Z-axis orientation

Chapter 01 | Getting Started

Aligning the tilted cylinder to the base's Z axis produces this result. Note that Align Orientation does not displace the object in space.

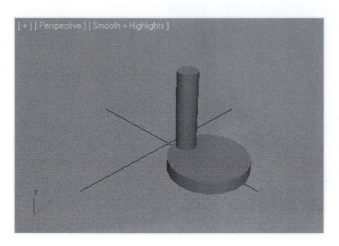

Two Cylinders with Z-axis oriented

Quick Align

The Align flyout on the main toolbar provides a number of tools for different types of alignments. One such tool is Quick Align, the second icon on the flyout.

The Align flyout

Quick Align works on the positions of the two objects' pivot points. It does not affect orientation.

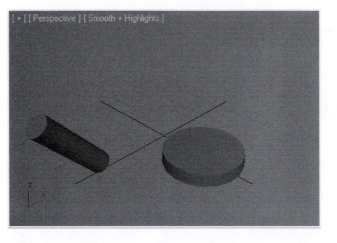

Before Quick Align

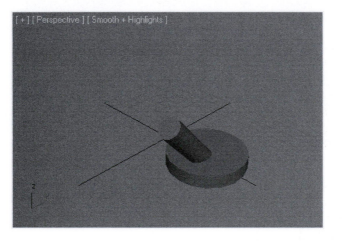

Quick Align aligns object's pivot points

Mirror

The Mirror transform takes an object and creates a symmetrical object along a mirror plane. You can choose to mirror about a number of different axes. The Mirror tool can be found in the Tools menu and on the Main toolbar.

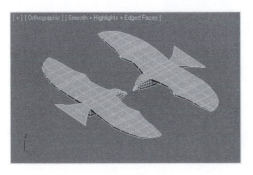

The Mirror tool on the Main toolbar and the Mirror dialog

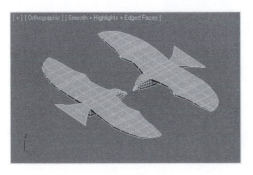

The Mirror tool creates a symmetrical object

Array

The Array tool makes multiple clones of objects in the X, Y, or Z direction. In more complex applications, you can use it to create multiple copies when you rotate and scale objects. You can find the Array tool in the Tools menu.

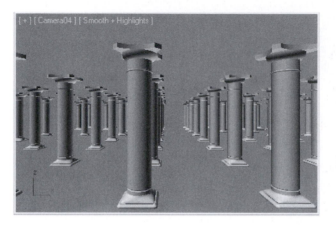

The Array tool creates clone objects in regular patterns

Spacing

The Spacing tool allows you to create multiple objects along a spline object. The objects can be separated based on distance or number of copies along the spline. The Spacing tool can be accessed in the Tools menu by selecting **Align** → **Spacing Tool**.

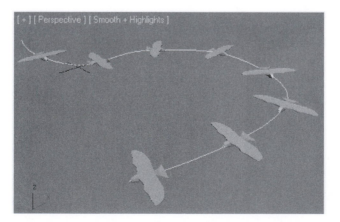

The Spacing tool allows you to create clones along a spline

Exercise | Transform with the Pick Coordinate System

1 **Open** the file *Tire Rack.max.*

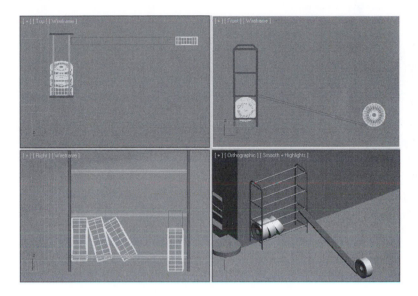

In the Tire Rack scene, a ramp has been constructed to facilitate the placement of tires on the rack. You'll want to make the tire follow the angle of the ramp.

2 Select the Tire To Move object.

3 Click the **Select And Move** button.

4 Right-click the **Front** viewport to make it active.

5 Try to move the tire up the ramp. It's a bit difficult because the tire does not follow the angle of the ramp.

6 Right-click to cancel the operation or undo any movement if necessary.

7 Make sure the **Move** tool is still active and the tire object is still selected.

8 From the **Reference Coordinate System** drop-down list, choose **Pick**.

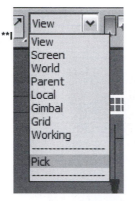

9 Click the *Ramp* object.

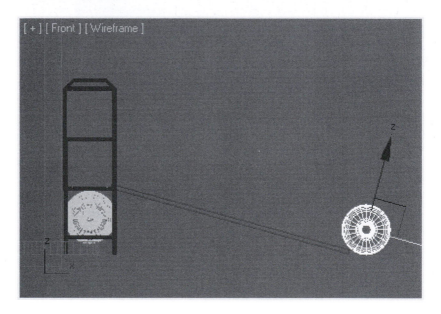

The tire's Move Transform gizmo now aligns with the Ramp object.

10 Move the tire along the ramp.

This is greatly facilitated by using the coordinate system of the ramp.

Exercise | Aligning Objects

In this exercise, you'll provide a bit more order to the layout of some pictures.

1   **Open** the file *Pictures01.max*.

A randomly spaced set of picture frames.

2   Select the *Tall Frame* object on the right.

3   On the main toolbar, click the **Align** button.

4   Click the *Regular Frame* object on the left side.

5   On the dialog that opens, make sure only **Y Position** is **on** (turn **off** X and **Y Position** if necessary), set both **Current Object** and **Target Object** to **Maximum**, and click **OK**.

Because you aligned the maximum values on the Y axis, the top edge of the Tall and Regular frames are now at the same level.

6   Select the *Elliptical Frame* object and click the **Align** tool.

7   Select the *Regular Frame* on the left.

Chapter 01 | Getting Started

8   On the **Align Selection** dialog that opens, make sure only **Y Position** is selected.

9   Set **Current Object** to **Center** and **Target Object** to **Minimum** and click **OK**.

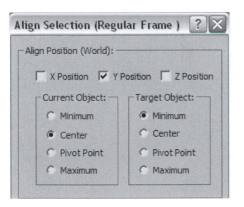

The Elliptical Frame is now centered on the bottom edge of the Regular frame.

10   Select the *Small Frame* object and click the **Align** tool.

11   Click the *Regular Frame* object.

12   In the **Align Position** group, turn on **X Position** only, set both **Current Object** and **Target Object** to **Minimum**, and click **OK**.

The Small Frame object is now left aligned with the Regular Frame object.

13   Make sure the *Small Frame* object is still selected, and click the **Align** tool.

14   Click the *Tall Frame* object.

15 On the **Align Selection** dialog, turn on **Y position** only and set both **Current Object** and **Target Object** to **Minimum**. Click **OK**.

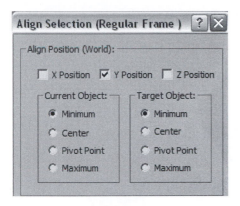

The picture frame layout is complete.

Lesson 06 | Object and Scene Organization

Introduction

In this lesson, you will learn about organization tools that are available in a scene. The organization tools allow you to easily operate or control the display on multiple objects. These organization tools will be especially useful as your scenes become more complex.

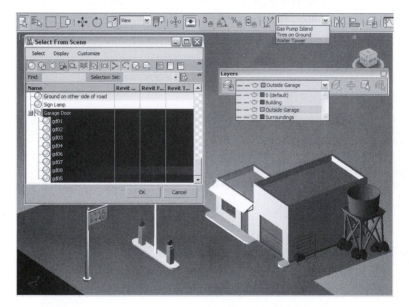

Organization Tools

Objectives

After completing this lesson, you will be able to:

- Use Selection Sets
- Assemble Objects into Groups
- Attach Objects
- Use Layers
- Manipulate the Display and Edit Status of an Object

Tools to Organize Objects in a Scene

Several tools are available to help you in organizing objects in your scene. In this section you will see three such tools, Selection Sets, Groups, and Layers.

Selection Sets

Using Selection Sets is the easiest way to organize a scene. This method does not affect your ability to transform and animate member objects. Selection sets can be created by entering a name in the Named Selection Sets drop-down list on the main toolbar. You can then use the list to choose each selection set.

Creating a Selection Set of Tires in a Scene

The Named Selection Sets dialog, accessible from the Edit menu and the main toolbar, enables you to create selection sets as does the Named Selection Sets drop-down list. In addition, this dialog lets you edit a selection set by adding and removing objects.

Named Selection Sets dialog

Groups

Naming objects and selection sets appropriately is a good starting point in a well-organized scene. Another method at your disposal is Groups. You might be able to see when these two are appropriate for given situations by looking at their relative advantages and disadvantages.

- Selection Sets always lets you pick objects in the set independently. There is nothing tying the objects together.

- A group is a single object that you select with a single click. Objects within a closed group behave as if they are one object.

- Objects in a selection set still appear separately in the Select From Scene dialog, giving you the choice of selecting them individually or as a set.

- Groups bring all the objects in the group into one named object. Twenty objects grouped together will be represented as one entry in the Select From Scene dialog.

- You must be careful when animating groups, as the group itself can be animated as well as the objects within it. Ungrouping will lose the animation of the group itself, leaving only the animation of the individual objects.

Groups are created by selecting the objects you wish to place in the group and by using the Group tool in the Group menu.

The Name you enter in the Group dialog will then appear in the Select From Scene dialog, replacing all the individual objects in the group with a single entry.

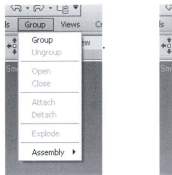

Group menu   A group displayed in the Select From Scene dialog

When you open a group, you gain access to all the individual members of the group. You can select these members in the viewport or through the Select From Scene dialog. As groups tend to be closed most of the time, you can save some time by not renaming all of the member objects in the group.

A Open Group Displayed in the Select From Scene dialog

Layers

Layers are like transparent overlays on which you organize different kinds of scene information. The objects you create have common properties including color, renderability, and display. An object can assume these properties from the layer on which you create it. Using layers makes it easier to manage the information in your scenes. Layers are used primarily to control the visibility of objects in your scene; however, they also control the objects' wireframe color and the hidden and frozen states of objects, among other options.

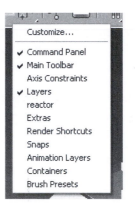

Accessing the Layers toolbar

Although layers can be used in any situation to organize a scene, they are often more popular with users coming from a CAD background. In fact, CAD files imported or linked using the .DWG™ format retain the layer information coming from applications such as AutoCAD® or Revit®.

The Layer toolbar can be toggled on or off with a right-click on an empty area of the main toolbar.

Layer States

When you import or link .DWG files to your scene, layers contained within the CAD files are retained and their hide/show state is visible in the layer list.

Icons in the Layer list of the Layers toolbar

Visible layers show no icon; hidden layers are grayed out and show a light bulb icon. A single click on the icon toggles between the two modes.

Creating Layers

Typically, you want to create your layering system before you start working on a project, but sometimes, you may need additional layers as you develop your work. One easy way to create a new layer and assign existing objects to it is to select those objects in the scene and then use the Create New Layer icon on the Layer toolbar.

Create New Layer icon in the Layer toolbar

This opens up a dialog prompting you for a new layer name but, more important, offers to move the selected objects to the new layer so that they inherit its properties.

Create New Layer dialog

The Layer Manager

As its name implies, the Layer Manager gives you the tools to manage the layers in the scene, with access to properties like visibility, freeze status, render control, and wireframe color, among others. You can also use the Layer Manager to create new layers, set a current layer, rename layers, or move objects from one layer to another.

The Layer Manager dialog

The Layer Toolbar

The Layer toolbar has less functionality than the Layer Manager but does provide you with the more common tools. You can use it to set the current layer active, change the visibility status of a layer, and create new layers in the scene. The various functions of the Layer toolbar are shown below:

The Layer toolbar

Layer Manager: Opens the Layer Manager

Layer List: Use this list to set a layer current or to change the visibility status of a layer

Create New Layer: Creates a new layer and by default moves the selected object(s) to that layer

Add Selection to Current Layer: Adds the selected object(s) to the current layer displayed in the Layer List

Select Objects in Current Layer: Selects all scene objects that are part of the current layer displayed in the Layer List

Set Current Layer to Selection's Layer: Picks up the selected object's assigned layer and makes it current

> **Note**: *By default in 3ds Max Design, an object's visibility, wirecolor, and other properties are controlled by the object's layer. If you need to control an object independently of its layer you can do this in the Object Properties dialog.*

Attaching Objects

Another strategy for organizing objects is to attach objects together into one object. When you attach objects, they lose their independence and become part of a single object. Unlike groups, which can be opened for temporary editing, attached objects must be detached to become independent again.

Hiding or Freezing Objects in a Scene

One of the reasons you organize scene objects is so that you can easily manipulate the visibility and editable status of the objects. Hiding objects will remove the objects completely from the display. Freezing objects prevents them from being selected as part of a potential selection set. When you need to hide or freeze objects in a scene, there are three main methods to accomplish this: by selection, by layer, and by category.

By Selection

You have a few choices on how you can hide or freeze objects by selection:

- You can select the objects you wish to hide and choose to hide or freeze the selection.

- You can select the objects and choose to hide or freeze all the objects except those selected.

- A hide or freeze by name option allows you to control the object from a dialog box where all the objects are displayed. This is similar to using the Select From Scene dialog.

- Hide or freeze by hit allows you to select one object at a time to be hidden or frozen.

You can access many of the operations listed above in the quad menu.

The quad menu and Hide/Freeze options

All of the Hide and Freeze tools can be found in the Display tab of the Command panel.

Hide/Freeze object rollouts in the Display panel

By Layer

The visibility and editability status of properly layered scenes can be easily manipulated in the Layers toolbar layer list or through the Layer Manager dialog.

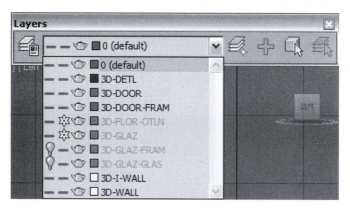

Hide/Freeze layers in the Layers toolbar

It should be noted that hiding and freezing layers and objects are somewhat independent of one another. An object can be hidden on a layer that is visible.

Layer Manager dialog showing a hidden object on a visible layer

Chapter 01 | Getting Started

By Category

Objects in 3ds Max Design can be hidden according to the object category they belong to in order to reduce display clutter. For example, while you are working on refining the geometry in a scenes you may not require the display of lights and cameras. Object categories can be hidden in the Hide Category rollout in the Display tab of the Command Panel.

Hide Category rollout in the Display Panel

Display Floater

The Display Floater dialog combines the Hide and Freeze object and category functions found above into a compact UI element that is most useful with multi-monitor systems. The Display floater can be accessed through the Tools menu.

The Display Floater Hide/Freeze and Object Level tabs

Isolate Mode

Isolate mode allows you to make a selection and quickly hide the objects not selected. This is most useful when you wish to clear your display of any objects other than the objects of interest. One of the big advantages of using Isolation mode is that it does not affect the Hide or Freeze status of objects, layers, or categories. Once you exit Isolation mode by clicking on the warning dialog, your scene returns to the same state as when you entered Isolation mode.

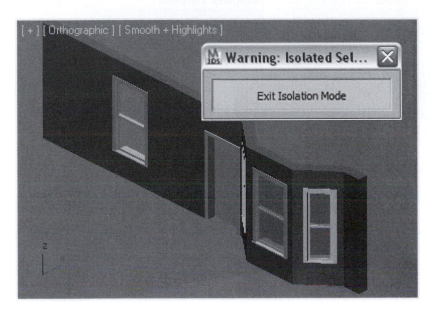

Isolation Mode warning dialog

Exercise | Selection Sets

In this exercise, you'll create a selection set and add objects to it.

1   **Open** the file *Blockout of Gas Station 03.max.*

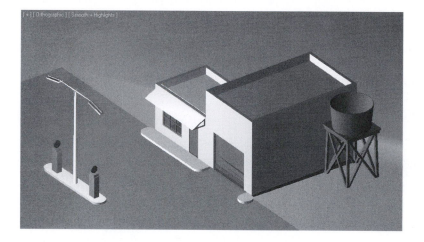

2   On the main toolbar, set the **Selection** mode to **Window**, and then use a rectangular region to select all the objects that comprise the water tower to the right.

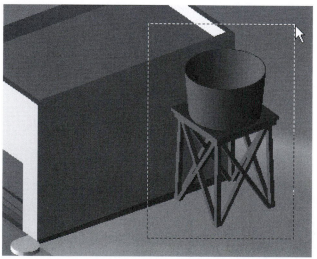

3   Go to the **Create Selection Set** drop-down list and enter *Water Tower*. Make sure to press **Enter** after you type the text. If you forget to press **Enter**, the selection set and its name won't be saved.

4   Deselect the *water tower* by selecting a different object in the scene.

5   Click the **Down** arrow at the right of the **Named Selection Sets** drop-down list, and then choose *Water Tower* from the list. The *Water Tower* is selected once again. The selection set simplifies the selection of the objects making up the water tower.

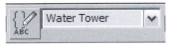

6   To the left of the **Named Selection Sets** drop-down list from the **Edit** menu, choose the **Edit Named Selection Sets** button.

7   The following dialog appears. The selection set you created appears in the **Named Selection Sets** dialog, as well as in the drop-down list.

Named Selection Sets
⊞ { } Water Tower
Ready

8   Move the dialog close to the gas pump island.

9   Select some of the objects in the gas pump island, using a **Window** region selection as shown
in the illustration. Most of the objects in the selection region will be selected except for the
island base and the left side of the light pole.

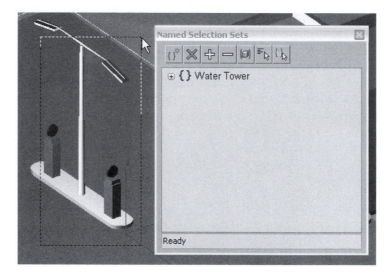

10   Click the **Create New Set** button in the **Named Selection Sets** dialog.

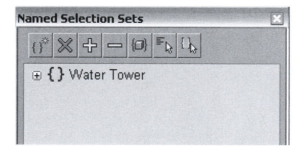

11 Enter *Gas Pump Island* in the **New Set** entry in the list.

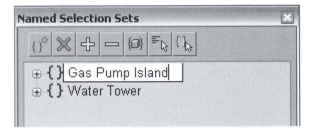

12 Click the plus sign (+) next to the *Gas Pump Island* entry to expand that selection set. Clicking the plus sign adjacent to the selection set name reveals all the objects in the selection set. This allows you to edit the contents of the set.

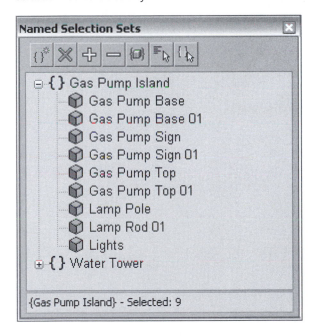

13 In a viewport, click the *Island Curb* object to select it.

14   In the dialog, click to highlight the *Gas Pump Island* selection set.

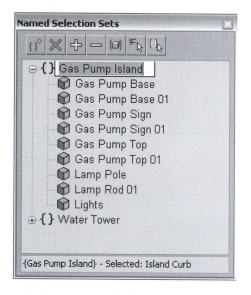

15   In the dialog, click the **Add Selected Objects** button.

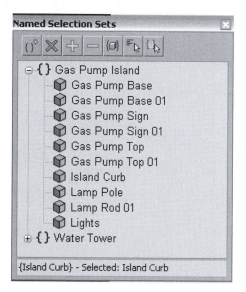

Chapter 01 | Getting Started

16 In a viewport, select the *Lamp Rod 02* and *Lights 01* objects by using a **Window** region selection as illustrated.

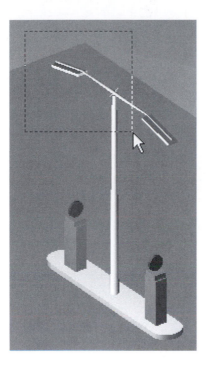

17 In the dialog, make sure the *Gas Pump Island Selection* set is still selected: then click **Add Selected Objects** once more.

18 In the dialog, click the **Select Objects by Name** button. The **Select Objects Dialog** appears.

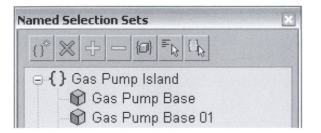

19   Select all geometric objects that begin with the word *Lamp* or *Lights*. Then click the
Select button.

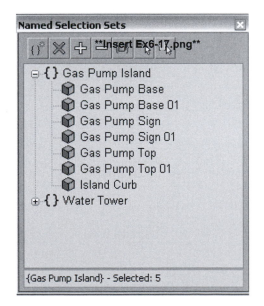

20   On the dialog, click the **Subtract Selected Objects** button to remove the lamps and lights
from the selection set.

Chapter 01 | Getting Started

21 Click the *Gas Pump Island* selection set once more.

22 Click **Select Objects in Set**.

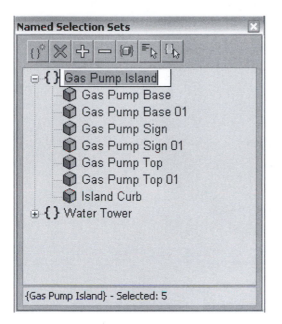

23 Only the *Gas Pump* and *Curb* objects are now selected.

Exercise | Groups

In this exercise, you'll organize objects in the scene into a group.

1   **Open** the file *Blockout of Gas Station 04.max*.

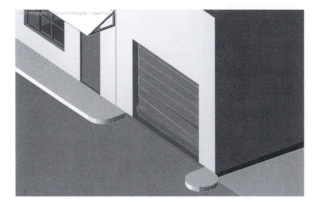

2   Press the **H** key. In the **Select From Scene** dialog, type *gd* into the find value. All objects whose name starts with *gd* are selected.

3 Click **OK**. All the garage door panels are now selected.

4 From the **Group** menu, choose **Group**.

5 On the dialog that opens, enter the name *Garage Door*.

6 Click **OK**.

7 Press **H** on the keyboard.

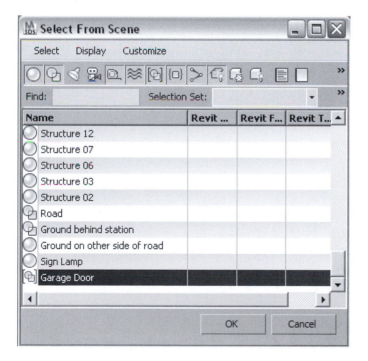

The Garage Door group appears as a single entry in the Select From Scene dialog. The objects that were used to create the group no longer appear in the Select From Scene dialog.

8   Click **OK**.

9   Click an empty area of the viewport to deselect the garage door panels.

10   Now click any one of the garage door panels. The entire garage door is selected.

11   From the **Group** menu, choose **Open**, which enables you to edit the group's individual objects.

12   Press **H** to access the **Select From Scene** dialog.

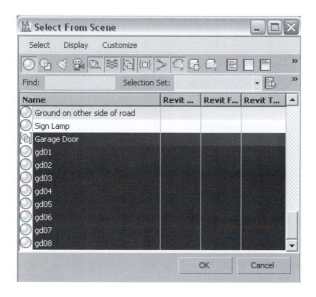

Notice how both the group and its members are displayed in the dialog.

13   In the **Select From Scene** dialog, choose **Display Children** from the **Display** menu.

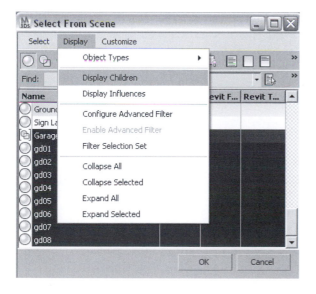

Notice how the Garage Door group now displays as a single entry with a small + sign next to it.

14 Click on the **+** sign to expand the group display.

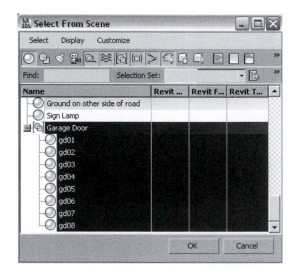

The Display Children option gives you a better idea of which objects belong to a group.

15 Select the *gd04* object from the **Select From Scene** dialog, and then click **OK**.

Note: *An open group displays a pink bounding box around the group in the viewport. You may need to switch the viewport display mode to wireframe to see this. You can now modify individual objects inside the group.*

16 On the main toolbar, click the **Select And Move** button.

17 Drag the blue vertical arrow downward. This moves the garage door panel down in the **Z** direction only.

18 Click to select the **fifth** panel of the group.

19 From the **Group** menu, choose **Detach**.

20 Press the **H** key.

21 Locate the *gd05* object. Notice how it is not part of the *Garage Door* group anymore.

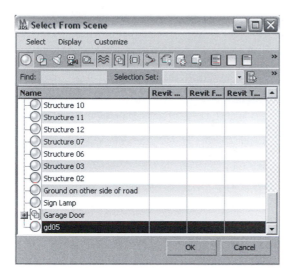

22 Click the object *gd05* in the **Select From Scene** dialog.

23 Click **OK**.

24 On the **Group** menu, choose **Attach**.

25 Press the **H** key, and select the *Garage Door* group from the **Attach to Group** dialog.

26 On the **Group** menu, choose **Close**.

27 Now that the group is closed, if you select any object in the group, the entire group will be selected as before.

Lesson 07 | Project Folders

Introduction

In this lesson, you will learn about Project folders. You can create Project folders as a way of facilitating the collection of files related to individual projects. Often a project can contain a multitude of individual files; in complex projects these files can exceed hundreds and thousands. Keeping these files organized is a major hurdle in getting the project completed efficiently.

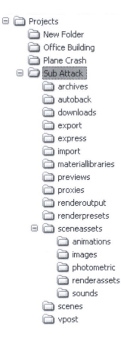

Project Folders

Objectives

After completing this lesson, you will be able to:

- Create a new Project folder
- Set a Project Folder as the Current Project

Creating a New Project Folder

You create new Project folders by using the Project Folder tool on the Quick Access toolbar.

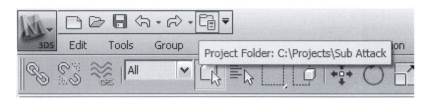

The Project Folder Tool

Once in the Browse For Folder dialog, you create new folders in the desired location and name them appropriately. Selecting a folder and clicking the OK button make that folder the current Project folder.

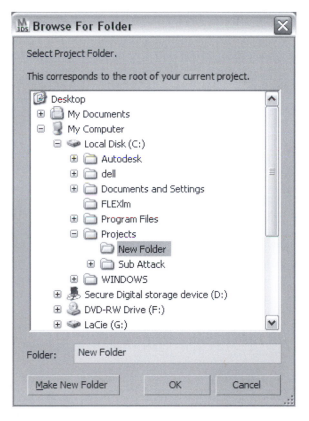

The Browse For Folder dialog

When a folder becomes a Project folder for the first time 3ds Max Design creates an underlying structure of sub folders that serves to organize the various files related to an individual project.

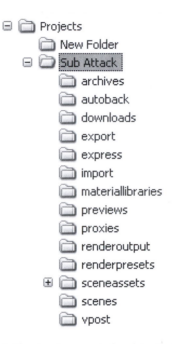

Folder structure created under a Project folder

File operations such as Save, Open, Import, etc., automatically default to this Project folder.

Save File As dialog

Changing the Current Project Folder

Switching the current project is a simple process. You select the Project folder button on the Quick Access toolbar, select the Project folder you wish to switch to, and then click OK in the Browse for Folder dialog. Your default folders are then switched to the new Project folder.

The Browse For Folder dialog

Chapter 02
Modeling

Introduction

This section is about modeling. Modeling is the first step in the design workflow. Regardless of whether you are designing buildings, or mechanical parts or laying out a golf course, you will typically model at least some of your design. There are many methods to create 3D geometry; the most important and essential methods are covered in the lessons that follow.

Objectives

After completing this section, you will be able to:

- Describe the Difference between Object Types in 3ds Max Design
- Create 3D Parametric Objects
- Use the Modifier Stack
- Use Some Essential Modifiers
- Clone Objects
- Create Low Poly Models
- Create Shapes
- Edit Splines
- Create Objects from Splines
- Create Compound Objects

Lesson 08 | Geometrical Object Types

Introduction

In this lesson, you will learn about different geometrical object types. This lesson is meant to clarify the differences between these object types and introduce you to the various sub-objects that make up these objects.

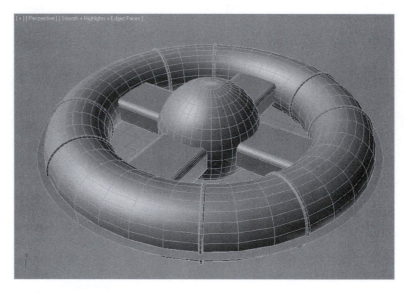

Different object types can be used to create a scene

Objectives

After completing this lesson, you will be able to:

- Describe the use of shapes.
- Describe the different 3D geometric object types
- Describe the difference between a base object and a parameter-driven object
- Attach and detach objects

Shapes

Shapes are mostly 2D spline objects with linear and curvilinear segments connecting two or more vertex points. Shapes can be made 3D, as vertex points can be distributed anywhere in space. Shapes can be defined with a thickness, thereby creating an object similar to a 3D mesh object.

The Shape object is the top-level object and contains the following Sub-Objects:

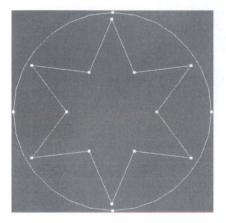

A Shape Object with Sub Objects identified

- **Splines**: A contiguous series of 2D or 3D segments between two or more vertices. A shape can contain multiple splines.

- **Segments**: A linear or curvilinear element defined by two vertices. Splines can contain one or multiple segments.

- **Vertex**: A point that defines an important location along a spline where the spline can potentially change direction. Vertices have different types that control whether a segment that starts or ends on it is linear or not. There are four types of vertex types: Linear, Smooth, Bezier, and Bezier Corner

Shape Creation

Shapes are created typically through the Create menu, or in the **Create Tab** →
Shapes of the Command panel.

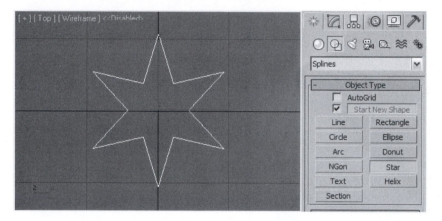

A default six-point Star Shape Object

In many cases Shape tools create parametric objects. This means that they can be adjusted through built-in parameters such as numerical inputs, check boxes, or radio buttons to change their appearance. A default six point star object can be changed to three points and have a radius at its corners rather than sharp edges.

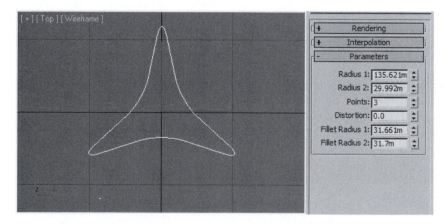

Adjusted Star Shape Object

While a shape maintains the ability to be edited by its defined parameters, you do not have direct access to the shape sub-objects. A shape must be converted to an editable spline. One way of doing this is through the right-click quad menu.

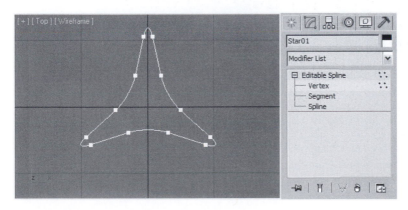

Converting to an Editable Spline

Once a shape is converted into an editable spline, the various sub-objects can be accessed.

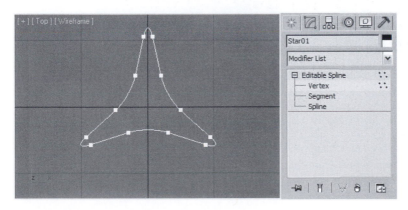

The Sub Objects of a converted Spline

A multiple spline shape is created when you use a Shape tool like Text or when you remove the check in the Start New Shape toggle in the Command panel.

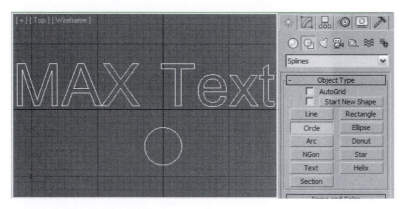

The Sub Objects of a converted Spline

By default, a shape does not render. A shape or editable spline has the ability to become renderable through a parameter in the rendering rollout.

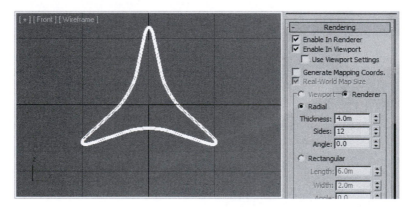

Parameters to make a spline renderable

NURBS Curves

A spline type that bears mentioning is the Non-uniform Rational B-Spline or NURBS Curves shapes found in the Create tab of the Command panel.

NURBS Curves tools

NURBS mathematics is complex; they were created specifically for digital 3D modeling. Shape curves such as the Line tool and other Shape tools are Bezier curves, which are a special case of B-splines.

3D Geometry Objects

3D geometry objects are similar to shapes in that there are parametric objects, different object types, compound objects, base objects, and sub-objects.

3D Parametric Objects

In the Create tab of the **Command Panel** → **Geometry** there are a multitude of tools that you can use to create either simple or complex parametric objects. These objects can range from a simple primitive like a sphere or cylinder to a complex foliage object found in the AEC extended rollout.

Parametric Foliage Object

Like a Shape object these parametric objects can be changed by adjusting parameters in the object's rollout.

Adjusting Parameters in the Foliage Rollout

3D Geometry Object Types

3D geometry also has different geometry types. A parametric object can be converted into a base object type in the same fashion that a shape is converted into an Editable Spline. One way of proceeding is though the right click quad menu.

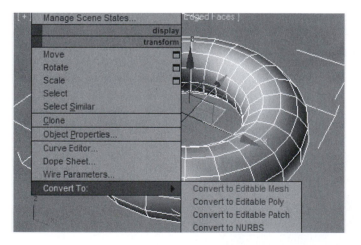

Converting 3D Geometry through the Right click quad menu

In the case of 3D geometry there are more options available. The following is a list of the geometry types available in 3ds Max Design. Most parametric objects can be converted into one or more of these object types and objects can be converted multiple times into different formats.
(i.e. an Editable Mesh can be converted into an Editable Poly and then back to an Editable Mesh)

Mesh

The basic 3D geometry object is a series of vertices and edges with the renderable surfaces of the object being either triangular or four sided (quads). The sub-objects contained in a mesh object include: Vertex, Edge, Face, Polygon, and Element.

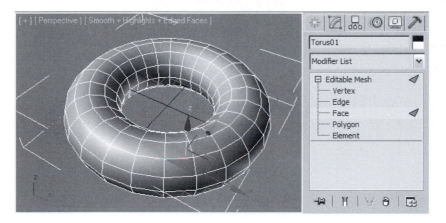

Sub Object Levels of an Editable Mesh Object

Polymesh

Similar to the Mesh object, the Polymesh object can contain polygons with any number of verticies and therefore be more than four sided. The sub-objects contained in a Polymesh object include: Vertex, Edge, Border, Polygon, and Element.

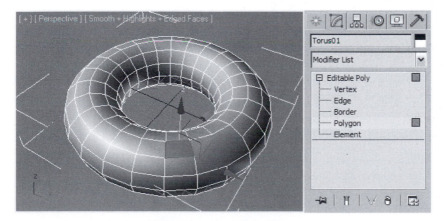

Sub Object Levels of an Editable Poly object. Note the multiple-sided polygon.

Bezier Patches

A Bezier Patch 3D object is made up of a framework of vertices and edges, with a surface. One of the unique elements in a Bezier Patch object is the handle present at each vertex of a patch. Like the vertex handle of a spline it can be adjusted to change the surface tangency and ultimately the shape of the surface. The sub-objects contained in a Bezier Patch object include: Vertex, Edge, Face, Polygon, and Element.

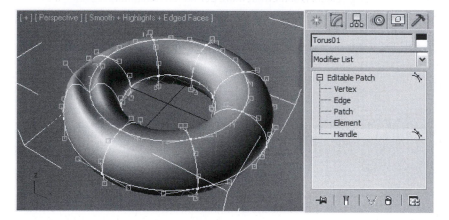

Sub Object Levels of an Editable Patch Object.

NURBS

As with the NURBS Curve, a NURBS Surface is a complex surface generated mathematically. While it is useful to know a bit about these objects, any detailed explanation about their behavior is beyond the scope of this book.

3D Object Types and Their Use

After being introduced to the various types of objects, you might be wondering which object you will want to use in various situations.

- When objects are simple and you wish to keep access to the parameters that create an object, you should use primitives and the parameter-driven objects found in the Create menu.

- When editing of objects is required at a sub-object level, you will, in most situations, want to change your object to an Editable Poly object.

There will, no doubt, be exceptions to these rules and alternative modeling strategies. This will be discussed in further lessons.

Attaching and Detaching Objects

Attaching Objects

Once you have created two or more objects you can collect your objects into a single object by attaching them. As opposed to other concepts of scene organization like the use of Selection Sets, Groups, and Layers, attaching objects is somewhat more permanent, and more it is difficult to access individual components. Occasionally, it is the only way to accomplish the intended goal.

When you attach one object to another, each object becomes a component of the whole. In the illustrated example, in the mock-up of a space station model, several objects have been attached together. The sphere at the center remains as an element of the newly formed object.

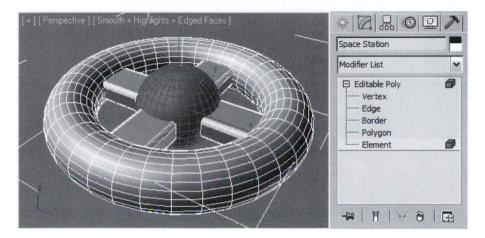

Sub Object Element

Detaching Objects

Whether you have attached objects or simply wish to extract some components from an object, you can use Detach to create a separate object from a series of sub-objects. In the illustrated example, a section of the torus's polygons has been selected.

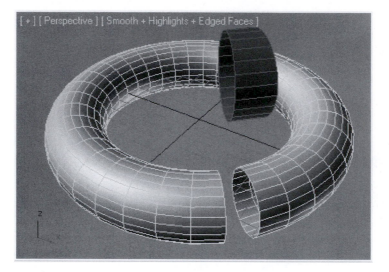

Detaching Sub Objects into a Separate Object

Note: *Attaching and detaching objects and sub-objects is only possible when objects are in their base form. Parameter-driven objects generally have to be converted to a base object before attaching or detaching or in some cases 3ds Max Design will do the conversion for you.*

Exercise | Geometrical Object Types

In the following exercise you will change object types, and attach objects together to create a simple stand-in object for a space station model.

1   **Open** the file, *Object Types_Start.max*.

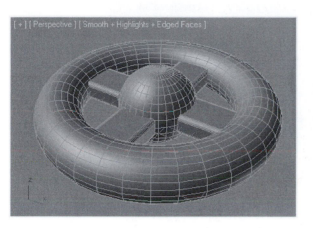

2   Select some of the 3D objects and note the object names and types.

3   In the **Perspective viewport** select the outer ring of the space station.

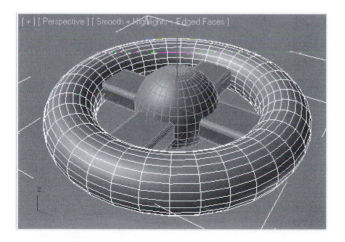

4   Right-click and select **Convert To** → **Editable Poly**.

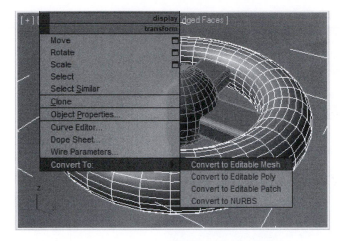

5   In the **Modify** panel, find the **Edit Geometry Rollout**.

6   Click on the small dialog button next to the **Attach** button.

7   Select all the Objects in the **Attach List** dialog and select **Attach**. All the selected geometry
is one object now.

> **Note**: *It was necessary to convert the first object from a parametric object to a base
> Editable Poly to gain access to the Attach tool. The objects you attach to the
> first object are converted by 3ds Max Design automatically. If you were to
> subsequently detach the sphere from the assembled object, its parameters
> would no longer be present.*

8   Right-click on a blank area of the **main Toolbar** and select **Layers** to display
the **Layers toolbar**.

9   Turn **off** the **Geometry** layer and turn on the **Shapes** layer.

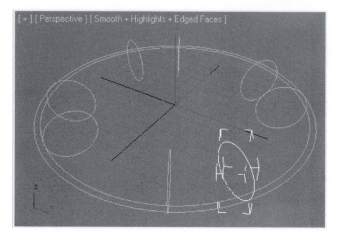

10   Make the **Shapes** layer current. The geometry of the model disappears, leaving some shapes. You will use these shapes to add detail to the model.

11   Select one of the circular shapes oriented vertically around the outside of the model.

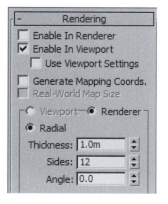

[+] [Perspective] [Smooth + Highlights + Edged Faces]

12   In the **Modifier** panel, open the **Rendering** rollout, and select the **Enable in Viewport** option.

13 Change the **Thickness** to **2m** and the sides to **6**.

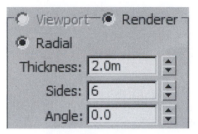

14 Select the outer Horizontal Circular shape.

15 In the **Modify** panel, **Geometry** rollout, select **Attach**.

16   Select the Inner Horizontal Circular shape. The splines are now joined together into one shape.

17   Click on the **Attach** button again to exit the tool.

18   Right -click the newly created shape.

19   Select **Covert To** → **Editable Poly**. The shape is converted to a Polymesh object.

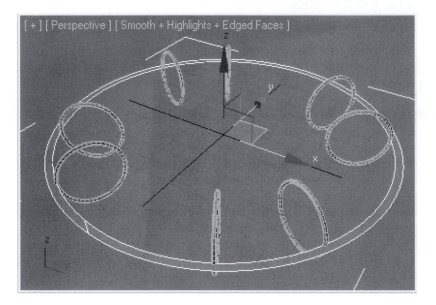

20   In the **Layer** toolbar, turn **on** the *Geometry* Layer.

21   Select the *Space Station* you attached previously.

22   In the **Geometry** rollout select **Attach**.

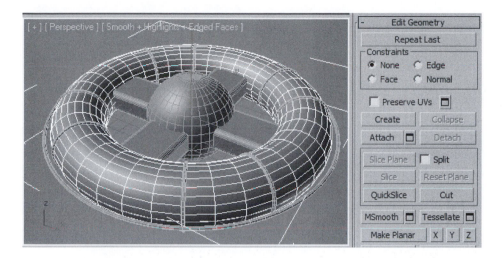

23   Select the *Horizontal Ring Platform*.

Note: *When you attach the Ring Platform to the main object, the geometry changes color. 3ds Max Design has changed the Ring Platform to the Geometry layer before attaching it to the main object.*

Lesson 09 | 3D Parametric Objects

Introduction

In this lesson, you will learn about the various 3D objects that are generated by parameters. While some of these parameter objects are simple, others are quite complex. This lesson will serve as an introduction to these objects.

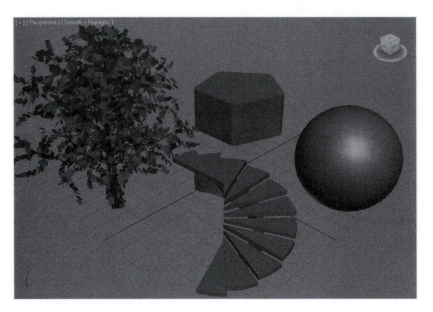

Examples of 3D Parametric Objects

Objectives

In this lesson, you will learn the following:

- How to access 3D Parametric Objects
- How to use 3D Parametric Objects
- Describe the Different Types of Standard Primitives

Accessing 3D Parametric Objects

The objects that are discussed in this lesson are contained in the Create tab > Geometry button of the Command panel, and in the Create menu. In the Command panel the geometry objects are organized by a list that appears in the Geometry panel.

The Create menu on the menu bar contains some of the same categories but organized a bit differently.

The objects that will be discussed in this section are: Standard Primitives, Extended Primitives, and AEC objects (Architecture, Engineering and Construction). Other categories in this geometry list or Create menu will be discussed in other lessons.

3D Parametric Objects in the Create tab Geometry panel

3D Parametric Objects in the Create menu

3D Parametric Objects

The following categories of 3D geometry are discussed in order of increasing complexity. In general, once the tool is selected, the object is created in the viewport by a simple click and drag process. Once you release the mouse button, the object is created. Some objects, however, will require further input. This usually requires that you move the cusor and click to establish the requested parameter.

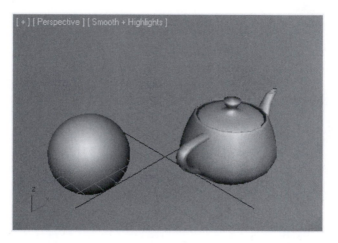

Standard Primitives that are created with a simple Click and Drag

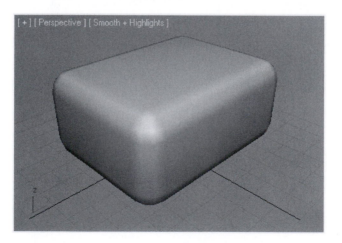

The Chamfer Box Extended Primitive that requires two additional parameters after the initial click and drag creation process.

Role of the Modify Panel

If you create a 3D Parametric object and you need to change its parameters at any time, recommended practice dictates that you go to the Modify panel. Some of the parameters in the Modify panel are not adjusted in the click and drag process -- for example, the number of segments which is used to create an object.

Generally you will adjust the number of segments in the Modify panel.

AutoGrid Feature

When you create objects, the objects are created by default in the construction plane of the viewport. With the AutoGrid feature, 3ds Max Design searches the scene for a surface and uses it as a temporary construction plane. The AutoGrid feature is turned on in the Create panel.

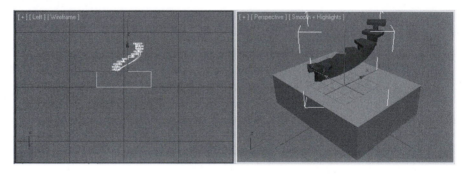

Enabling the AutoGrid Feature

Creating a Spiral Stair on top of a Box Object, note the temporary grid that appears on the top surface of the box.

Standard Primitives

Standard primitives are 3D parametric objects of the most basic variety. With the exception of the Teapot object, which has some historical significance in the 3D computer graphics industry, all the objects included in the Standard Primitives group are simple.

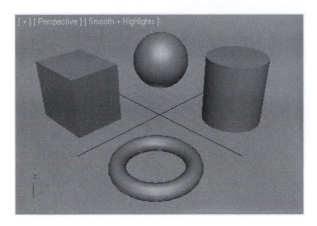

Examples of Standard Primitives

Often the standard primitives are used as starting points in creating models using polygon modeling techniques. Primitives can also be used as operands in boolean operations, or in other compound objects, or they can be modeled using modifiers in the Modifier stack.

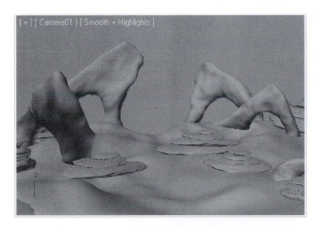

Much of this scene was developed using Standard Primitives as a starting point.

An object such as a simple sphere can be used as a basis of a more complex and organic form.

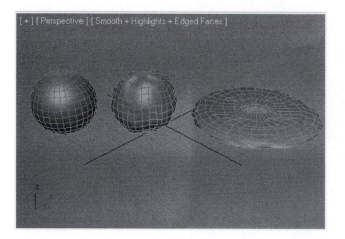

A flat rock created from a standard sphere

Extended Primitives

Extended primitives in some cases take standard primitives one step further and add some new parameters to their creation.

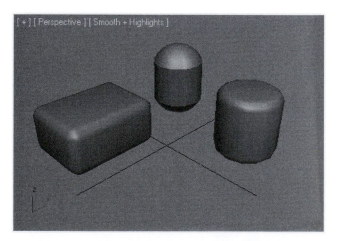

A Chamfered Box, An Oil Tank, and A Chamfered Cylinder

In other cases Extended Primitives offer a completely different object type with very different uses.

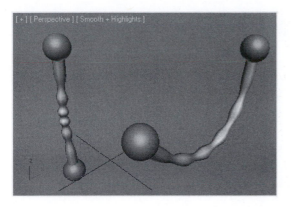

A Hose Object attached to two spheres. In this case the Hose is bound to the sphere.

AEC Objects

AEC objects appear both in the Create menu and in the Command panel. In the Create menu these objects are organized into one sub menu, while they are distributed into different categories in the Command panel.

AEC objects in the Create Menu

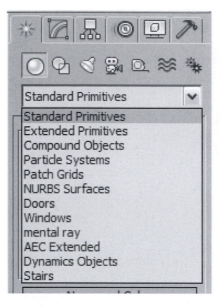

AEC objects in the Command panel

The use of AEC objects is oriented to the AEC industry, and often geometry for buildings is better created in vertical market programs like Autodesk AutoCAD Architecture or Autodesk Revit Architecture. The objects you can create with AEC objects are as follows:

- **Foliage**: This is the most generic object in the AEC objects. Although many exterior scenes of Architectural visualization require some sort of foliage to enhance the image, foliage can be used in any situation where landscapes are being created.

- **Wall**: This object creates a series of box-shaped objects that can be chained together. Walls act as parent objects for doors and windows. If the wall is transformed, the door or window will follow the wall.

- **Doors and Windows**: these objects come in a variety of types common in the AEC industry. Typically they will be inserted into a wall.

- **Stair**: The stair object creates a complex series of geometry to represent stairs.

- **Railing**: A railing object can be used in conjunction with a stair object or independently. Used independently railings can create fences over terrains.

A Scene Created using AEC Objects

Exercise | Using Parametric Objects

In this exercise, you will create a lamp post using some standard primitives.

1   Start or reset 3ds Max Design.

2   Type **Alt** + **W** to switch from a single to the four-viewport configuration.

3   In the **Create** tab of the **Command** panel select **Geometry** and then click on the **Cylinder** tool.

4   In the approximate center of the grid, click and drag out a cylinder.

5   In the **Modify** tab, change the **Radius** and **Height** of the cylinder to **6** and **6**.

6   Change the Number of **Sides** to **24**.

7   Click on the **Select and Move** tool on the **Main Toolbar**. Then **right-click** on the same button. The **Move Transform Type-In** will appear.

8   **Right Click** on the **Spinners** adjacent to the **Absolute World X** and **Y** values to change the values to **0**.

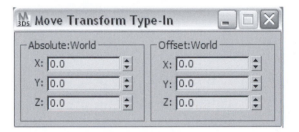

9   Your cylinder will now be centered on the origin of the **World Coordinates**.

10   Click on the **Zoom Extents All** button in the **Viewport** controls.

11   In the **Create** tab Click on the **Cone** tool.

12   **Enable** the **AutoGrid** toggle.

13   Bring your cursor to the top surface of the cylinder, and click and drag out the base of the cone, the height and the radius of the top of the cone.

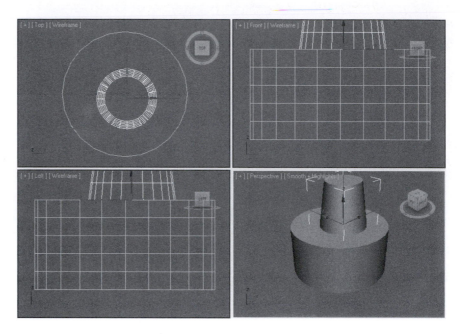

You will note that the cone places itself on top of the cylinder automatically rather than on the XY-plane.

14   Go to the **Modify** tab and change the following values for the cone:

Radius 1: 5.5
Radius 2: 2.5
Height: 3.0

15   Your **Move Transform Type-In** should still be floating on your screen. **Zero out** the **X** and **Y** values of the **Cone**.

16   In the **Create** tab, click on the cylinder, using **AutoGrid**, and the techniques above create a cylinder centered and on top of the cone **Radius 2.0 Height 108**.

17   Zoom Extents all Viewports.

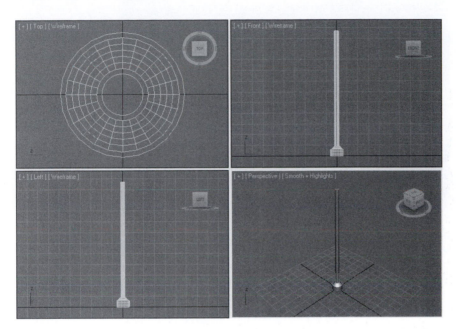

18   Zoom into the top of the cylinder in the **Perspective** viewport.

19   With **AutoGrid On**, create a **Box** on top of the cylinder of the following dimensions:

    Length: 8.0
    Width: 8.0
    Height: 16.0

20   Next, create a **Pyramid** on top of the **Box** with the following dimensions:

    Length: 16.0
    Width: 16.0
    Height: 4.0

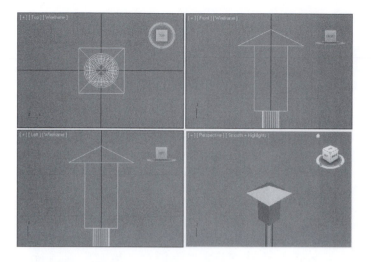

To complete the lamp you will create a spherical ornament on the top of the pyramid. To place it on the apex you will use Snap modes.

21   Dismiss the **Move Transform Type-In** dialog.

22   Right-click on the **Snaps** toggle on the main toolbar.

23   In the **Grid and Snap Settings** dialog, set the **Snaps** to be **Vertex** only and dismiss the dialog.

24 In the **Create** tab of the **Command** panel, select the **Sphere** tool.

25 Turn **Off** the **AutoGrid**.

26 Click on the **Snaps** toggle to turn it **On**.

27 Click and drag a sphere from the apex of the pyramid. When you click to set the radius, be careful not to snap on the Apex point again.

28 In the **Modify** panel change the **Radius** of the sphere to **1.5**.

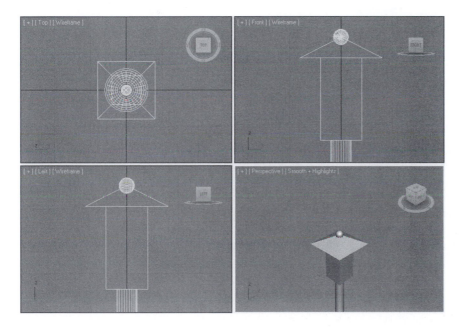

29 **Save** your file.

Exercise | Adjusting a Foliage Object

In this exercise, you will create a Foliage object and adjust its parameters to reduce the number of polygons used to the minimum possible.

1   Start or reset 3ds Max Design.

2   In the **Create** tab of the **Command** panel, in the **Geometry** pull-down list, select **AEC Extended**.

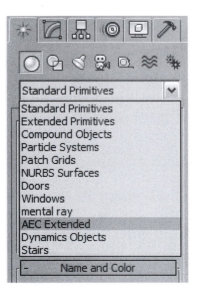

3   In the **AEC Extended** panel, select **Foliage**.

4   In the **Favorite Plants** rollout scroll down until you find the **Japanese Flowering Cherry, Spring plant**.

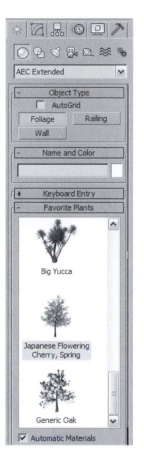

5 Click and drag the plant to the **Perspective** view. Zoom out so the plant fills the screen.

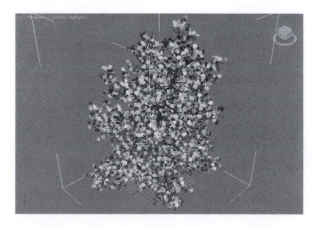

6 Right-click the foliage object and select **Object Properties** from the **Quad** menu.

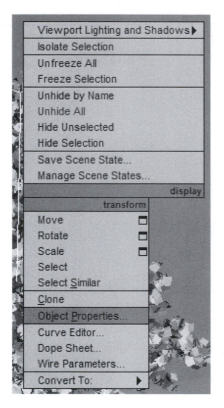

7 Note the **Faces** value at the top of the **Object Properties** dialog.

Chapter 02 | Modeling

The Faces value will be in the range of approximately 36,000 faces for this single object. An average building model may contain 100,000 faces. If you add 10+ trees to the landscape around a building, you can dramatically increase the size and rendering time of the model. You can make adjustments to the Foliage object to reduce the impact on the scene.

8   Click **OK** to exit the **Object Properties** dialog.

9   In the **Modify** tab of the **Command** panel, make the following changes to the tree:

Density:	0.4
Pruning:	0.25
Level of Detail:	Medium

10   Check the number of faces in the **Object Properties** dialog.

The number of faces should be in the 9-10,000 range. You have reduced the complexity of the object by almost 75%.

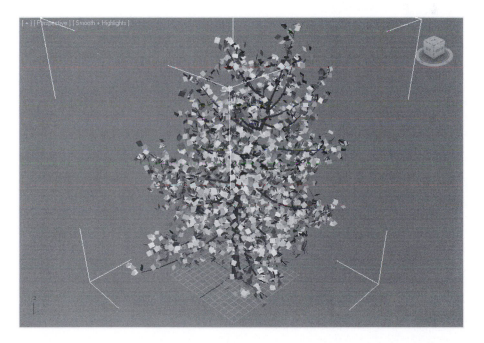

Lesson 10 | Using the Modifier Stack

The modifier stack is one of the more powerful modeling tools in 3ds Max Design®. It gives you the ability to model without destroying the original object. In addition, you can continue to tweak your model at any level of the modifier stack.

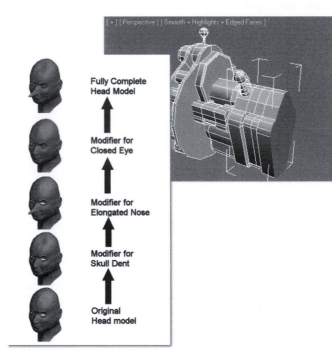

The Modifier Stack Concept

Objectives

After completing this lesson, you will be able to:

- Understand the concept of the modifier stack
- Manipulate basic controls in the stack
- Understand modifier stack order

Basic Concepts

Concepts of the Modifier Stack

Imagine a sculptor being able to add and subtract from a model without committing to any of the changes made to the model. Take a piece off here, add a piece there, and adjust this section over here. Hmmm, I don't like the piece I took away originally. I'll simply remove that action from the changes. Consider the following images, which show a series of changes or modifications to a head model made in chronological order.

The original head model

First change: original head with added dent in skull

Second change: dented head with Pinocchio effect

Third change: head with the left eye winking

In 3ds Max Design, you can make each of these three changes to the basic head object with separate modifiers. The modifiers are added, or stacked, one on top of the other. Here's how the modifiers are interpreted by the application:

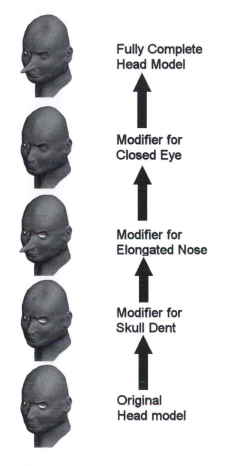

**Fully Complete
Head Model**

↑

**Modifier for
Closed Eye**

↑

**Modifier for
Elongated Nose**

↑

**Modifier for
Skull Dent**

↑

**Original
Head model**

A schematic on how the modifier stack works

The resulting head model and the applied modifiers would look like the following in 3ds Max Design. This sequence of modifiers is known as the modifier stack. The stack works from bottom to top, adding modifiers to the already modified geometry.

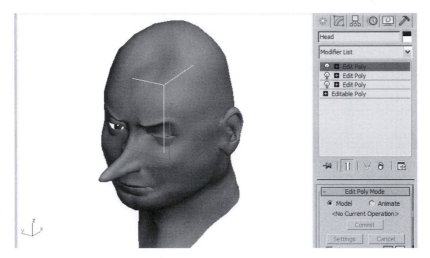

The modifier stack displaying the three modifiers applied to the original head.

As with objects, you can rename modifiers. Above is how the modifier stack might look with renamed modifiers that make it easier to remember what each modifier does.

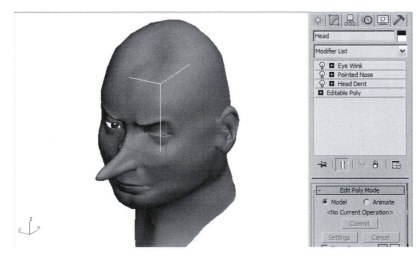

Modifier stack with renamed modifiers.

Operations

Navigation in the Modifier Stack

When you want to make a change to a modifier in the modifier stack, you'll need to return to that level in the stack. For example, if you wanted to change the length of the character's nose, you would need to select the modifier named Pointed Nose.

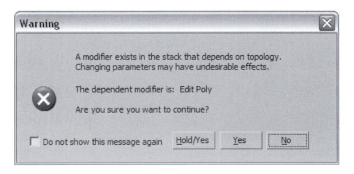

The modifier that affects the nose of the character.

Depending on the type of work you're doing, you might receive the following warning message when moving to a modifier that's lower in the stack:

Warning dialog for the modifier stack.

It's a good idea to click Hold/Yes on this dialog. This saves your work to a temporary file using the Hold command from the Edit menu.

Many modifiers have a plus (+) button in the stack that lets you expand the modifier, revealing its sub-objects.

Three modifiers applied to the original head.

Showing End Result and Turning Off Modifiers

Frequently, when you work on an object with a number of modifiers, you may want to see the result of the modifiers to a certain point in the stack. You may also want to temporarily turn off the results of one or more modifiers in the stack.

The Show End Result toggle lets you turn on/off the modifiers from the current position to the top of the stack.

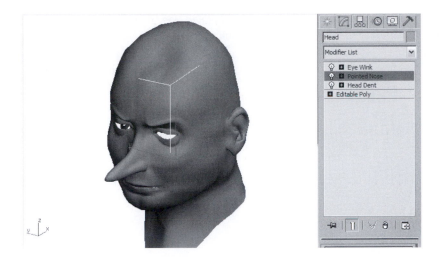

The Show End Result Toggle

Turning off the end result when you're positioned at the Pointed Nose modifier removes the result of the Eye Wink.

Next to each modifier is a small light bulb icon for controlling the visibility of the effect of a modifier on an object in the viewport. Clicking this icon turns the modifier on or off.

Visibility Icons for Modifiers

With Show End Result on, removing the visibility on the Pointed Nose modifier lets you see how the object appears with the Head Dent and the Eye Wink only.

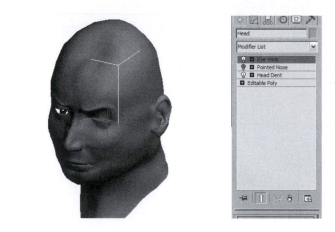

Turning off a single modifier in the stack

Copying and Pasting Modifiers

You can copy and paste modifiers from one object to another. You copy modifiers though a right-click menu in the modifier stack or by dragging and dropping the modifier.

The following illustration depicts copying and pasting modifiers on simple objects. The object on the left is a cylinder with no modifiers and the object on the right is a box with Taper and Bend modifiers. When you copy and paste the modifiers through the right-click menu, you have the option of pasting either a regular independent copy or an instanced duplicate of the modifier. Highlight the modifier to copy and then right-click in the modifier stack to open the menu.

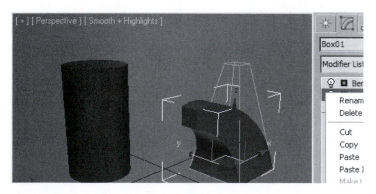

Copying a modifier to the clipboard

Select the target object, right-click the modifier stack, and choose Select Paste or Paste Instance.

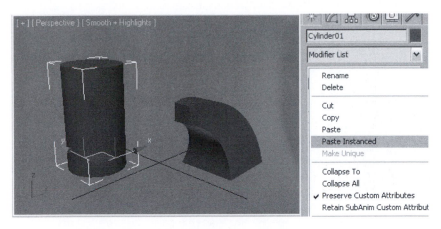

Pasting a modifier from the clipboard

When a modifier is instanced, both the original and the instanced modifiers become dependent.

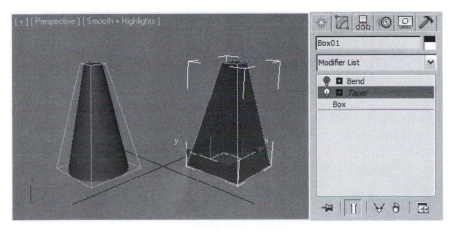

Instanced modifiers

You can drag a modifier from one object to another. If you press the **Ctrl** key and then drag, you create an instance of the modifier.

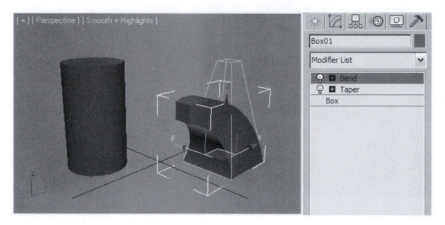

Drag the Bend Modifier from the box to the cylinder

Modifier Order

The order of modifiers in the modifier stack is important. Modifiers are added one on top of another, and the current modifier acts on the result of all evaluated modifiers before it.

We'll use a simple example to illustrate this principle. Here are two cylinders: one with the Bend modifier, the other with Taper.

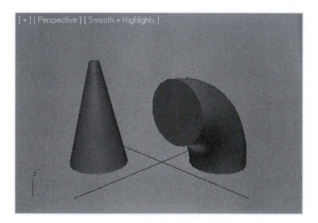

Start the process with different modifiers

Chapter 02 | Modeling

If you bend the tapered cylinder and taper the bent cylinder, you get completely different results.

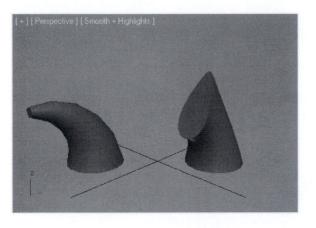

Add alternate modifiers

If you find that a modifier is not in the proper position, you can move it by dragging in the modifier stack.

Dragging a Modifier in the stack

Edit Poly Modifier and the Edit Mesh Modifier

In a previous lesson, you saw how a parametric object could be converted into a base object and the advantages of each object type. With a parametric object like a sphere you can access the radius of the sphere and change it. If the Sphere was converted to a Base Editable Poly object you can then access individual Verticies, Edges, Faces, and Elements and edit them.

You can combine the advantages of a parametric object with the advantages of an Editable Poly or Mesh through the use of the Edit Poly modifier or the Edit Mesh modifier. When you add an Edit Mesh modifier to an object you create two levels in the stack, one with the parametric object and a second where you can add edits to the parametric object as if it was converted to a base object.

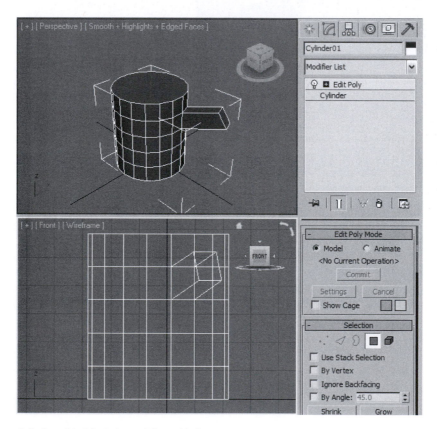

Cylinder with Edit Poly modifier Added

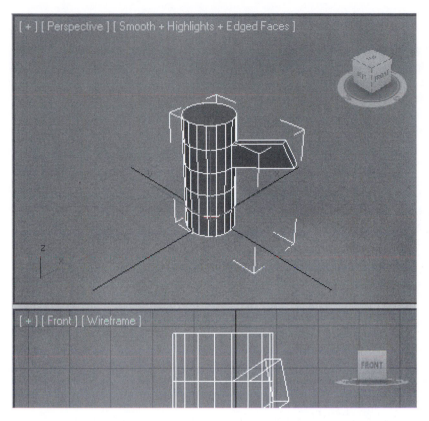

Accessing and changing the cylinder parameters

While this may appear to be an ideal scenario of combining the advantages of both types of objects, there are some things to note about working in this manner.

- A parametric object with an Editable Poly or Mesh modifier requires more computational overhead than a base object. While this may not be a problem with a single object, if many objects in the scene are constructed in this fashion, it may enlarge the file size and slow down overall performance.

- Although some parameters of a base object can be changed, this must be limited to parameters that do not change the topology (i.e. number of verticies and faces) of the parametric object.

Collapsing the Stack

There might come a time when it's no longer necessary to maintain the complexity of an object's modifier stack. The process of converting an object and all its modifiers to a single object is called collapsing the stack. When you collapse an object, it becomes one of a few base object types. It should be noted that collapsing the stack removes the ability to control an object through its base and modifiers' parameters. Therefore this should be done only when you no longer expect to modify the object with those parameters.

Collapsing the Stack

When collapsing the stack, you can combine modifiers to a given point in the stack or collapse them all. The following illustration shows a base editable poly object and three modifiers.

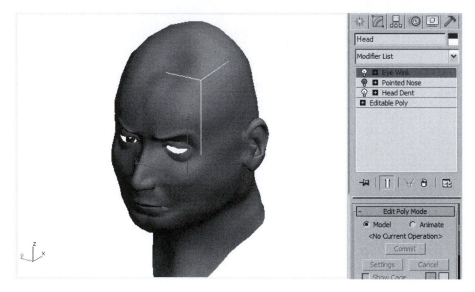

Object with 3 Modifiers

The Head Dent modifier is the highlighted level in the stack. Show End Result is off, so the effects of the Pointed Nose and Eye Wink modifiers are not visible.

If you choose to collapse to a given location in the stack, modifiers are removed up to that point, and a new base object is created.

Right-click Menu in the modifier stack.

When you collapse to the first modifier in the stack, the Head Dent modifier becomes incorporated into the new base object.

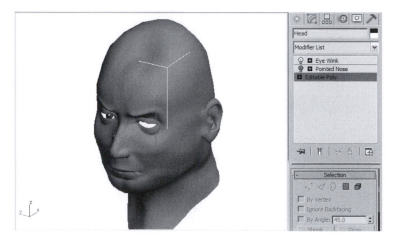

Collapsing to a point in the stack.

The result of collapsing the entire modifier stack is a new base object, with all modifiers removed from the stack.

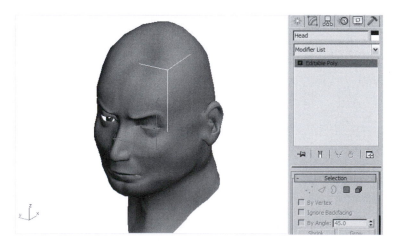

Collapsing the entire stack.

Note: *Because the Pointed Nose modifier was off when the stack was collapsed, it was not incorporated into the new base object.*

Chapter 02 | Modeling

Exercise | Accessing Sub-Object Levels

1 Open the file *LowPoly_Modeling_Start.Max*. If the **Units Mismatch** dialog appears, click **OK** to accept the default option and continue.

2 Select the object named *Energy_Globe_04*. This is a primitive sphere object.

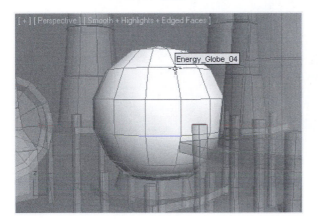

3 From the **Modify Panel** → **Modifier List**, choose **Edit Poly**.

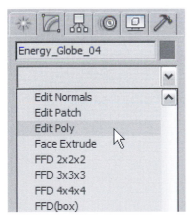

By applying this modifier, your object is no longer simply a primitive sphere. It is a sphere with the ability to access Poly object sub-objects.

4   On the **Modify Panel** → **Modifier Stack Display**, click **Sphere**. The rollouts return to their previous state, back to the primitive object level.

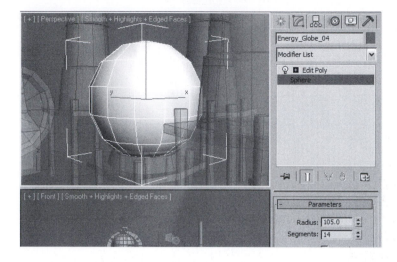

5   Change the **Radius** parameter to **100.0**.

6   In the modifier stack, right-click. Select **Collapse All**.

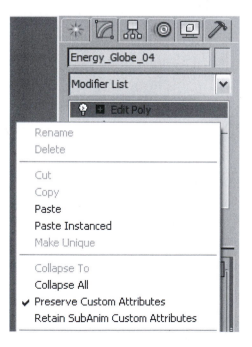

Chapter 02 | Modeling

The object is collapsed into an Editable Poly object and the definition of the primitive sphere
is lost. You can also collapse the modifiers in the modifier stack by right-clicking in the viewport
and selecting from the Quad menu **Convert To** → **Editable Poly**.

transform	
Move	☐
Rotate	☐
Scale	☐
Select	
Select Similar	
Clone	
Object Properties...	
Curve Editor...	
Dope Sheet...	
Wire Parameters...	
Convert To: ▶	Convert to Editable Mesh
	Convert to Editable Poly
	Convert to Editable Patch

Exercise | Working at Sub-Object Levels

1   Open the file *Low_Poly_Engine.max*.

2   Press the **H** key and select the *Engine_Part_01* object.

3   Go to the **Modify** panel.

4   On the **Selection** rollout, click **Vertex**.

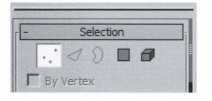

*There are several ways of making selections at the sub-object level. You can select a vertex in the viewport by clicking it, and you can select multiple vertices by dragging a region selection around the vertices. You can add vertices to a selection with **Ctrl** + **click**.*

5   In the **Front** viewport, drag a region selection box to select the vertices at the right most edge of the object, as shown in the following illustration.

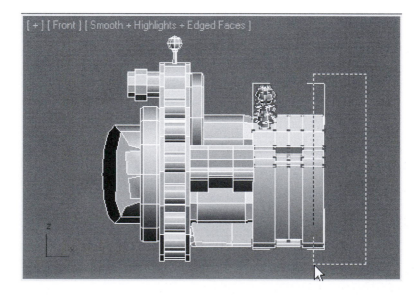

6   Move the vertices on the **X**-axis to see how this action affects the mesh.

7   Press **Ctrl** + **Z** to undo the last transform.

8   On the **Modify Panel** → **Selection** rollout, click the **Polygon** button. Click a polygon to select it. Select additional polygons by holding the **Ctrl** key and clicking to add polygons to the selection. You can also drag a region to select a group of polygons.

9   In the **Perspective** viewport, select the polygons that form the right end of the engine.

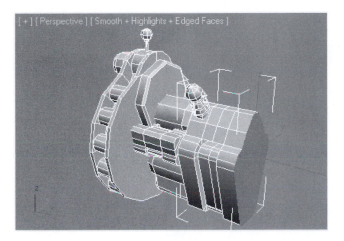

10   Hold the **Ctrl** key and click the **Edge** icon on the **Modify Panel Selection** rollout. This converts the sub-object selection; in this case, from polygons to edges. This is a good way to quickly select components at the sub-object level.

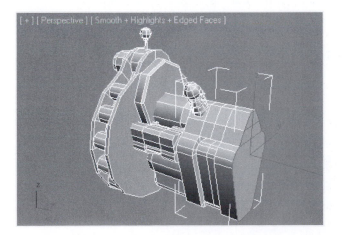

Note: *3ds Max Design offers additional options for converting selections among vertex, edge, and polygon sub-object levels. For example, by using the **Shift** key, you can convert a polygon selection into an edge selection around the perimeter of the selected polygons. Using **Shift** + **Ctrl** simultaneously lets you select the edges inside the perimeter defined by the polygon selection.*

11   Click on the **Polygon** button in the **Selection** Rollout.

12   **Shift** + **Click** the **Edge** icon to select all edges on the perimeter of the selected polygons.

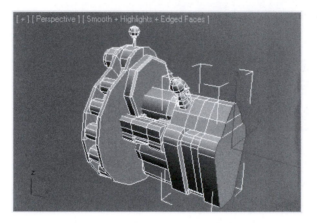

13   Click on the **Polygon** button in the **Selection** Rollout.

14   **Shift** + **Ctrl** + **Click** the **Edge** icon to select all edges inside the perimeter of the selected polygons.

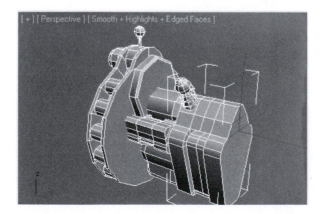

15 Go to the Polygon sub-object level. With the polygons still selected, click the **Grow** button on the **Selection** rollout. This expands your selection by adding adjacent polygons to the original. You can use the **Shrink** button to do the opposite, that is, remove the outermost polygons from the selection.

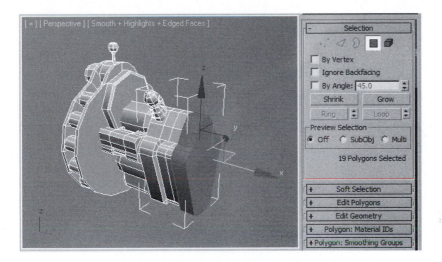

16 Click the **Element** button on the **Selection** rollout, and click the small sphere on the body of the engine. You have selected an element in the same Poly object.

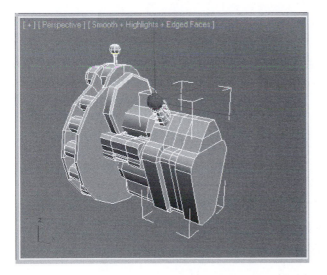

This object comprises four elements.

Lesson 11 | Essential Modifiers

Introduction

In this lesson, you will learn about several modifiers that are used frequently with 3ds Max Design. Almost every modifier has a specialized function, with the exception of a few whose functions are similar. With the compounding effect of the modifier stack, adding two or more modifiers can result in unique results every time.

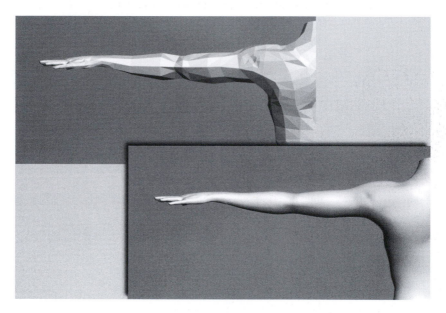

TurboSmooth Modifier

Objectives

After completing this lesson, you will be able to:

- Describe the function and use of some essential modifiers
- Use some of the basic modifiers
- Manipulate the modifier stack using multiple modifiers

Essential Modifiers

Throughout this section you will see a number of modifiers in action. Some of the modifiers used will have fairly simple parameters; others will be quite complex.

Bend

Bend is a fairly straightforward modifier. As its name suggests, it allows you to bend an object. Like most modifiers, you can animate Bend parameters. Some simple applications might be to bend a cylinder or create a dancing can, although it can be used on any kind of mesh object representing geometry, such as an animal, creature, or human. You can limit the bending to only part of an object.

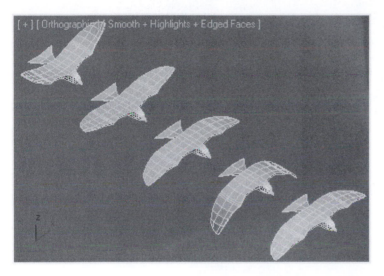

Bend can be used on an animal model, such as a bird.In this case, Bend is used to simulate flapping wings.

Taper

You can adjust the Taper modifier to create some interesting forms. You can apply a curve and limit the effect to only part of an object.

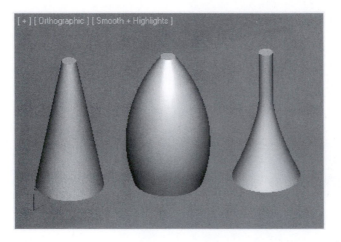

The first cylinder has a straight taper applied. On the second cylinder, the taper has been curved. On the third cylinder, the taper is limited to the lower part of the object.

Twist

The Twist modifier is a fairly straightforward modifier. It applies a helical motion to an object's vertices about a chosen axis.

A basic application of Twist

You can adjust Twist parameters to produce more complex results. The example shown here, uses the Limits settings to apply twisting to part of the box. Adjusting the Bias value produces the result on the right, shifting the twist effect away from or closer to one end of an object.

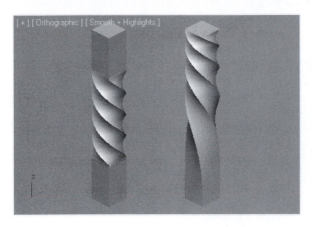

A more complex application of Twist

Normal

The Normal modifier lets you flip the renderable side of a surface of a geometric object. By default, the surface modeling in 3ds Max Design renders the outside of an object such as a box or sphere. If you positioned a view, so that you were looking from the inside of the object, flipping the normals would be necessary.

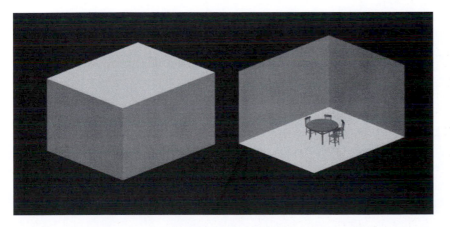

The box on the left has no modifier; the one on the right has the Normal modifier applied

Noise

The Noise modifier is useful for introducing irregularity to your geometry. You can also apply Noise to animate irregular motion, such as a lightning bolt or the effects of an earthquake. Noise works on the vertices of an object, producing different results on low and high polygon count objects.

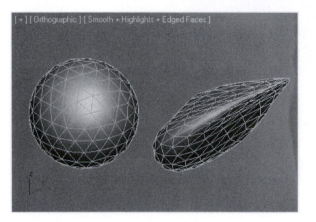

A sphere primitive turned into an irregular form (a rock or an asteroid, perhaps) after the Noise modifier is applied.

Shell

The Shell modifier allows you to take a paper-thin surface model and create a double-sided model, or "shell."

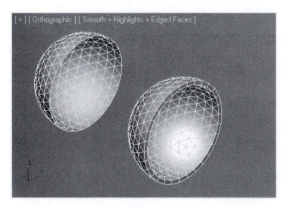

A surface model, like the hemisphere on the left, can be easily converted into a shell of the same form

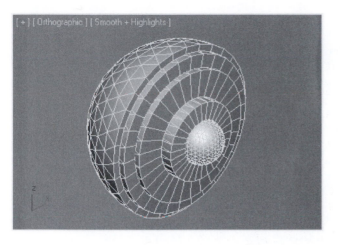

You can combine concentric spheres to create a cross-sectional model

Lattice

The Lattice modifier places geometry at an object's edges and vertices. Struts are placed along the visible edges of the geometry, and joints are placed at the vertices. You can use Lattice to create complex geometry from simple primitives.

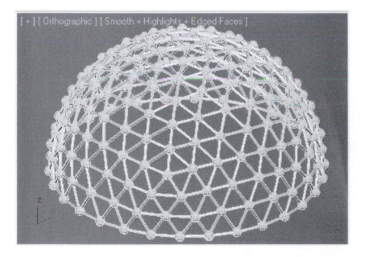

Lattice applied to a half geosphere

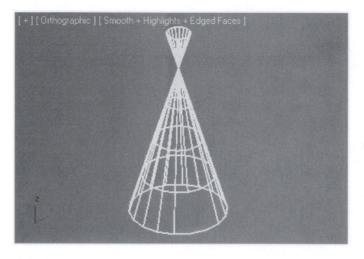

Skeletal structure quickly modeled with the aid of Lattice, using struts only

FFD

The Free Form Deformation (FFD) modifier family lets you change object shapes in a flowing manner and produce organic forms. The FFD modifier acts as a lattice with control points that you manipulate to push or pull a geometric form. You can use FFD to create complex shapes from simple objects.

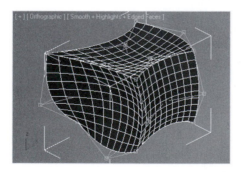

A box is deformed to create this free-flowing object. Note the locations of the control points of the lattice

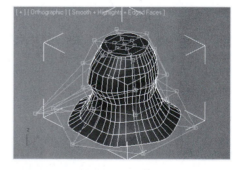

A cylinder is deformed by a cylindrical FFD modifier

TurboSmooth

You use TurboSmooth to smooth geometry in your scene. Turbo Smooth produces a Non-Uniform Rational MeshSmooth object (NURMS), similar to a NURBS object. Another modifier MeshSmooth, provides additional control over the surface of the object through adjusting weights of each control vertex.

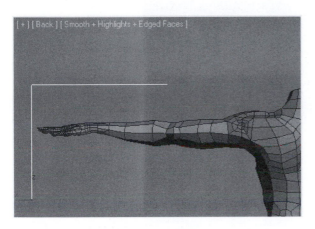

Mesh model before TurboSmooth modifier applied

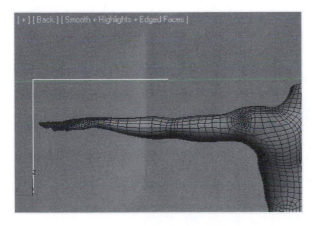

Mesh model after TurboSmooth modifier applied

Slice

The Slice modifier lets you create a cutting plane that generates new verticies at the intersection of the geometry and the plane. These new vertices can be used to refine the geometry, or split the mesh into parts.

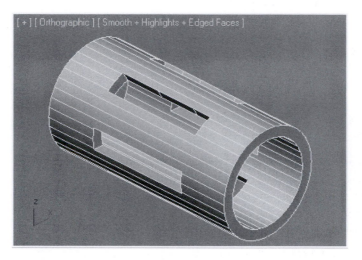

Object before application of Slice modifier.

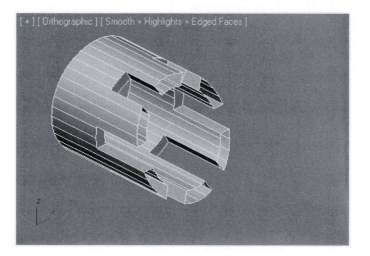

Slice modifier with slice plane moved and rotated.

Chapter 02 | Modeling

MultiRes

MultiRes is a modifier that will simplify the complexity of a model by decreasing the number of verticies and polygons used to create the object. Often while you model, you may need to create a high-resolution mesh. MultiRes gives you the ability to reduce the complexity in a mesh and allow you to adjust the level of complexity with a percentage or vertex count values.

In the example, the body of the submarine was reduced from its initial face count of 4200 to a final face count of 1048 by reducing the vertex count to 25% of the original. Note the differences in the mesh geometry, and at the same time the minor difference in the appearance of the rendered object.

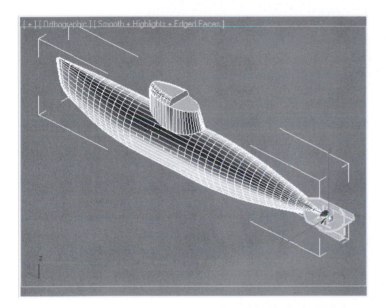

Original sub body model

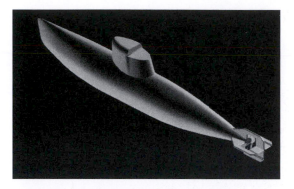

Rendering of original sub body model

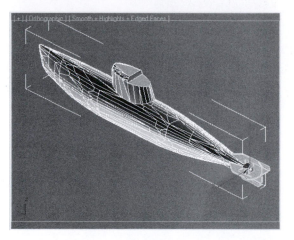

Sub body model verticies reduced to 25%

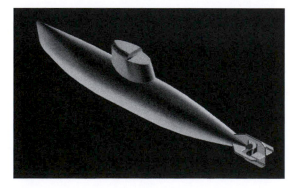

Rendering of lower-res sub body model

Exercise | Basic Manipulations of the Modifier Stack

1   Open the file *Basic Objects.max*.

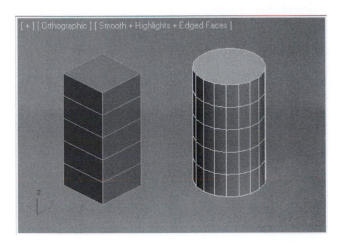

There are two simple primitive objects. Each object has five height segments.

2   Select the **box** object on the left.

3   On the **Modify** panel, click the **Modifier List**.

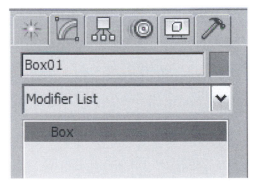

4   Near the bottom of the list, select **Taper**. A new **Taper** modifier is applied to the base object.

Subdivide
Substitute
SurfDeform
Symmetry
Taper
Tessellate
TurboSmooth
Turn to Mesh
Turn to Patch
Turn to Poly

5   On the **Parameters** rollout, decrease the **Amount** value to make the object narrower at the top.

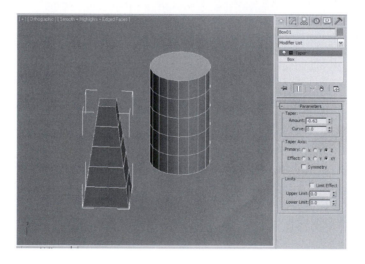

6   From the **Modifier List**, choose **Twist**. A **Twist** modifier is applied on top of the **Taper** modifier.

7   Change the **Angle** value to approximately **45** degrees.

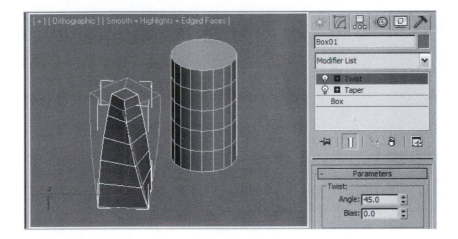

8   Add a **Bend** modifier to the top of the stack.

9   Change the **Angle** value to approximately **–90** degrees.

10   Right-click the **Bend** modifier entry in the stack and choose **Rename**.

11   Rename the modifier to *Bend 90* and press **Tab** to exit the value.

12   Select the **Twist** modifier in the stack.

13   Increase the **Angle** value to **360**.

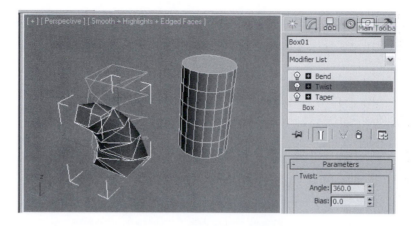

A twist angle of 360 causes distortion in an object with this number of faces. The box needs more height segments.

14   Select the *Box* entry in the modifier stack.

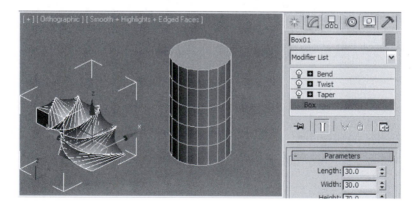

15 Change the **Height Segs** value to **30**. The twisted form looks better now.

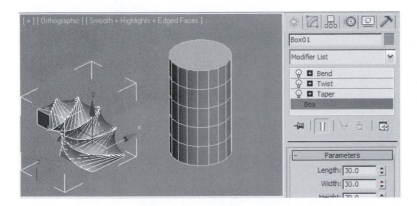

16 Click the *Bend 90* entry in the stack.

17 Drag the *Bend 90* modifier onto the cylinder.

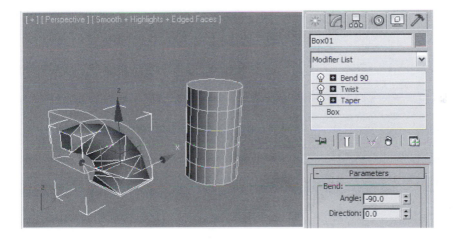

18 The **Bend** modifier is copied from the box object and applied to the cylinder.

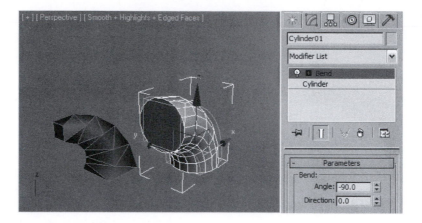

19 Select the modified box object.

20 Click the **Taper** modifier in the stack.

21 Right-click the stack and choose **Copy**.

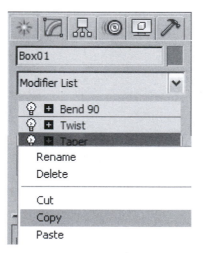

22 Select the Cylinder object.

23 Right-click the stack and choose **Paste Instanced**.

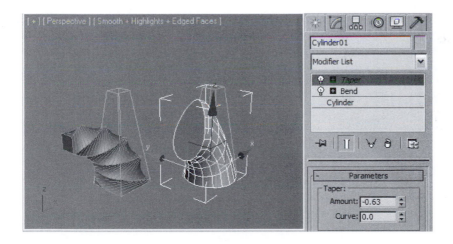

The bent and tapered cylinder doesn't look right. You'll compare it to the bent and tapered box by temporarily turning off the box's Twist modifier.

24 Select the box.

25 Click the **light bulb** icon next to the **Twist** entry.

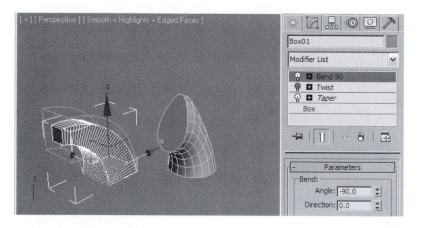

The Twist modifier now has no effect on the box. The objects look different due to the order of the Taper and Bend modifiers in the stack.

26 Select the cylinder object.

27 Click the **Bend** entry and drag it above the **Taper** entry.

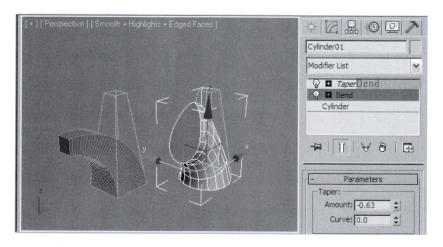

The Taper and Bend modifiers on the cylinder object are now in the correct order.

28   Select the box object and click the **light bulb** icon next to the **Twist** modifier to activate it.

29   Click the **Taper** modifier. Note that it's italicized to remind you that this modifier is instanced in the scene.

30   Change the **Amount** value of the **Taper** modifier to **-0.8**. Both the Box and Cylinder objects are affected.

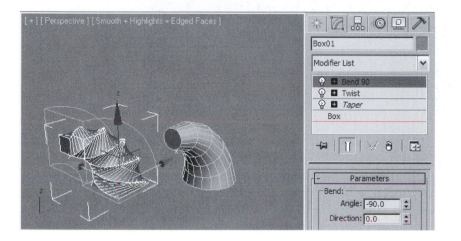

The Taper amount changed on both objects because the modifier was instanced when it was pasted.

Exercise | Modeling with Modifiers

1   Open the file *Cactus.max*. The scene contains a basic cactus object. You'll be building a tumbleweed with a primitive and two modifiers, as well as improving the cactus with a modifier.

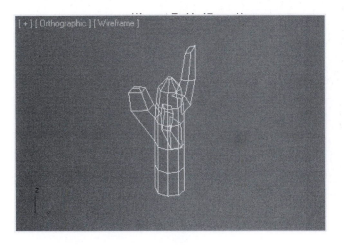

2   On the **Create** panel, click the **GeoSphere** button.

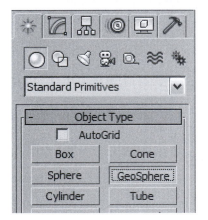

3   Turn on **Base To Pivot**.

4   In the **Orthographic** viewport, drag out a **geosphere** of approximately **20** units in radius.

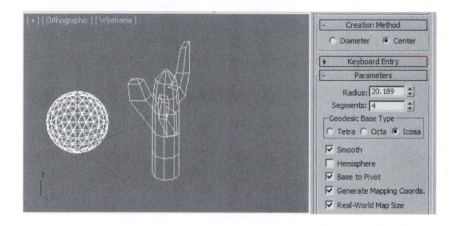

5   Go to the **Modify** panel, and from the **Modifier List** choose **Noise**.

6   Change the **Seed value** to **1**.

7   Set the **Strength → X/Y/Z** values to about **30**. You'll start to see some distortion in the sphere.

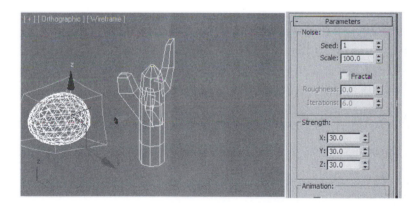

8   Turn on **Fractal**.

9   Change the **Roughness** value to **0.2** and **Iterations** to **8.0**.

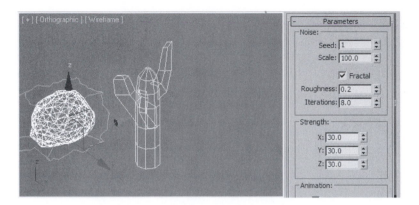

10   The Fractal mode and parameters make the noise pattern more irregular.

11   Rename this object *Tumbleweed*.

12   Press the **F3** button to set the **Orthographic** viewport to **Smooth + Highlights** display.

13   From the **Modifier List**, choose the **Lattice** modifier.

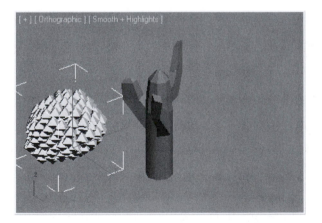

To make the distorted sphere look like a tumbleweed, you'll need to adjust the Lattice modifier's values.

14 On the **Parameters** rollout, choose **Geometry → Struts Only From Edges**.

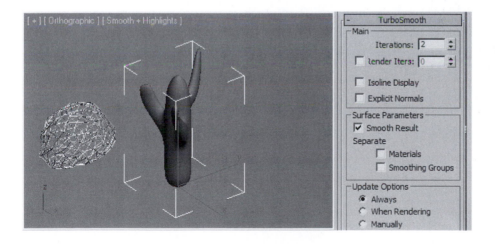

15 Change the **Struts → Radius** value to **0.2**.

16 Select the **Cactus** object.

17 From the **Modifier List**, choose **TurboSmooth**.

18 Change the Iterations value to **2** or **3** to see the result, and then return the value to **1**, which is adequate for this exercise.

> **Note:** *Typically it's not a good idea to set an Iterations value larger than **3**, as this dramatically increases the number of faces on an object.*

Lesson 12 | Object Cloning

Introduction

In this lesson, you will learn about the duplication of objects in 3ds Max Design, referred to as object cloning. There are three methods you can use when you clone an object; copy, instance, and reference. Each of these methods will have implications in how the duplicated objects behave if they are subsequently modified.

Object Cloning

Objectives

After completing this lesson, you will be able to:

- Describe the different object clone types
- Use the various clone tools
- Create and modify clones of objects

Basic Clone Types Explained

You use cloning to duplicate objects. One way to clone an object is to hold down the **Shift** key while moving, rotating, or scaling an object. Another is the Clone Selection command on the Edit menu. In 3ds Max Design, you can create a clone in one of three states: Copy, Instance, or Reference.

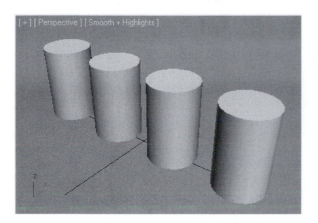

Duplicated Cylinders

The behavior of cloned objects when modified differs depending on which clone option is chosen.

Copy

When you make copies of objects, the new objects and the source objects are completely independent of one another.

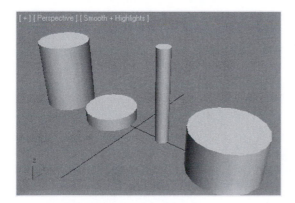

Copied Cylinders

Objects that are copied when cloned have complete independence. In the above illustration, each cylinder's Radius and Height values were adjusted, affecting the others.

Instance

When you choose to instance objects as you clone them, all the objects are linked together. Any change to one is reflected in the others.

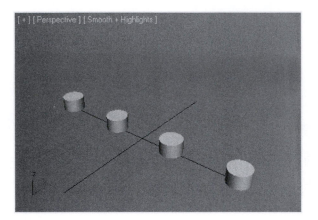

Instanced Cylinders

Objects that are instanced when cloned have complete dependence on one another. If you change the Height or Radius value of one cylinder, the others change as well.

Reference

When you choose to reference objects as you clone them, you create a link between objects that allows some flexibility in the cloned objects.

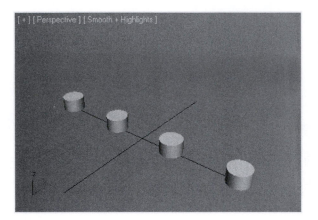

Reference in the Modifier Stack

Objects that are cloned with the Reference option display a gray horizontal bar in the modifier stack - in this case, just above the cylinder.

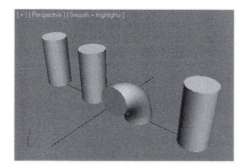

Reference Cylinder and with a bend modifier added

Modifiers applied when the gray bar is highlighted appear above the bar and are unique to that object.

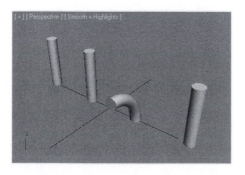

A Bend modifier is added to one of the referenced cylinders

Modifications to the base object or modifiers applied below the gray bar will affect all objects. In this case, the radius of the initial cylinder has been changed.

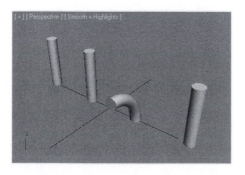

Parameters of the referenced cylinder are changed

Clone Tools

Make Unique

When you're working with instanced and referenced objects and you want to make a duplicate that is independent of the others again, you can use the Make Unique tool found on the Modify panel. Make Unique converts an instance or reference to a copy.

Make Unique button in the Modifier panel

Select Dependents

When you work with instance and reference objects, you may want to know which objects in your scene are dependent. You can check Select Dependents by using a toggle in the Select menu of the Select from Scene dialog.

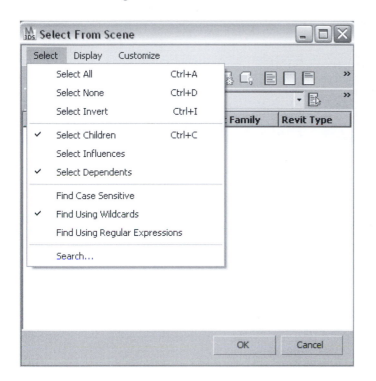

Select Dependents toggle

When Select Dependents is on, clicking any of the referenced cylinders highlights all of them.

Instanced or referenced objects are selected with Select Dependents on.

Copy and Instance Modifiers

Modifiers can also be copied and instanced. Refer to the lesson on the modifier stack for further information.

Clone and Align

The Clone and Align tool lets you distribute source objects to a selection of destination objects. For example, you can populate several rooms simultaneously with the same furniture arrangement by replacing 2D temporary symbols with 3D chair objects.

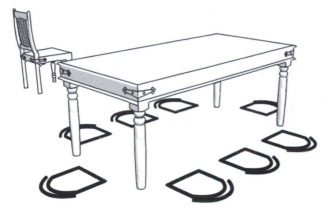

Prior to the Clone and Align tool being applied.

Temporary 2D symbols are placed around the dinner table as placeholders for the Clone and Align tool. This is done so the scene is less geometrically heavy (that is, it contains fewer polygons), potentially speeding up viewport interaction. The Clone and Align tool is found in the Tools menu under the Align selection.

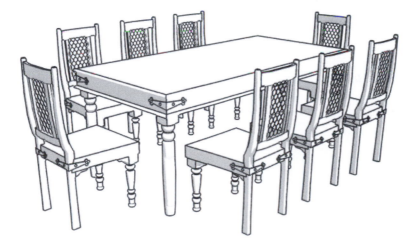

After the Clone and Align tool is applied, the 3D chairs are distributed around the table.

Exercise | Cloning Objects

1   **Open** the file *Bird.max*. The scene shows a low-resolution version of a bird.

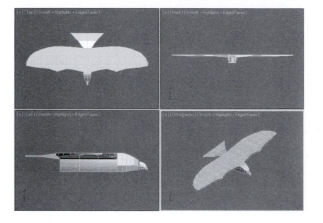

2   Zoom out all the views, so that you see plenty of space around the bird.

3   Select the bird.

4   Click the **Select And Move** button.

5   Hold the **Shift** key down and drag the bird down along the **Y-axis**. When you release the mouse button, the **Clone Options** dialog appears.

6   In the *Object* group, select **Copy** and change the **Number of Copies** to **2**.

7   Maximize the **Orthographic** viewport and then **Zoom Extents**.

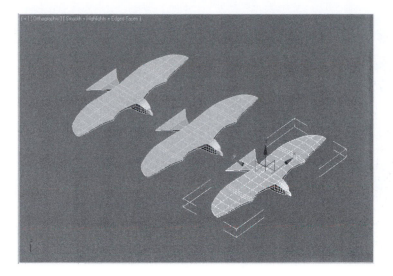

The clones you just made are separate copies of each other and entirely independent. For example, if you add a modifier to one of these birds, the remaining birds will be unaffected by it.

8   Select the bird closest to you.

9   In the **Modify** tab of the **Command** panel, select the **Bend Modifier** from the **Modifier** pull-down list.

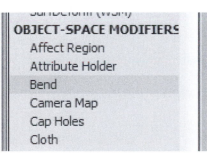

10   Change the **Bend Angle** to **60**.

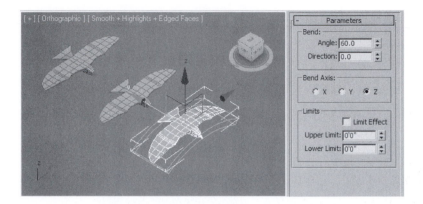

 Note: *The front bird is changed while the remaining two are unaffected.*

11   Access the **Top** view. Zoom out so there is enough room to the right of the viewport to make two additional copies.

12   Verify the front bird is still selected. If not, select it.

13   Hold the **Shift** key down and drag a clone of the bird to the right.

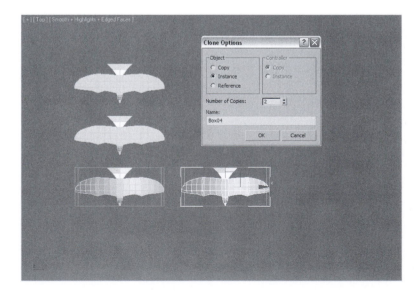

Chapter 02 | Modeling

14   In the **Clone Options** dialog, select **Instance**.

15   Change the **Number of Copies** to **2** and click **OK**.

16   Access the **Orthographic** view.

17   Click the **Zoom Extents** button.

18   Change the **Bend Angle** using the spinners. All three instanced birds are affected by the change in the bend parameters.

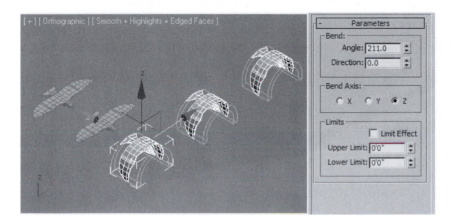

19   Go back to a **Top** view.

20   Create two clones of the birds along the second row, selecting **Reference** in the **Clone Options** dialog.

21   Create two clones of the birds along the third row, selecting **Copy** in the **Clone Options** dialog.

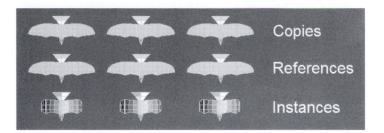

Copies are independent; Instances are completely linked. The references' underlying structure is linked, but other elements added to the referenced object are independent of the base object.

22   Switch to an **Orthographic** view.

23   Select the bird in the second row on the right.

24   In the **Modifier** panel, add a **Bend** modifier to it.

25   Change the **Bend Angle** to **-90**.

The Bird's Bend Modifier along the second row is completely independent. It has not been added to the other objects.

26   Select the bird in the second row on the left side.

27 In the **Modifier** panel, click the pull-down list and add a **Stretch** modifier to the bird.

Spherify
Squeeze
STL Check
Stretch
Subdivide
Substitute
SurfDeform

28 In the **Stretch** parameters, change the **Stretch** value to **-0.2**.

Parameters

Stretch:

Stretch: -0.2

Amplify: 0.0

Stretch Axis:

X   Y   Z

29 All the birds in that row now have a smaller wing span.

The second row illustrates the relationship between reference objects. If the base object is modified, all of the reference objects are modified. You have the flexibility to add modifiers to a reference object's clones; the modifications are independent of the base object.

Lesson 13 | Low Poly Modeling

Introduction

Of the various 3D modeling techniques, low poly modeling is the one that is perhaps most widely used in game production. Low poly modeling is important in the design industry as well in order to keep complex models from generating too many polygons and slowing down screen responsiveness and rendering times.

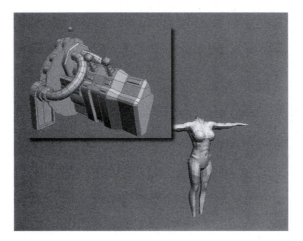

Low Poly Models

Objectives

After completing this lesson, you will be able to:

- Identify types of surfaces
- Navigate the various mesh sub-object levels
- Understand mesh sub-object modeling versus modeling with modifiers
- Make selections at the sub-object level
- Use the Polygon Counter utility
- Use smoothing
- Create a simple 3D environment
- Use subdivision surfaces

Objects and Sub-Objects

In a previous lesson, object types were discussed and sub-objects were identified in each object type. In this lesson, we further discuss sub objects and provide illustrations of how these sub-objects can be manipulated to produce low polygon models.

A complex object can be represented with a small number of polygons if carefully constructed.

In this lesson, you'll learn about the fundamental sub objects that make up geometry and how to manipulate them. When you model in 3ds Max Design, you can create a complex object by refining a primitive object. An example of this is box modeling This is a modeling technique that starts with a box that you edit to create a rough draft of the final model. The primary function of box modeling involves extruding and scaling the flat planes (polygons) that make up your model. You can fine-tune the model by editing the edges that bind the polygons, or vertices—points in space typically placed where edges intersect. To access the sub-objects mode on an object, you can either add a modifier, such as Edit Poly to your object, or turn the object into an Editable Mesh or an Editable Poly by collapsing the stack.

The difference between an Editable Mesh and an Editable Poly are subtle, as they have some of the same sub components like Vertices, Edges, and Polygons. Historically, Editable Meshes came first but Editable Polys are the better solution as they provide you with better tools to create 3D models.

It should be noted that once you begin editing an object's sub-objects, you cannot transform the object as a whole until you exit the sub-object level.

Sub-Object Levels

Each sub-object level in an editable poly object is appropriate for specific modeling tasks. There are five sub-object levels, including Vertex, Edge, Border, Polygon, and Element.

Vertex: Vertices are points in space defined by XYZ coordinates. They make up the structure of an object at its most basic level. When you move or edit vertices, the faces they form are also affected.

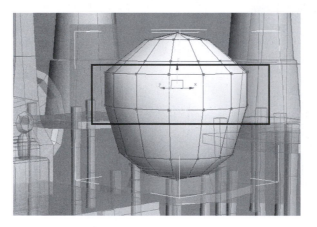

Sub-Object Vertex mode

Edge: An edge is a line that connects two vertices, forming the side of a face. Two faces can share a single edge and can be visible or invisible. Edges can be manipulated in much the same way as vertices, but they have their own set of unique parameters.

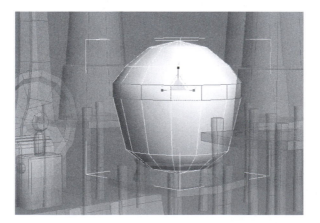

Sub-Object Edge mode

Border: A border is a continuous series of edges that surrounds an open hole in geometry. This is usually a sequence of edges with polygons on only one side. For example, a box doesn't have a border, but if you create an object, such as a box or a cylinder, and then delete an end polygon, the adjacent row of edges forms a border.

Polygon: A polygon is comprised of all the faces in an area surrounded by visible edges. Polygons offer a more robust method of dealing with object surfaces.

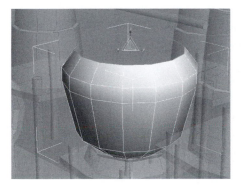

Sub-Object Border mode

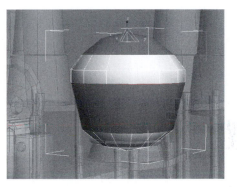

Sub-Object Polygon mode

Element: An element is an individual poly object (that is, a group of contiguous faces) that's part of a larger object. When a separate object is joined to a poly object with the Attach function, it becomes an element of that poly object.

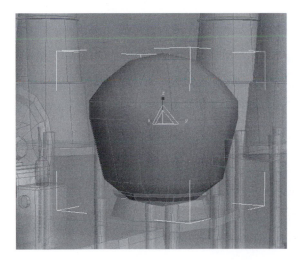

Sub-Object Element mode

Smoothing Groups

Smoothing is a rendering trick that blends between faces to produce an even, curved surface from flat polygons. This is a concept that is used as an integral visual component, for example, when you model a curvilinear mechanical part and want to give it a smooth appearance. This can be accomplished by applying smoothing groups to different parts of the model. The result is a better-looking model without additional geometry.

As you model, you'll notice that each time you create a new 3D primitive, the default object is smoothed. However, when adding polygon geometry with an Edit Poly modifier, the new polygons created are not automatically smoothed: They require manual intervention.

Using Subdivision Surfaces

As you build low poly models, there will be occasions when you'll want to create a high poly model. This brings up the question of what kind of surface you want to work with. You can use splines or patches or start with a primitive and apply modifiers to model the shape you want.
For many modelers, it's preferable to start modeling a low-resolution version and then add detail to generate a high-resolution version.

You can increase the resolution of a low poly model by adding modifiers. The modifiers available to increase resolution are:

- **MeshSmooth**: increases the resolution of geometry by adding faces at corners and along edges and blending them together.

- **TurboSmooth**: is a condensed version of the MeshSmooth modifier. It is faster and more memory efficient, but has fewer parameters.

- **HSDS (Hierarchical Subdivision Surfaces)**: is meant as a finishing tool. Use this modifier to add detail and adaptively refine the model in specific areas.

- **Tessellate**: adds geometry by subdividing polygons.

Exercise | Basics of Low Poly Modeling

In this exercise you will take a partially complete model and add some details by transforming some of the scene objects. Remember that maintaining a low poly count is your main goal.

1 Open the file *Low_Poly_Engine.max*.

2 Click the **General Viewport** label (**+** sign at the upper left of the viewport), and choose **Configure** at the bottom of the menu.

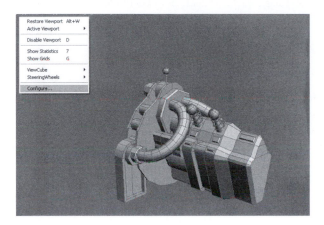

3 Click the **Statistics** tab in the **Viewport Configuration** dialog.

4 Set the **Setup** option to display the **Total + Selection** and click **OK**.

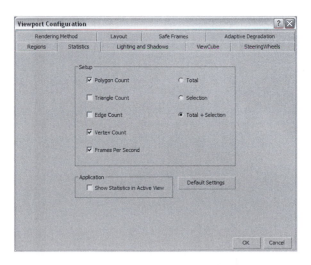

This setup option controls the viewport polygon counter that you will display momentarily. Statistics for both the selected object and the whole scene will be displayed.

5   Activate the polygon counter in the viewport by pressing the **7** key on your keyboard. The polygon counter below the viewport labels shows the scene statistics.

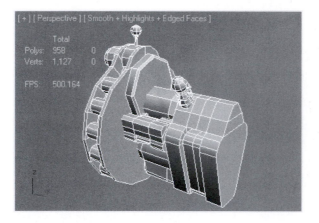

6   Press the **H** key to open the **Select From Scene** dialog.

7   Select *Engine_Part_01* object and press **OK**.

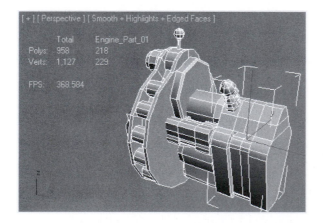

Note the display of the selected object in the viewport polygon counter.

8   Go to the **Modify** tab of the **Command** panel.

9   Click on **Polygon sub-object level** and select the front polygons in the **Perspective** viewport.

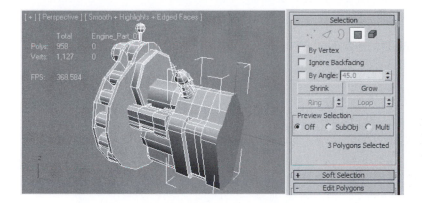

10   On the **Edit Polygons** rollout, click the **Extrude** button.

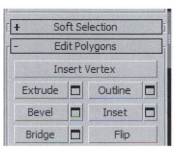

11   Place the cursor over the selected polygons, and click and drag upwards to set the extrusion height. You have created an extrusion of the selected faces.

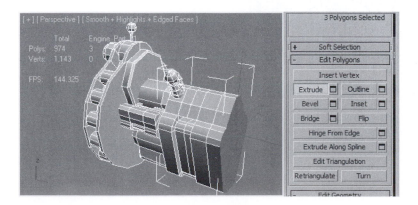

12 With the polygons still selected, click **Outline** on the **Edit Polygons** rollout.

13 Place the cursor over the selected faces, and then click and drag downward to perform the outline operation.

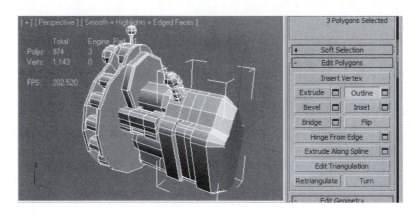

Note: *The Outline operation scales the selected polygons in their own plane. Be careful not to let edges cross.*

14 Click the **Settings** button next to the **Extrude** button to open the **Extrude Polygons** dialog.

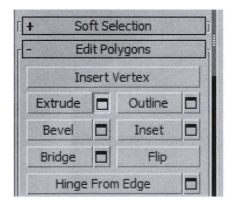

15 Set **Extrusion Height** to **50.0** and click **OK**.

Extrude Polygons ✕

┌─ Extrusion Type ─┐   Extrusion Height:
    ⦿ Group   ┌─────────┐ ▲
    ○ Local Normal   │ 50.0   │ ▼
    ○ By Polygon   └─────────┘

   [Apply]   [OK]   [Cancel]

> **Note:** *Many functions have a Settings button. These dialog boxes are modelless, letting you test your work before committing to it. An extrusion using the Settings button can also be more precise than dragging in the viewport, because you can specify the exact value.*

16 Click the **Bevel** button. Drag the selected polygons slightly as when performing an extrusion, release the mouse button, and then move the mouse vertically to outline the extrusion. Click to finish.

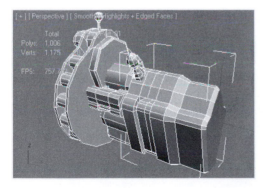

> **Note:** *You may find that you have coincident vertices that were created after using the extrude tool. Coincident vertices are two vertices that lie on top of each other but are not welded in any way. If this happens you will need to weld them together using the Weld tool; otherwise, you may get unexpected results when trying to Bevel the geometry.*

Exercise | Adding Detail to the Engine and Optimizing the Mesh

1.   Open the file *Low_Poly_Engine_00.max*.

2.   Using the **Ctrl** key, select the **5** polygons as shown in the illustration.

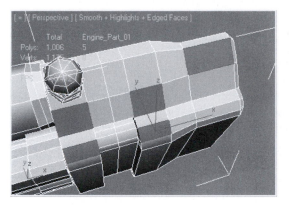

3.   On the **Edit Polygons** rollout, click the **Inset** button, and then drag vertically on any polygon to inset it. With multiple polygons selected, dragging on any one insets all selected polygons qually.

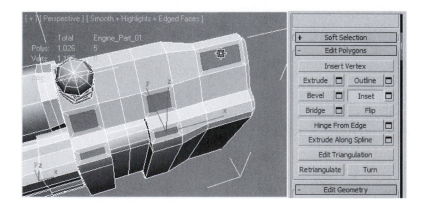

4.   Use the **Inset** button to perform a bevel with no height within the plane of the polygon.

5   Without deselecting the currently selected polygons, click the **Bevel** button. Click and drag to create an initial extrusion, and then move the mouse gently to outline the selected faces.

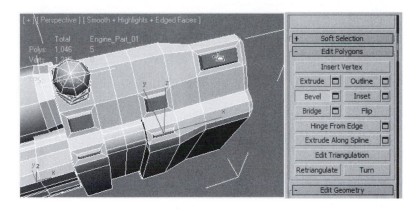

6   Now that you've added some detail to the object, you might want to optimize it a little. Deleting faces you won't see is a simple way to reduce the polygon count of a model.

7   Go to the **Edge** sub-object level.

8   Select the edges on the side of the engine as shown in the illustration.

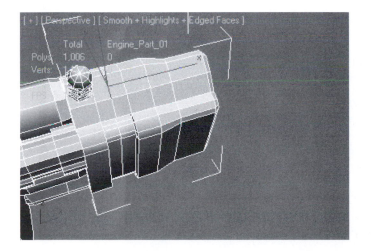

9   On the **Selection** rollout, click **Loop**. This function extends your current edge selection by adding all the edges aligned to the ones originally selected.

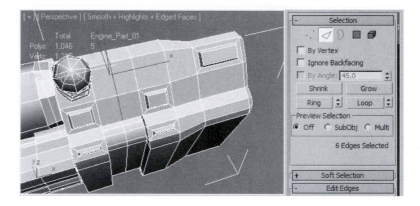

10   Hold the **Ctrl** key and click the **Remove** button on the **Edit Edges** rollout.

Note: *Holding the **Ctrl** key performs a "clean" remove, deleting the edges and removing any superfluous vertices that would have remained if you used the standard Remove function.*

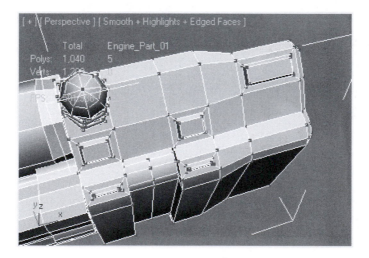

Notice how unwanted vertices are cleaned in correct illustration.

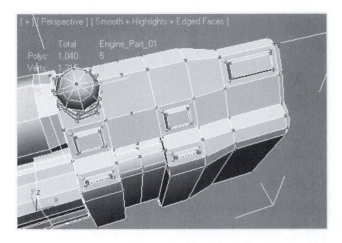

11   Right-click the *Engine_Part_01* object in the viewport, and choose **Isolate Selection** from
      the Quad menu. This temporarily hides all other objects in the scene while you work on the
      selected one.

12   Orbit around the object to see the polygons that are in contact with the rest of the
      engine parts.

13   Go to the **Polygon** sub-object level, and using the **Ctrl** key, select the three inner
      polygons as shown.

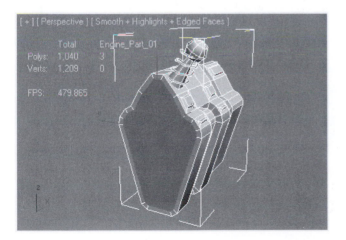

14 Expand the polygon selection to those around the perimeter by clicking **Selection Rollout** → **Grow**. Note the number of Polygons used to create a back face of this part.

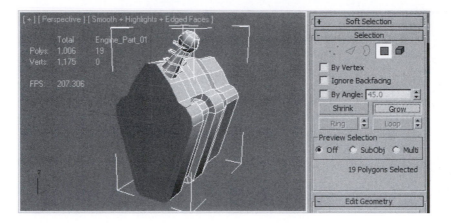

15 Delete the selected faces by pressing **Delete** on your keyboard.

16 Go to **Border** sub-object level and select the new border as shown below.

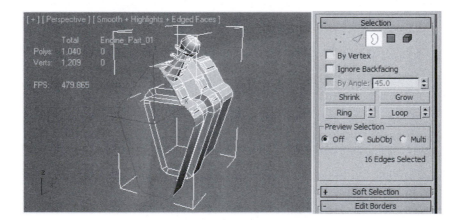

17 On the **Edit Borders** rollout, click the **Cap** button. The border is now capped with a single polygon. The total number of Polygons in the model is reduced.

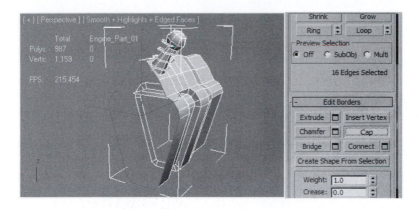

18 Go to the **Element** sub-object level.

19 Select the small sphere, spring, and cone elements.

20 Clone the selected elements by **Shift** + **dragging** the elements to the position shown below. On the **Clone Part of Mesh** dialog, click **OK** to accept the defaults.

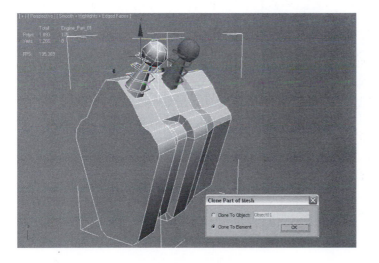

21 Exit the sub-object level and then exit **Isolation** mode.

22 Use the **Save As** command to save your progress. Name the new file *My_Low_Poly_Engine.max*.

Exercise | Modeling with Modifiers

In this exercise, you'll be adding components to the engine by reshaping objects with the help of modifiers. Keep in mind that to obtain satisfactory results when deforming with modifiers, some objects might need additional subdivision.

1   Open the file *Low_Poly_Engine_01.max*.

2   Go to the **Create panel** → **Geometry** → **Standard Primitives** category and click the **Cylinder** button.

3   Turn on the **AutoGrid** option.

Note: *AutoGrid lets you automatically create, merge, or import objects based on the surface of another object by generating and activating a temporary construction plane based on the normals of the face you click. This serves as a more efficient way of stacking objects as you create them, rather than building objects and then aligning them as a separate step.*

4   Position the cursor on the octagonal plate in the **Perspective** viewport. Notice how the axis tripod adapts to the orientation of the various faces in that area.

5   Create a cylinder on that plate. Note the temporary construction grid that allows you to align the cylinder base to the face of the plate.

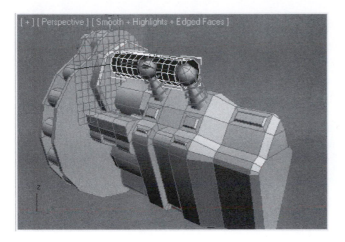

6   Go to the **Modify** panel and adjust the parameters of the cylinder. Set **Radius** to **20.0**, **Height** to **250.0**, **Height Segments** to **12,** and **Sides** to **10**.

7   Right-click the **Select and Move** icon.

8   In the **Move Transform Type-In** change the **Y** value to **50**, the **Z** value to **-167.5**. Exit the Dialog.

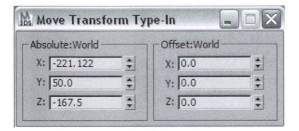

9   Add a **Bend** modifier. Set **Angle** to **180.0**.

10 Press the **A** key to enable **Angle Snap**. This lets you rotate the object in 5 degree increments.

11 In the **Perspective** viewport, rotate the cylinder by **–135** degrees on the **X**-axis, represented by the red circle on the Rotate gizmo.

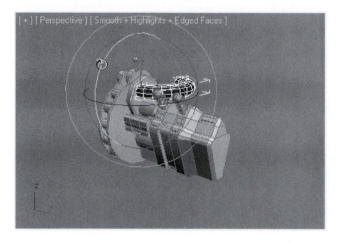

As you rotate the bent cylinder, note that there are two places where you can keep track of the angle of rotation.

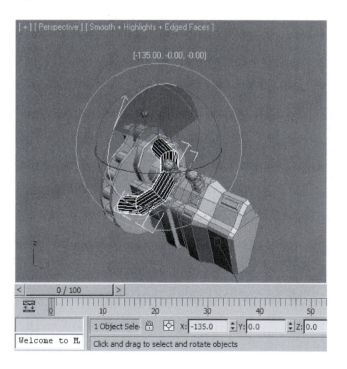

12 In the modifier stack display, click **Cylinder** to adjust the cylinder's creation parameters.

13 Set **Radius** to **15.0** and **Height** to **235.0**.

14 Click **Bend** in the modifier stack display.

15 Add an **Edit Poly** modifier.

16 Go to the **Polygon** sub-object level.

17 Change the **Perspective** viewpoint so it resembles the following illustration, and then select the top polygon of the cylinder.

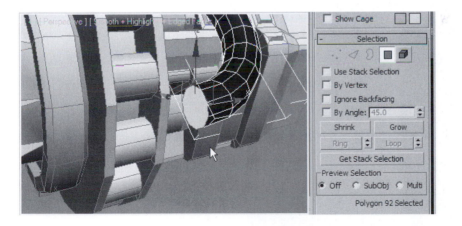

18 Click the **Extrude Settings** button. **Extrude** the polygon by **20** units and click **OK**.

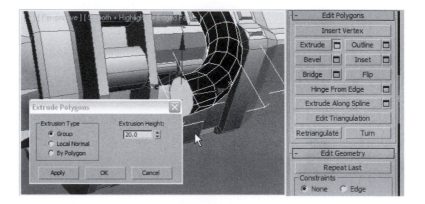

19 Press **Delete** on the keyboard to delete the selected polygon.

20 In the **Front** viewport, select the newly extruded polygons.

> **Note:** *Since you are in a sub-object mode you need not worry about selecting other objects or their sub-objects. Sub-object mode locks selection to the current object only.*

21 Click the **Extrude Settings** button again.

22 Choose the **Local Normal** option, set **Extrusion Height** to **7.0**, and click **OK**.

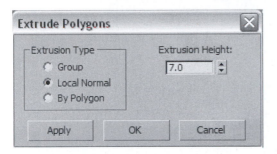

23 Go to the **Edge** sub-object level, and select the edge shown in the following illustration.

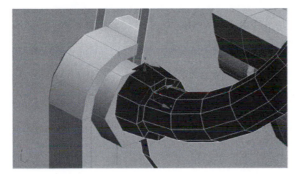

24 Click **Loop** on the **Selection** rollout to quickly select the edges around the cylinder.

25 On the **Edit Edges** Rollout, click the **Chamfer** button. This tool lets you cut off the selected edges and create a new set of faces in their place.

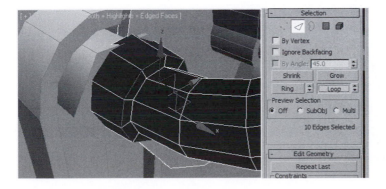

26   Place the cursor over the selected edges and click and drag gently upward.

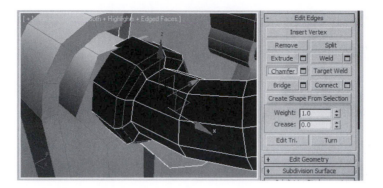

27   Click on the **Edit Poly** entry in the **Modifier** stack to exit sub-object mode.

28   Right-click in the **Top** viewport to activate it.

29   Activate the **Mirror** tool. In the **Clone Selection** group, choose the **Copy** option. This duplicates the object to the other side of the engine.

30   Set the **Mirror Axis** to **Y**, the **Offset** to **40**, and click **OK**.

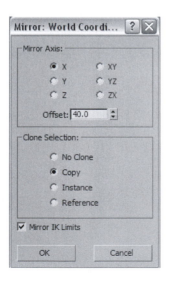

31   Select the *Engine_Part_03* object.

32   On the **Edit Geometry** rollout, click the **Attach List** button.

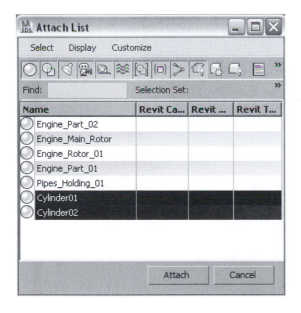

33   In the **Attach list** dialog, select *Cylinder01* and *Cylinder02*.

34   Click **Attach** to accept the changes and exit the dialog. The two cylinders are now attached to *Engine_Part_03*.

35 Right-click in the viewport to activate the Quad menu. Choose **Unhide All** to unhide the *Pipes_Holding_01* object.

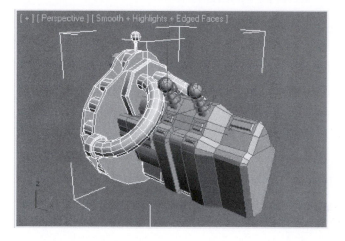

36 Save your progress. Name the new scene *My_Low_Poly_Engine_01.max*.

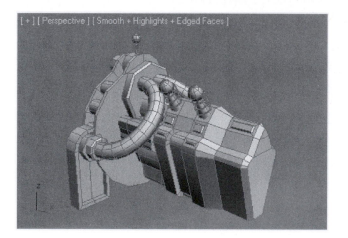

Exercise | Repairing the Broken Part

In the following exercise, you'll encounter a small problem. The original engine mesh supplied for this lesson has a broken rotor, that you'll have to fix.

1   Open the file *Low_Poly_Engine_02.max*.

2   **Arc** rotate around the object, in the **Perspective** viewport to look at the left part of the engine. Select the *Engine_Main_Rotor* object.

3   Right-click the selected object and choose **Isolate Selection** from the **Quad** menu.

4   Go to the **Polygon** sub-object level. In the **Front** viewport, region-select all the irregular polygons that make up the rotor cap.

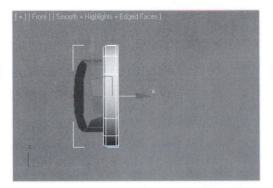

5   **Delete** the selected polygons.

6   Go to the **Border** sub-object level, and click a point on the circle that was left vacant when you deleted the polygons in the last step.

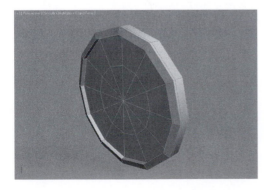

7   In the **Front** viewport, hold the **Shift** key and move the selected edges to the left (on the **X**-axis) to extrude the rotor cap.

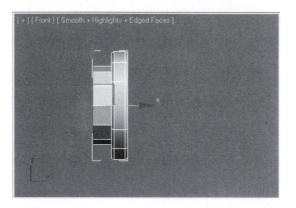

8   On the **Edit Borders** rollout, click **Cap**. This caps the entire selected border with a single polygon.

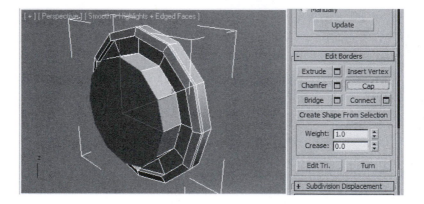

9   Go to the **Polygon** sub-object level, and select the new polygon.

10   Use **Extrude** and **Bevel** the selected polygon as you learned to do earlier to add the finishing touches to the rotor part.

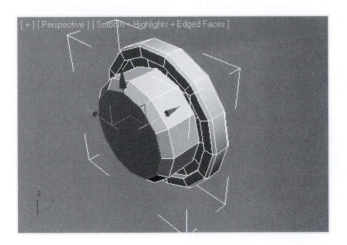

11   Exit the sub-object level, and then exit **Isolation** mode. The engine is now completed.

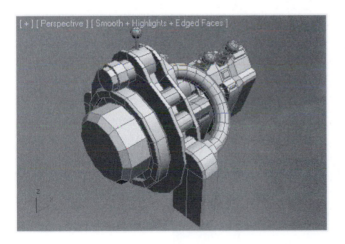

12   Save your progress. Name your new scene *My_Low_Poly_Engine_02.max*.

Exercise | Using Smoothing Groups

1   Open the file *Girl_Model.max*. If the **Units Mismatch** dialog appears, click **OK** to accept the default option and continue. The model is faceted as no smoothing has been applied yet.

2   In the **Perspective** viewport, select the *Girl_Model* object.

3   Go to the **Modify** panel.

4   Set the sub-object level to **Element**.

5   Select the model element by clicking on it. The model is made of only one element.

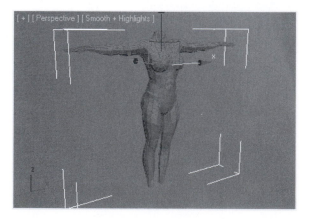

6   On the **Polygon: Smoothing Groups** rollout, click the **1** button. The smoothing on the model has changed.

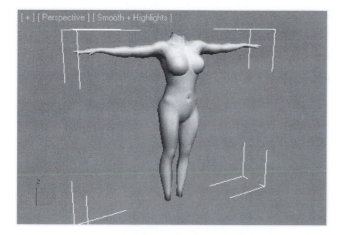

7   In the viewport, click anywhere in an empty area of the viewport to deselect the element.

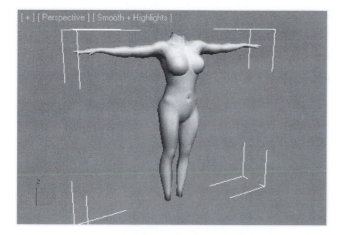

8   Set the sub-object level to **Polygon**.

9 **Arc** rotate the viewport as necessary to see the polygon at the bottom of the right leg, and then select the polygon.

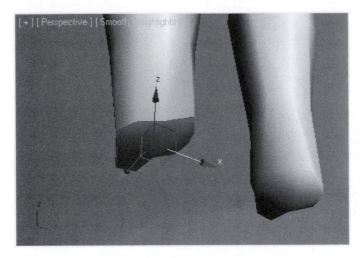

10 On the **Edit Polygons** rollout, click **Extrude**.

11 Drag the selected polygon to extrude it. The new polygons are not smoothed. You must assign them to a smoothing group in order to make them smooth.

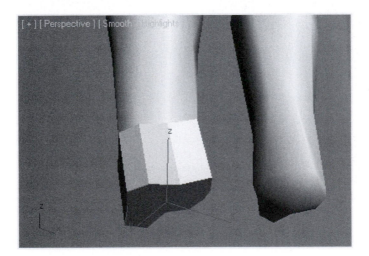

12 Set the sub-object level to **Element**.

13 Click the model to select the element.

14 On the **Polygon: Smoothing Groups** rollout, click the button where the **1** appeared previously.

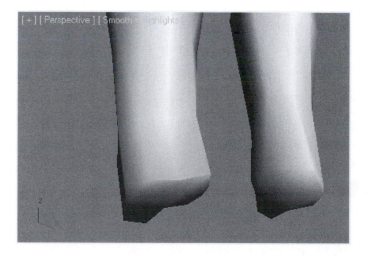

15 This reapplies the smoothing on the leg; the new polygons are now smoothed with the rest of the leg.

Exercise | Smoothing a Low Poly Model

1   Reopen the *Girl_Model.max* file you worked on in the previous exercise. Do not save the changes you have done so far as you need to work on the original model.

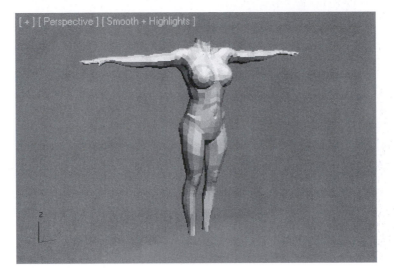

2   In the **Perspective** viewport, select the character.

3   Press **7** on your keyboard to activate the **Poly Count** option. The character currently has approximately 3,600 polygons.

4   Go to the **Modify** panel.

5   From the **Modifier List**, choose **TurboSmooth**.

Taper
Tessellate
TurboSmooth
Turn to Mesh
Turn to Patch
Turn to Poly

6 The Face Count has increased to almost 30,000 faces. The result is a rounder, smoother object.

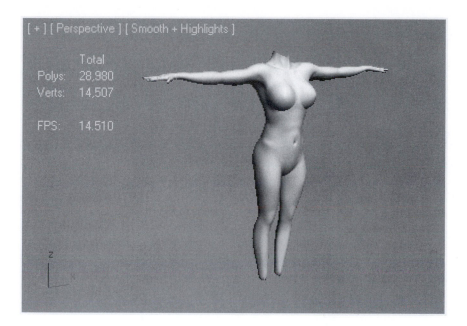

> **Note:** *The TurboSmooth modifier smoothes the geometry to which it's applied. It subdivides the geometry while at the same time interpolating the angles at vertices and edges. By default, the modifier applies a single smoothing group to all the faces in the object.*

7 On the **Subdivision Amount** rollout, make sure **Iterations** is set to **1**. The **Iterations** value determines the number of times the mesh is subdivided.

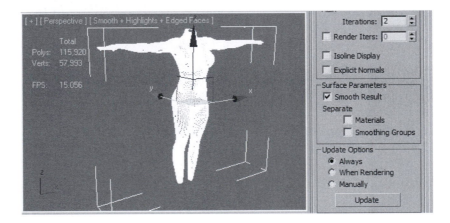

8 Press **F4** to turn on **Edged Faces** in the viewport to see the level of detail that corresponds to the Iterations setting.

9 Set the Iterations value to **2** and notice the polygon count has increased significantly.

> **Note:** *Do not try to increase Iterations to too high a value; 3 should be the maximum setting for most models. High Iterations will slow down your computer and make it harder to work on your model.*

10   Turn on **Isoline Display**. When this option is active, TurboSmooth adjusts the geometry to the Iterations amount while maintaining the visible edges of the low poly model.

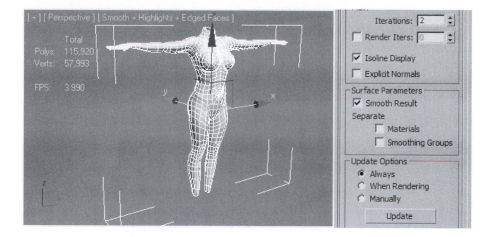

Lesson 14 | Creating Shapes

Introduction

Shapes are both 2D and 3D objects that can take on linear and curvilinear forms. Shapes are useful in the creation of more complex 3D geometry as well as in creating renderable objects of themselves. In this lesson you will see how to create shapes and some basic shape manipulation.

Shapes

Objectives

After completing this lesson, you will be able to:

- Create shapes.
- Convert shapes to editable splines.
- Use the Edit Spline modifier.
- Extract Shapes from 3D objects.
- Work with shape parameters.

Creating Shapes

There are a few basic tools available to you to create shapes. The first is through the use of the Line tool. The second is by creating parametric shapes. Whichever way you start, you will probably wind up modifying the shape in some manner. Shapes are found in the Create menu, under Shapes or Extended Shapes. The Create tab of the Command panel contains panels for Shapes and Extended Shapes.

Accessing Shape commands from the menu bar

Accessing shape commands from the Command Panel

Line Tool

The Line tool is the most basic shape creation tool. It creates the most fundamental shape without parameters that would control its size or number of points as in the Star shape tool. You draw lines by placing verticies in the scene. Based on how you place the vertex and the settings in the Creation Method rollout, you will get a straight corner, smooth, or Bezier curve.

- When you simply click to place a vertex point, it creates a vertex of the type selected under Initial Type. This can be either a Corner or Smooth vertex, which will create a straight edge or a rounded one, respectively.

- When you click and drag the vertex when placing it in the scene, it will create a vertex like the one selected in the Drag Type area. One additional option, not available when you click and drag, is to obtain a Bezier vertex. You would need to edit your vertex to obtain this vertex type.

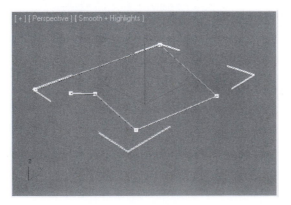

Creation Method Rollout

When the options set in the Creation method rollout are as pictured in the illustration, you can create straight lines and sharp corners simply by clicking to place your verticies.

Creating splines with Corner vertices

If you place verticies using click and drag operations to create Bezier curves, you can obtain a spline with curves. The Bezier vertex allows you to control the tangent of the curve at the vertex point.

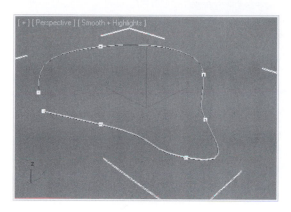

Creating Splines with Bezier vertices

If you choose to use the Smooth option to place the line, you will obtain lines that are curvilinear but will not have control over the tangency of the curve at the vertex. In the illustration you see 2 curves side by side created using the same number of verticies placed approximately at the same locations. On the left, the smooth vertex option is used. On the right, Bezier curves are created by clicking and dragging at each vertex. A more complex curve can be created with Bezier verticies by controlling the tangencies of the curve.

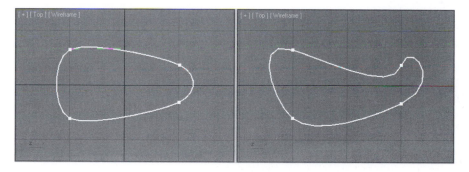

Splines with Smooth and Bezier vertices

When you are trying to draw horizontal or vertical line segments with the Line tool, you can restrict the movement of the cursor by holding down the Shift key while selecting vertices.

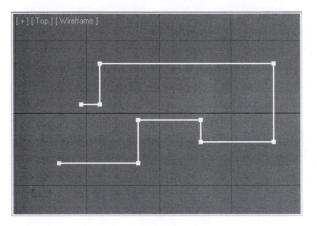

Use the Shift Key for Horizontal and Vertical Line Segments

 Note: *You can remove the last segment of a line without exiting the tool by using the Backspace key on the keyboard.*

When you select a line you created in the scene and go to the Modify panel, you will note the interface of the panel is much like the base Editable Spline object.

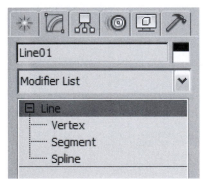

Modify panel display of the Line object

Chapter 02 | Modeling

Parametric Shape Objects

In addition to the Line tool, there are a series of standard parametric shapes that are generally created in the viewport through click and drag operations. There are two groups of these shapes. They are organized in the Create menu under Shapes and Extended Shapes, and in the Command panel under Splines and Extended Splines.

Splines in the Command panel

Extended Splines in the Command panel

Some of the parameters to adjust splines are simple and limiting. The Circle, for example, has a single Radius value to adjust its size.

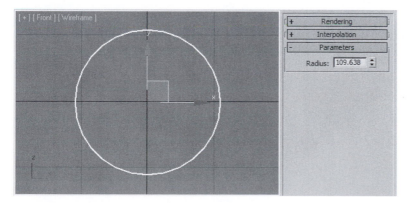

Circle Parameters

More complex shapes such as the Rectangle have several parameters that can be adjusted through numerical parameters.

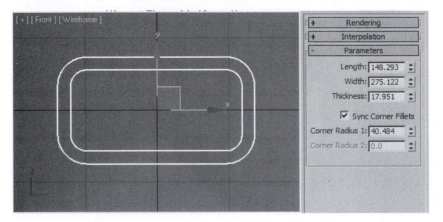

Rectangle Parameters

Basic Spline Manipulation

There are many ways that splines can be adjusted. Many times this starts with the conversion of parametric splines to an Editable Spline or the application of an Edit Spline modifier. The behavior of parametric splines and Editable Splines, or the parametric spline with an Edit Spline modifier, is similar to the behavior of parametric Meshes, edtiable Meshes, or Parametric Meshes and the Edit Mesh modifier.

Conversion to an Editable Spline

As discussed in a previous lesson, conversion of parametric splines is a process that eliminates the parameters available in parametric splines. The new way of adjusting a spline after conversion is at a sub-object level. For many tasks that require that you edit your spline at a sub-object level, this is sufficient.

Edit Spline Modifier

As with the parametric meshes and the Edit Mesh or Edit Poly modifiers, you can use the modifier stack to add a series of modifiers onto a spline. In the illustration, two modifiers have been added to the parametric circle. Each of these modifiers was used to create an additional spline. These modifiers can be removed if you change your mind about the eventual shape.

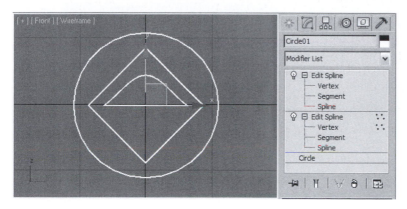

Edit Spline modifiers in the Modifier tab of the Command panel

As with Editable Poly meshes, you can collapse the modifier stack of a spline in a similar fashion. A right-click menu in the modifier stack allows you to collapse the stack. Collapsing the entire stack would result in an Editable Spline.

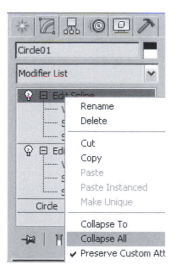

Right-click Menu in the Modifier Stack

Extracting Shapes from 3D Objects

You may wish to create a shape based on some geometry in your scene. Tools in the Editaible Poly and Editable Mesh objects allow you to select segments of a mesh and extract them to a separate spline object. In the example you see edges selected on a hemisphere form.

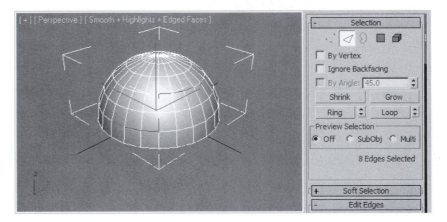

Edges Selected in an Editable Poly Object

In the Edit Edges rollout, the Create Shape From Selection button creates the shape.

Extracting the Shape

Chapter 02 | Modeling

You can use the shape for a variety of purposes; in this case the shape has been made renderable to add some detail to the hemisphere.

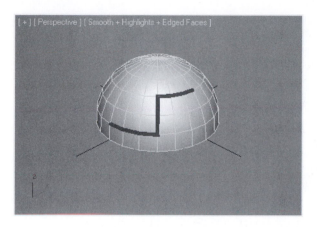

Resulting Shape with Rendering Settings on

Shape Steps

When you create a shape, 3ds Max Design displays curved segments with straight-line components called steps. The greater the number of steps, the smoother the curve. You can adjust the number of shape steps on the Interpolation rollout.

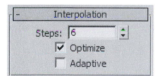

Interpolation Rollout

The default Steps value of 6 produces fairly smooth results, but the segmentation is evident when you zoom in to the scene.

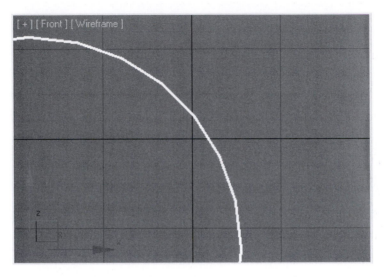

Segmentation of Circle zoomed in to Viewport

Note the difference among these three concentric circles. The inner circle has a Steps value of 2, while the outer circle uses a Steps value of 12. The center circle uses the default (6).

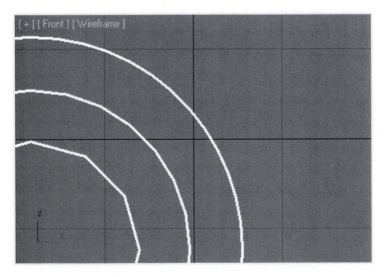

Circles with different shape step values

Shape steps are calculated between vertices. A shape with many vertices looks smoother than a shape with fewer vertices and the same number of steps. In the illustration, the inner circle shows four vertices with a Steps value of 4, while the outer circle contains two vertices with the same Steps value of 4.

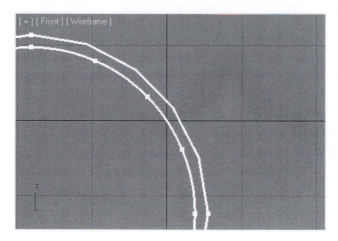

Shape Steps are calculated between verticies

The Interpolation rollout contains two check boxes worth noting:

- **Optimize**: Removes shape steps where they're unnecessary, usually on a straight-line segment. Optimize is on by default.

- **Adaptive**: Controls the distribution of shape steps. It removes steps in linear segments and distributes steps in curved segments based on the angle of the curve. Adaptive is off by default. When enabled, both Steps and Optimize are unavailable.

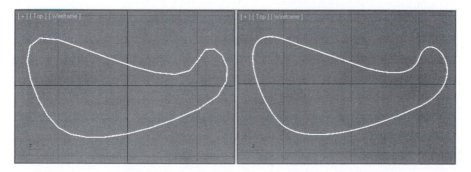

Identical splines: The left one has a Steps value of 6, while the right one has Adaptive on

Exercise | Creating a Simple Shape

In this exercise, you'll be creating shapes that represent a logo.

1   Start or reset 3ds Max Design.

2   Right-click the **Front** viewport to make it active.

3   Press the **G** key to remove the grid.

4   On the **Create** tab of the **Command** panel, click the **Shapes** button.

5   Click the **Circle** object type button.

6   In the **Front** viewport, drag out a circle.

7 Click the Star object type button.

8 Drag out a star (approximately) centered on the circle.

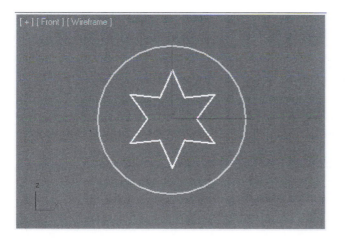

9 With the star selected, click on the **Align** tool, and select the circle.

10   Align the pivot points of the two objects in **X** and **Y**.

M3DS Grid and Snap Settings			
Snaps	Options	Home Grid	User Grids

Standard ▾   Override OFF

☐ ☐ Grid Points   ☐ ☐ Grid Lines
人 ☐ Pivot   [ ] ☐ Bounding Box
⌐ ☐ Perpendicular   ○ ☐ Tangent
+ ☑ Vertex   ☑ ☐ Endpoint
☐ ☐ Edge/Segment   ☑ ☐ Midpoint
△ ☐ Face   ▽ ☐ Center Face

Clear All

11   Select the circle and go to the **Modify** panel.

12   On the **Parameters** rollout, change the **Radius** to **60**.

Parameters

Radius: 60.0

13   Select the **Star** object.

14   On the **Parameters** rollout, change the **Points** value to **5**, **Radius 1** to **50.0**, and **Radius 2** to **21.0**.

Parameters

Radius 1: 50.0
Radius 2: 21.0
Points: 5
Distortion: 0.0
Fillet Radius 1: 0.0
Fillet Radius 2: 0.0

15   With the **Star** object still selected, click the **Select and Rotate** button.

16   Rotate the star until one of the tips is pointed up.

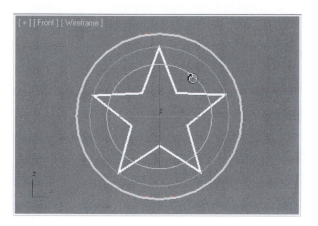

17   Right-click the **Snaps** toggle button.

18   On the **Grid and Snap Settings** dialog, turn on **Vertex** and turn off any other options.

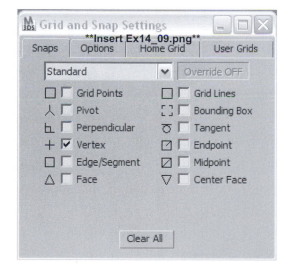

19   Close the dialog.

20   Click the **Snaps** toggle button to enable it. The button turns blue.

21   On the **Create** tab of the **Command** panel, click the **Shapes** button.

22   Click the line object type button.

23   Set both **Initial Type** and **Drag Type** to **Corner**.

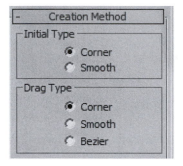

24   Draw a line connecting the outer points of the star.

25   After you've drawn the line to each star point, click the first point again.

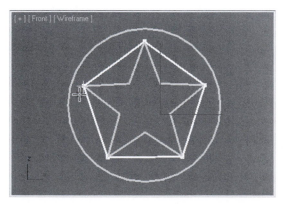

26   You are prompted to close the spline. Click **Yes**.

27   Click the **Select Object** button and return to the **Modify** tab.

Chapter 02 | Modeling

28 Select the star, and set **Radius 1** to **45.0** and **Radius 2** to **17.0**.

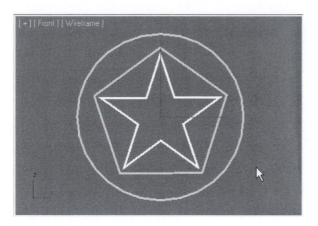

29 Select the circle.

30 From the **Modifier List**, choose **Edit Spline**.

31 In the **Selection** rollout, click the **Segment** sub-object button; it turns yellow.

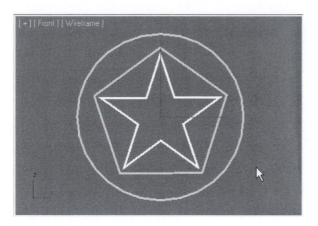

32 Select the two lower arcs of the circle. You can use the **Ctrl** key to make multiple selections.

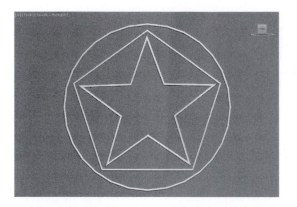

33 Right-click to open the Quad menu, and choose **Line** to turn the arcs into linear segments.

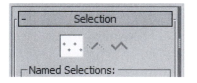

34 On the **Modify** panel, switch to the **Vertex** sub-object level.

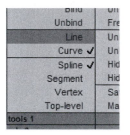

35 Click the **Select and Move** button on the toolbar, and select the vertex at the bottom of the shape.

36 Turn off **Snaps** toggle.

37 Drag the vertex downward until the shape resembles the following illustration.

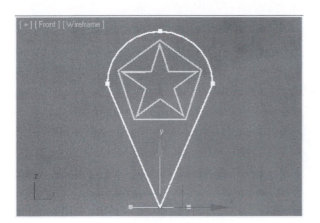

38 Click the **Vertex** sub-object button to turn it off. It turns gray.

39 In the **modifier stack**, click the **light bulb** icon next to the **Edit Spline** modifier. The modifier's effect is turned off.

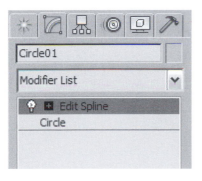

40 Click the light-bulb icon next to the **Edit Spline** modifier again to turn the modifier back on.

41 Save your file as *mylogo.max*.

Lesson 15 | Spline Editing

Introduction

Splines are important objects in the creation of most scenes. Learning how to edit them is an important element in your successful use of these objects. This lesson will go into more depth about the possibilities of editing splines. You will learn how to use some of the more common editing tools at the various sub-object levels.

Editing Splines

Objectives

After completing this lesson, you will be able to:

- Differentiate between shapes and splines
- Use basic transformations of Shape sub-objects
- Edit shapes at the Spline sub-object level.
- Edit shapes at the Segment sub-object level
- Edit shapes at the Vertex sub-object level

Chapter 02 | Modeling

Shapes and Splines

The difference between shapes and splines can sometimes be confusing. Remember that a Shape is a collection of one or more splines joined together as one object. Consider the logo that was made in the previous lesson.

A logo made of splines

By just looking at the scene you might think that these objects should be a single object, but once you display the Select From Scene dialog, you will note that there are three objects in the scene. Selecting one of the objects does not select all three splines. In this situation you have three shapes with a single spline each.

Splines are in separate shapes

When you use these three shapes, they will behave independently. Should you wish to change how they behave together, you can attach or detach splines from shapes.

Adding Splines from a Shape

When a shape is in Editable Spline form or has an Edit Spline modifier applied to it, you can add splines to the selected shape with the Attach tools found on the Geometry rollout.

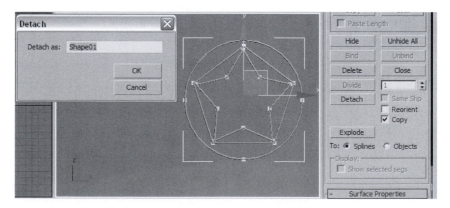

Splines attached into one shape

Once attached, the objects loose the parameters of any parametric shapes that were used to create them. In this case, the circle object retained its name, but it is now the root of the entire complex shape.

Detaching Splines from a Shape

When you select a spline in a multi-spline shape, you have the option to detach it from the shape. When you detach a spline, you can keep the original and make a copy. The spline must be selected before these tools become available.

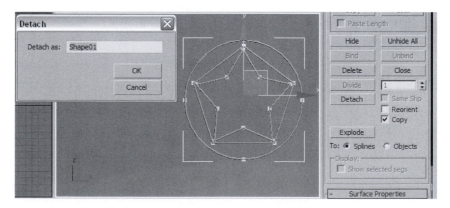

Detaching a spline as a new shape

Basic Transformations of Sub-Objects

Move Rotate and Scale

You can edit shape sub-objects (Vertex, Segment, and Spline) with the Move, Rotate, and Scale transforms. These transforms are not only important in enabling you to adjust sub-objects in a shape, but also because you can use them combined with the Shift key to copy sub-objects within the same shape.

For example, you can select the star spline in the center of the multiple spline shape, use the Select and Move tool with the Shift key down, and get a result as illustrated. A second star spline is created, but it is still contained within the original shape object.

Copying a spline sub-object within a shape

Spline Editing

Mirror

You can use mirroring to create symmetrical splines within a shape. After selecting a shape and accessing the Spline sub-object level, you use the Mirror tool found on the Modify panel.

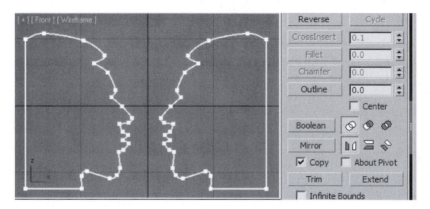

Mirroring a face profile within the same shape

Boolean

Booleans let you create geometry by combining 3D geometry and 2D splines in various ways. Booleans can make complex modeling tasks easier than conventional methods. With splines, you can use Union (add), Subtract (remove), and Intersect (common area) Boolean operations. First, you must ensure that all of the splines are part of the same shape. Booleans work at the Spline sub-object level.

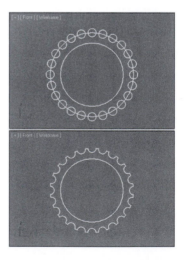

A shape before and after a Boolean operation. Subtracting the outer circles creates a gear shape

Outline

Outline is a tool that allows you to create a duplicate spline parallel to the one selected. It can be used to quickly create an identical object parallel to another, or walls or paths, creating the inner side of a bottle object as shown below.

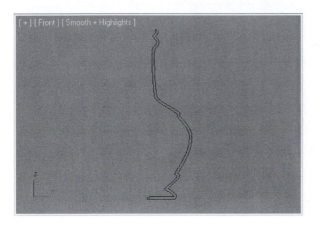

[+] [Front] [Smooth + Highlights]

A single curvilinear profile can be quickly converted into the inner and outer walls of a bottle using the Outline tool.

Segment Editing

A segment can be detached from a shape. This is accomplished with the same Detach tool you use with splines, only here it's used at the Segment sub-object level.

Hide	Unhide All
Bind	Unbind
Delete	Close
Divide	1
Detach	☐ Same Shp
	☐ Reorient
	☐ Copy
Explode	
To: ◉ Splines	○ Objects

The Detach tool in the Geometry rollout

In this example, a segment of the inside of the gear has been detached and scaled; it's no longer part of the original shape. It was then scaled to make it smaller.

The Detach tool in the Geometry rollout

Refining a Segment through the Addition of Vertices

When you create a shape, you may need to add detail in certain segments of the shape. The Refine tool at the Segment or Vertex sub-object level provides a quick way of adding vertices to add detail to the shape.

The Refine tool in the Geometry rollout

In the example, a curvilinear shape is formed of three fairly smooth sides. The fourth side has been created using Bezier corner vertices which create a complex curve. At the default Shape Steps of six this side looks jagged. Increasing the Shape Steps to an adequate level will add unnecessary complexity to the entire shape. Using Refine to add a single vertex in the curve smooths out the problem side.

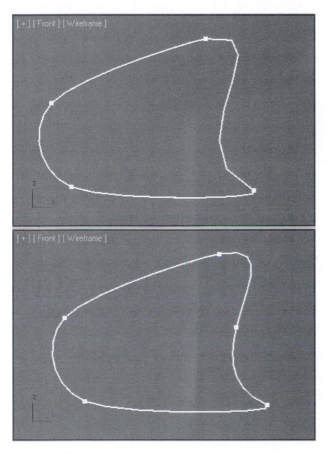

Segment smoothness improved by using the Refine tool

Vertex Editing

The vertex is the most fundamental of spline elements. A considerable amount of editing is possible at the Vertex sub-object level. In fact, re-shaping splines is easiest at this level.

Deleting Vertices

When you delete a vertex, you remove it. 3ds Max Design then creates a segment between the two adjacent vertices. Both the circle and the star have had a vertex deleted at the top of the shape. The circle creates a curved segment, while the star creates a straight segment between the two inner radius points.

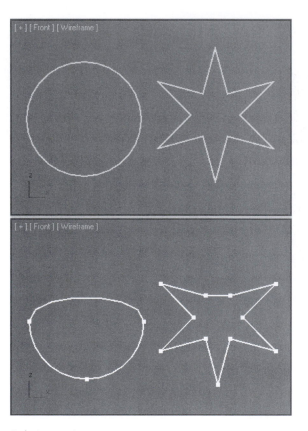

Deleting vertices

You can find the Delete tool near the bottom of the Geometry rollout, or more conveniently, you can simply select the desired vertices and use the Delete key on the keyboard.

Delete tool in the Geometry rollout

Welding Vertices

Welding vertices is different from deleting a vertex. When you weld vertices, two or more vertices are combined into a single vertex, reducing the number of vertices. The Weld tool is found on the Geometry rollout.

The Weld tool

The numerical value on the right is a threshold value; vertices farther apart than this value are not welded.

Consider the following spline. Welding the two open vertices creates a single vertex at the midpoint between them and closes the shape. The vertices to weld must be selected and they must be closer than the defined weld threshold value.

When you select vertices on a spline, the number of selected vertices is displayed on the Selection rollout.

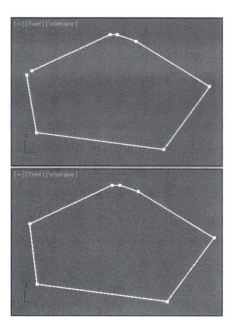

The Weld tool

Selected Vertices displayed in the Selection rollout.

Occasionally, you will need to work with splines that have been created by other software programs and imported into 3ds Max Design. In such situations, you may have splines that contain too many vertices. Welding is a quick way of reducing the number of vertices.

In the example, three vertices were placed close together at the top of the spline, and the spline is open. If you select all the vertices in the spline, you can close the spline and reduce the three vertices to one with the careful selection of a proper weld distance.

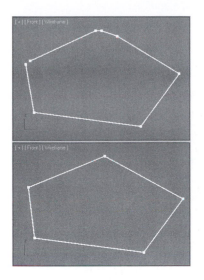

Welding is used to close and reduce vertices in a spline.

Connecting Vertices

Using the Connect tool at the Vertex sub-object level, you can close the gap between open segments. You can connect two vertices with the Connect tool by clicking and dragging from one open vertex to another. In the example, line segments are added between the end points of the arcs when you connect the vertices.

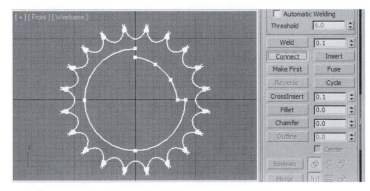

Connecting vertices creates a new segment in between open vertices.

Vertex Controls

Each spline vertex can take on the properties of one of four types: Bezier Corner, Bezier, Corner, and Smooth. Switching vertex types is done through the Quad menu.

Unbind		Viewport Lighting and S
Bezier Corner		Isolate Selection
Bezier		Unfreeze All
Corner	✓	Freeze Selection
Smooth		Unhide by Name
Reset Tangents		Unhide All
Spline		Hide Unselected
Segment		Hide Selection
Vertex	✓	Save Scene State...
Top-level		Manage Scene States...
tools 1		
tools 2		transform
Create Line		Move

Quad Menu, Vertex controls

After selecting one or more vertices, choose a new type from the Quad menu.

Often a vertex is created as the Corner type. This type is characterized by a sharp linear change in direction at any angle.

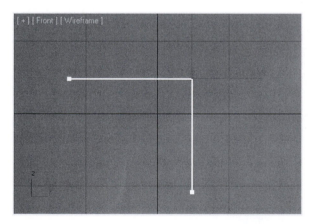

Corner-Type vertex

Changing the vertex to the Smooth type will smooth the spline curvature at that vertex location.

A Bezier vertex provides a curved shape you can control with handles. With the Bezier vertex type, you can adjust the length of the handles and their directions symmetrically.

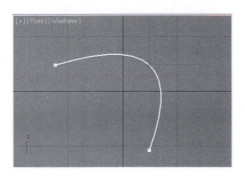

Smooth vertex

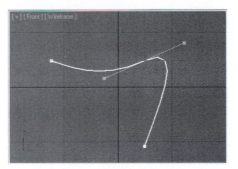

Bezier vertex

A Bezier Corner vertex lets you control the tangents going into and out of the vertex asymmetrically.

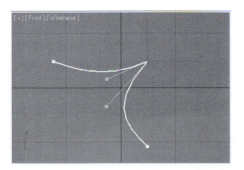

Bezier Corner vertex

Fillet and Chamfer

Occasionally you might need to round off or slice off corners of a shape. You can easily do this with the Fillet tool for rounded corners and the Chamfer tool for straight edges.

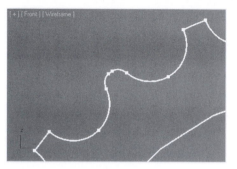

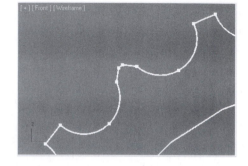

Filleting the vertices at the corners of the gear's teeth produces a rounded effect.

Chamfering the vertices produces an angular effect.

Importance of the First Vertex

The first vertex, as its name suggests, is the first vertex on a spline. It is used as a starting point in the creation of geometry. In animation applications, such Path constraints, the first vertex is the starting point of the path.

First vertices on splines are indicated by yellow squares. You can customize this default yellow color to your liking. You can change the location of the first vertex by selecting a vertex and clicking the Make First button.

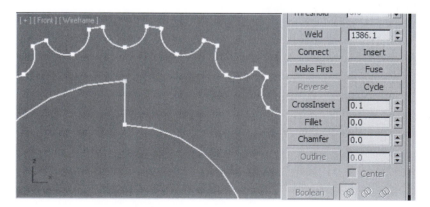

First Vertices on two closed splines of the gear shape

Chapter 02 | Modeling

The Make First tool resets the first vertex. On a closed spline, the first vertex can be anywhere. On an open spline it has to be at either end.

The presence of more than one first vertex signals a potential problem in a shape. A typical problem could be multiple splines when you think there is only one. Usually, welding the vertices in the spline will correct the problem. In the illustration, a shape is drawn using the Line tool with Smooth Vertices set for the creation type. While the shape was drawn, the process of drawing was interrupted and restarted. This will lead to multiple splines and, as you can observe, angular corners where first vertices appear.

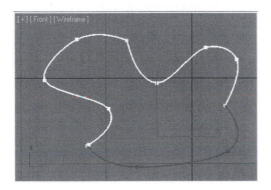

A shape drawn with separate segments, multiple first vertices

Welding all the vertices and then checking that all vertices are of the smooth type will give you the following result.

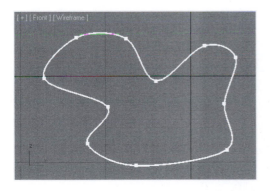

Single Spline, all smooth vertices

Exercise | Creating a Profile for an Oil Can

1   Reset 3ds Max Design.

2   Open the file *Oil Can.max*.

3   In the **Create** panel, click the **Shapes** button and click the **Line** button.

4   Draw a spline in the **Front** viewport following the approximate size determined by the grid. Don't forget the angled bead in the lower right corner. Hold down the **Shift** key when you want to draw horizontal or vertical lines.

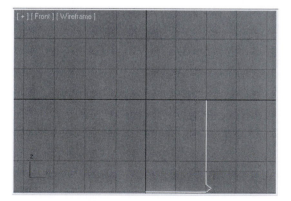

5   Press the **G** key to turn off the grid.

6   Zoom in to the angled bead area.

7 Go to the **Modify** panel and expand the Line base object entry.

8 Go to the **Vertex** sub-object level.

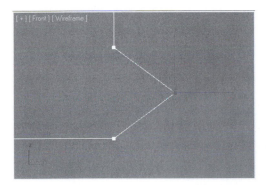

9 Select the **Vertex** at the tip of the angled bead.

10 Right-click to open the **Quad** menu and then choose the **Bezier** option.

11   Switching to the **Bezier** vertex type produces a curve that needs adjusting.

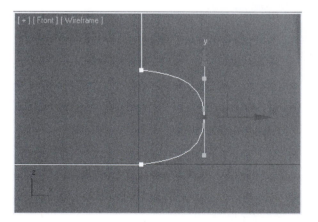

12   Next you will change the curve, by adjusting the curve handles.

13   On the **main** toolbar, click the **Move** button.

14   Move the bottom vertex handle so that the entire handle is approximately vertical.

15   Click the **Vertex** entry in the modifier stack to exit the sub-object level.

16   In the **Front** viewport, zoom out to see the entire spline.

17 Click **Spline** in the modifier stack to access the **Spline** sub-object level.

18 Select the spline in the view. It turns red.

19 On the **Modify** panel, turn on **Copy** below the **Mirror** button.

20 Choose the **Mirror Vertically** option, and click the **Mirror** button.

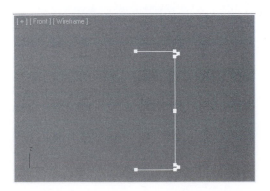

21 Move the newly created spline upward, so that it just meets the existing spline at the middle.

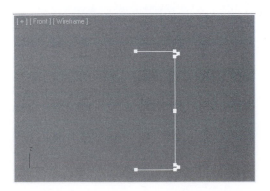

22 Go to the **Vertex** sub-object level and select the two vertices created at the juncture of the top and bottom of the can.

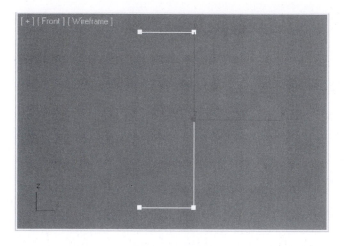

 Note: *The existence of two vertices at the center of the profile indicates that they're two separate splines. No automatic welding occurred during the mirror process.*

23 Increase the **Weld** threshold value to **0.5**.

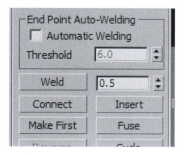

Chapter 02 | Modeling

24   Click the **Weld** button.

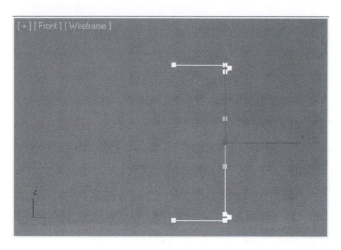

Now only one vertex exists at the center of the profile. In addition, because the Weld process converted two splines into one, it also left only one first vertex.

25   Save the file and name it *My Oil Can Profile.max*.

In a later exercise, you'll be using the Lathe tool to create a 3D object.

Exercise | Creating a Profile for a Bottle

In this exercise, you'll be drawing the profile of a bottle to create the inner and outer edges.

1   Reset 3ds Max Design.

2   Open the file *Bottle.max*.

3   Select the **Line** tool.

4   Set the **Creation Method** to **Initial Type** = **Corner, Drag Type** = **Bezier**.

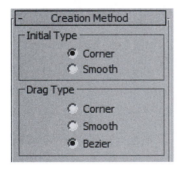

5   Use the **Line** tool to start drawing your profile. Position the cursor near the center of the bottom of the bottle and click the first point.

> **Note:** *Normal viewport zoom and pan does not work during the spline creation function. If you need to zoom in do at the beginning. Then you can press the I key on your keyboard to use the Pan Viewport function. This will allow you to pan the viewport should your spline go off the screen. It's a great way of retaining your current spline creation.*

6 Hold down the **Shift** key to draw a horizontal line, and then click the second point.

7 Place your third point at the curved edge of the base, but this time click and drag to create a small curve.

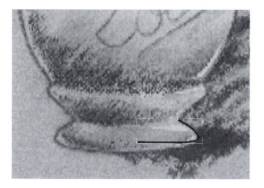

8 Click a fourth point to complete the base. You do not need to be very precise as you create your curve; you can make adjustments later.

9 Proceed up the side of the bottle, picking up the detail of the smooth center area and the cap top.

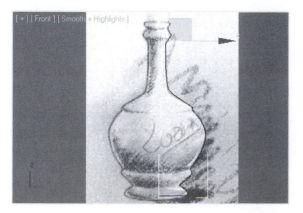

10 Make sure the line is still selected.

11 On the **Modify** panel, expand the **Line** entry.

12 Go to the **Vertex** sub-object level.

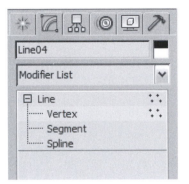

13 Zoom into the base of the bottle sketch.

14 The first three vertices look pretty good, so select the fourth vertex at the top of the base.

15 Right-click and choose **Bezier Corner** from the **Quad** menu.

16 Adjust the **Bezier** handles, so they look similar to the illustration.

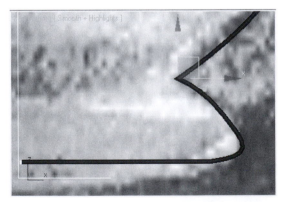

17 Pan the **Front** viewport down and zoom in to the fifth and sixth vertices.

18 Select both vertices and convert them to **Bezier Corner**.

19 You might need to adjust both the vertex locations and the tangent handles to get the desired form. Zoom in more if necessary.

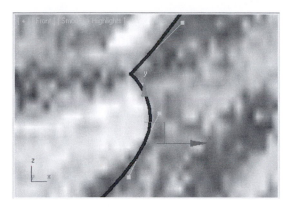

20 Move up the profile, making adjustments where necessary, and stop when you arrive at the top of the bottle.

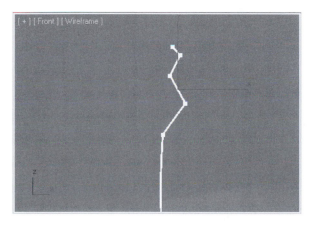

The profile displayed without the background for clarity

21 In the **Modify panel** → **Modifier stack**, access **Segment** sub-object level.

22 Select the third segment from the top.

23 At the bottom of the Geometry rollout, click the **Divide** button, leaving the default value at **1**. This will insert a vertex in the middle of the segment.

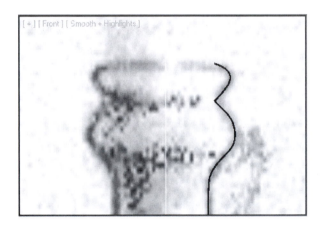

24 Go back to the **Vertex** sub-object level.

25 Continue to adjust the vertices curvature until the top of the bottle is complete.

The completed curve at the top of the bottle

26 Continue working on the bottle profile or open *Bottle01.max*.

27 Make sure the bottle profile (*Line01*) is selected.

28 On the **Modify** panel, go to the **Spline** sub-object level, if necessary.

29 Select the **Spline**. It turns red in the viewport.

30 In the numeric field next to the **Outline** button, enter the value **0.075** and press **Enter**. It's not necessary to click the **Outline** button.

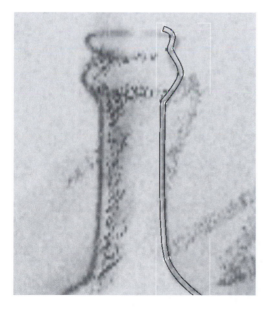

31 Go to the **Vertex** sub-object level of the shape.

32 Zoom in to the top of the bottle.

33 After outlining the profile, the inside of the bottle has some distortion and is excessively detailed.

34 Select the four vertices on the inside, as illustrated.

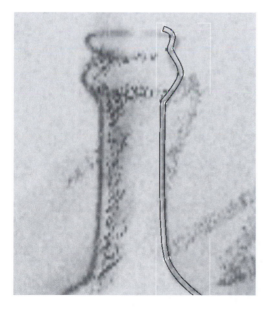

35   Click the **Delete** tool in the Geometry rollout. After deleting the extra vertices, adjustments to the curvature are necessary.

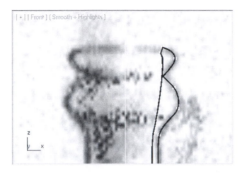

36   Select the second vertex from the top on the inside of the bottle.

37   Move the bottom vertex handle until the inside profile looks something like the illustration.

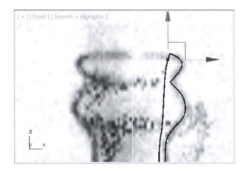

38   Pan down the profile until you get to the first notch in the bottle, just below the bottle neck. It has two vertices. The notch on the outside of the bottle has created a notch on the inside that should not be there.

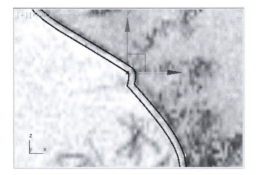

39 Select the upper vertex on the inner notch and delete it.

40 Convert the remaining vertex to a **Bezier** type and adjust it as shown.

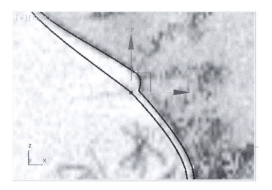

41 Repeat this process for the notch above the base.

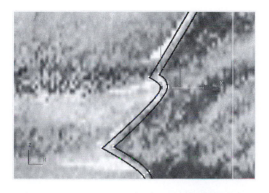

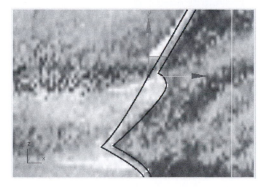

42 Save your file as *My Bottle Profile.max*.

Lesson 16 | Creating Objects from Splines

Introduction

In this lesson, you will learn about creating 3D Objects from Splines using modifiers made specifically for this purpose. Splines are often created to define objects that otherwise might be difficult to model directly in 3D. Creating objects by extrusion or by revolving a profile about an axis of rotation are two such examples.

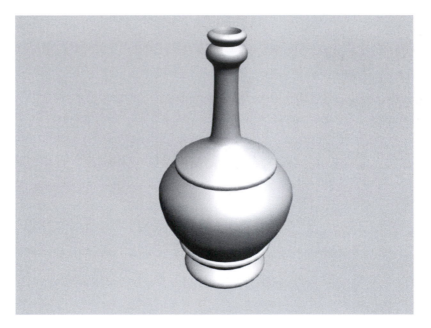

A Bottle Formed from A Spline

Objectives

After completing this lesson, you will be able to:

- Use several modifiers on splines to create 3D objects

Shape Modifiers

Several modifiers can be used with shapes. Here are some of the more common modifiers and the results they produce.

Extrude

Extrude is a fairly straightforward modifier. It allows you to take an open or closed shape and create a 3D object with a thickness.

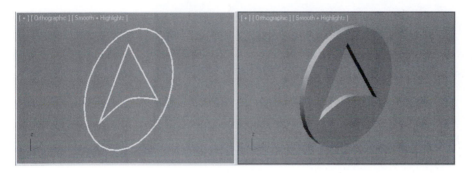

A medallion created with Extrude

Lathe

Lathe is also a fairly straightforward modifier but normally requires some adjustment to get the desired result. Lathe takes a profile, such as that of a bottle, and rotates it about an axis. Lathe rotates about an axis that goes through the pivot point of the shape. You can set the axis of revolution to X, Y, or Z, and adjust the location of the axis in the modifier.

A bottle created with Lathe

Bevel

You can use the Bevel modifier instead of Extrude when you need to produce geometry with angled or curved edges. Objects in reality that might appear to be simple extrusions do in fact have subtle rounded or angled edges at their ends. Beveled edges conveniently catch highlights generated by light sources in the scene.

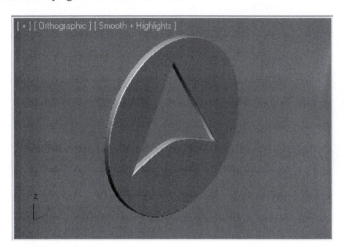

A medallion created with Bevel

From the same shape used in the medallion above, a curved medallion with a recessed area can be created with changes to the values of the Bevel modifier.

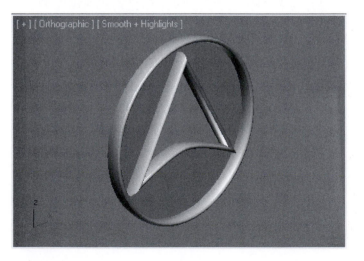

Changing Bevel modifier values alters the medallion dramatically

Bevel Profile

Bevel Profile works like Bevel but uses a profile or path instead of entered values to generate a 3D object. Bevel Profile can be used to create a relatively simple form like this gas bar island. The rounded rectangular base is shaped to fit the profile.

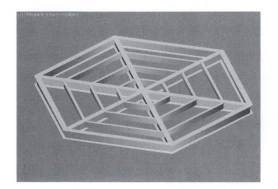

Bevel Profile

Sweep

The Sweep modifier takes a profile and extrudes it along a path. You can use built-in profiles or draw a profile of your own.

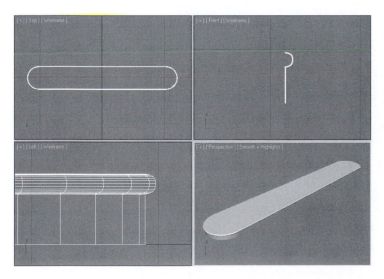

A complex floor structure platform is quickly created with the Sweep modifier

Exercise | Using the Lathe Modifier

1   Open the file *Bottle and Can Profile.max*. These profiles were previously created; you'll turn them into 3D geometry using Lathe.

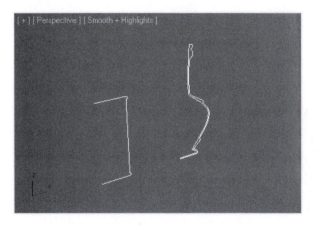

2   Select the *Can Profile* object on the left side of the **Perspective** viewport.

3   Go to the **Modify** panel, and from the **Modifier List** choose **Lathe**.

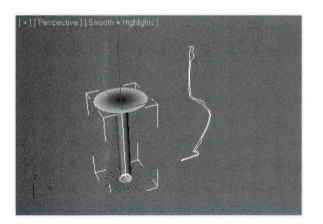

The Lathe modifier has been applied but did not produce the anticipated results. Lathe has rotated the profile about the Z-axis of its pivot point, where the desired axis is the minimum edge (left side) of the profile.

4   Click the **Min** button in the **Align** group of the **Parameters** rollout (Min is short for Minimum).

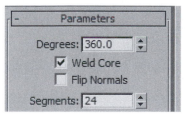

The overall shape of the can looks OK now but the top of the can is distorted as a result of the core vertex of the can not being welded.

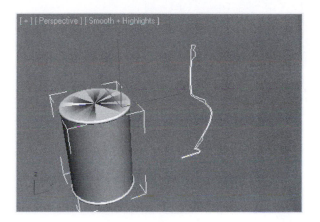

5   Turn on the **Weld Core** option to remove the rendering problem at the top of the can.

6   Select the *Bottle Profile* object.

7   Apply a **Lathe** modifier.

8   Click the **Min** button in the **Align** group of the **Parameters** rollout.

9   Verify that **Weld Core** is **on**. The two geometric objects are complete.

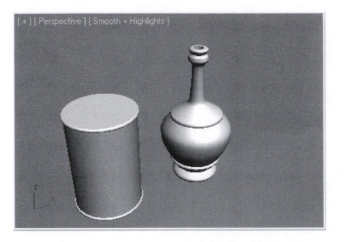

10   Make the **Perspective** viewport current and press **F3** to switch to wireframe mode.

11   Click on the **General Viewport** label (the [**+**] at the top left of the viewport).

12   Select **Configure** from the **Menu** that appears.

13   In the **Viewport Configuration** dialog, select the **Statastics** tab.

14 Set the **Setup** to **Polygon Count** only, and **Selection**. Click **OK** to exit the dialog.

Viewport Configuration

Rendering Method	Layout	Safe Frames	Adaptive Degradation
Regions	Statistics	Lighting and Shadows	ViewCube	SteeringWheels

Setup
- ☑ Polygon Count   ○ Total
- ☐ Triangle Count   ● Selection
- ☐ Edge Count   ○ Total + Selection
- ☐ Vertex Count
- ☐ Frames Per Second

Application
- ☐ Show Statistics in Active View

Default Settings

OK   Cancel

15 Select the lathed can and then press the **7** key on the keyboard to make the **Face Counter** active in the viewport. There are approximately 992 polygons in the Can object.

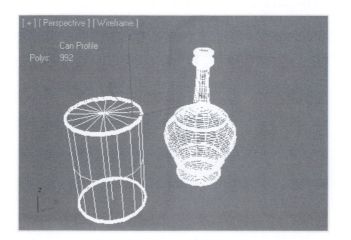

[+] [Perspective] [Wireframe]

Can Profile
Polys: 992

16 The **Face Counter** shows the number of faces that the selected object uses. It is better to keep the face count low while preserving good rendering quality.

17 With the can still selected, go to the **Line level** in the modifier stack.

18 Click the **Show End Result** button. This lets you see the completed 3D object as you edit the profile.

19 On the **Interpolation** rollout, change the **Steps** value to **2**.

20 Go to the **Vertex** sub-object level.

21 In the **Front** viewport, select the vertex at the middle of the profile of the can.

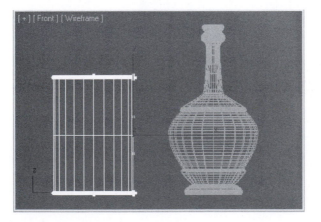

22 Click the **Delete** button on the **Geometry** rollout.

23 In the **Modifier** stack, select the **Lathe** level of the can.

24 Change the **Segments** value to **24**.

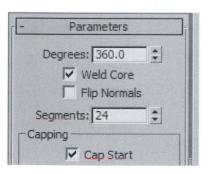

The face count should now be 672. You have managed to reduce the number of faces and improve the appearance of the object. If this object was in the distance you would make further adjustments to their values to further reduce face count. If you have time, make similar adjustments to the bottle object.

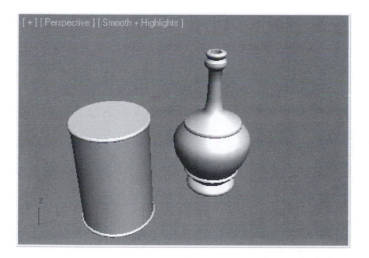

Exercise | Creating a Medallion with Bevel

1   Open the file *Bevel Medallion.max*.

2   Select the shape and go to the **Modify Panel**.

3   From the **Modifier List** choose **Bevel**.

4 Under **Level 1** set both **Height** and **Outline** values to **1.0**.

5 Turn on **Level 2** and enter a **Height** value of **8.0**, leaving the **Outline** value at **0.0**.

6 Finish by turning on **Level 3** and entering a **Height** of **1.0** and an **Outline** value of **-1.0**.

7   Zoom in on the Left viewport to see the profile of the medallion more clearly. Compare the profile to the level values you entered. Positive Height values produce added thickness; positive Outline values produce a larger radius; and negative Outline values produce a smaller radius.

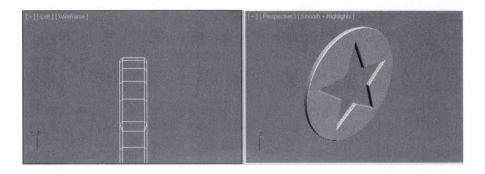

8   Reset all the level values to **0.0**. You'll try another bevel that will produce a relief medallion.

9   Set the **Level 1 Height** value to **10.0** and leave **Outline** at **0.0**.

10   Leave the **Level 2 Height** value at **0.0**, and set the **Outline** value to **-5.0**.

11   Set the **Level 3 Height** value to **-8.0**, and leave **Outline** at **0.0**.

12   In the **Surface** group of the **Parameters** rollout, choose the **Curved Sides** option.

13   Change the **Segments** value to **4**.

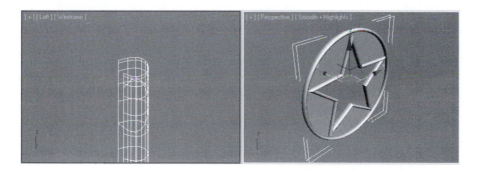

14   Finish by turning on **Smooth Across Levels**. The changes to the parameters produce an interesting curved form.

Exercise | Recreating the Gas Station Island with Bevel Profile

In this exercise, you'll replace the existing gas station island with a more detailed object that has a bull-nosed edge at the top. You'll use Bevel Profile to create the new object.

1   Open the file *Gas Station Island Curb.max*.

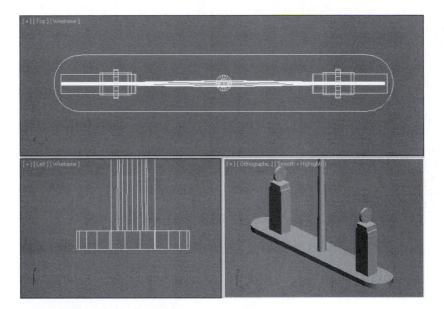

2   On the **Create** panel, click **Shapes** → **Rectangle**.

3   In the **Top** viewport, drag a rectangle to approximately encompass the existing island.

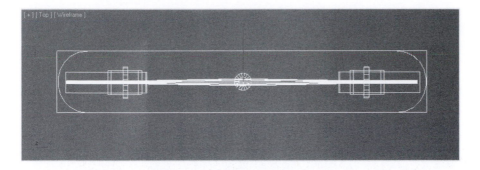

4   Go to the **Modify** panel and adjust the **Corner Radius** value, so it rounds off the two ends of the island. A value of about **16** should work well. The new rectangle with its rounded corners approximately follows the existing island base.

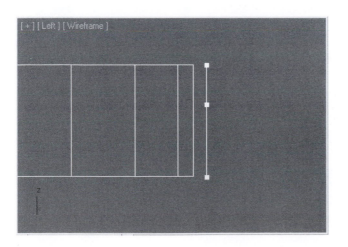

5   In the **Left** viewport, zoom in on the right side of the base of the island.

6   Draw a line with three corner vertices: one at the bottom, another two-thirds of the way to the top, and the last at the top. Use the **Shift** key to help you draw the line straight.

7   Go to the **Modify** panel, and go to the **Vertex** sub-object level.

8   Select the two top vertices of the new line.

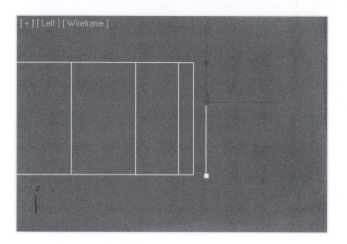

9   Right-click the vertex and choose **Bezier Corner** from the **Quad** menu.

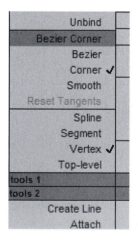

10   Select the topmost vertex, and activate the **Select and Move** tool.

11   Adjust the handles as shown in the illustrations.

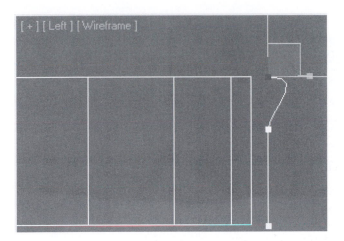

> **Tip:**   *If you need to, press **F8** to switch between the different axies constraints.*

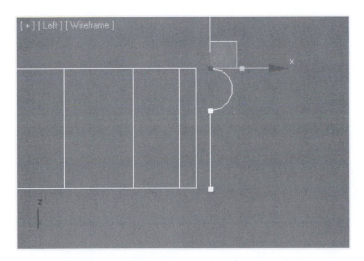

12   Exit the sub-object level.

13   Select the *Gas Island Curb* object and delete it.

14   Select the rectangle shape you created earlier, and from the **Modifier List** choose **Bevel Profile**.

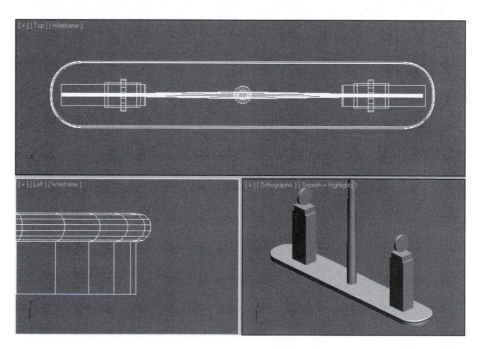

15   Click the **Pick Profile** button.

16   Click the profile you just created in the **Left** viewport. The new Gas Island Base with bull-nosed top is complete.

Exercise | Using the Sweep Modifier to
Create a Wainscoting

In this exercise, you'll be drawing a spline and using Sweep to create wainscoting along the wall.

1   Open the file *Walls Doors and Windows.max*.

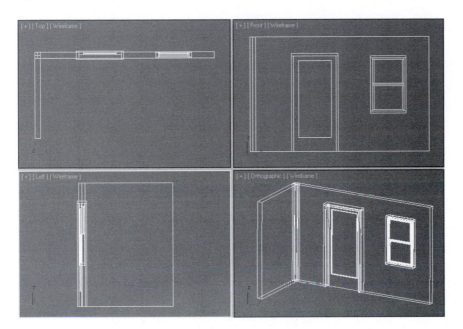

2   Activate the **Line** tool from the **Create panel** → **Shapes** category.

3   Right-click the **Snaps Toggle** on the **main toolbar**.

4   On the dialog that opens, turn on **Vertex** only and close the dialog.

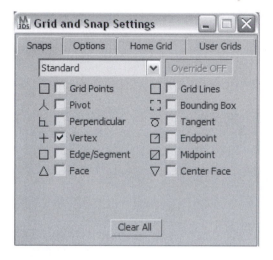

5   On the **main** toolbar, click the **Snaps Toggle** button to turn on **Snaps** mode. The button turns Yellow.

6   Draw a line along the inside base of the wall to create a straight L-shaped line. When setting the corner of the L, be sure to pick the vertex at the inside corner of the wall.

7   On the **main** toolbar, click the **Select and Move** button.

8   Right-click the **Select and Move** button. The **Transform Type-In** dialog opens.

9   Enter **42** in the **Absolute World Z** value field to move the line up to a height of **42** units.

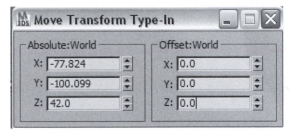

10   Close the **Move Transform Type-In** dialog. Press the **S** key to turn off **Snaps** toggle.

11   On the **Modify** panel, go to the Vertex sub-object level.

12   Click the **Refine** tool. In the **Front** view, select points along the wall where the spline intersects the window and door frame.

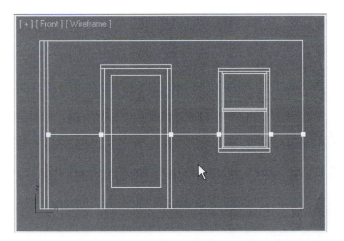

13   Although accuracy is not 100% crucial, you can zoom in to the view to select the points.

14   Click the **Refine** tool again to exit the **Refine** mode.

15   On the **Modify** panel, go to the **Segment** sub-object level.

16 Select the two segments inside the door and window and delete them. Exit the **Segment** sub-object level when done.

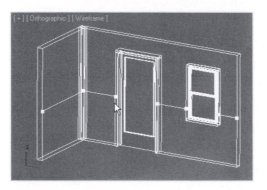

17 If you have trouble creating the spline, you can open the file *Sweep.max*.

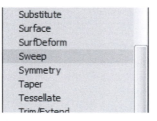

18 Make sure the line is selected. From the **Modifier List**, choose the **Sweep** modifier.

19 On the **Section Type** rollout, open the **Built-In Section** list and choose **Half Round**.

20 Switch the **Rendering Mode** of the **Orthographic** view to **Hidden Line**.

21 You'll need to make some adjustments to orient and size the **Half Round** profile properly.

22 On the **Parameters** rollout, change the **Radius** to **2.0**.

23 On the **Sweep Parameters** rollout, change the **Angle** value to **-90.0**. The wainscoting is properly oriented on the wall.

Lesson 17 | Using Compound Objects

In this lesson, you'll learn about a set of creation tools known as compound objects. Typically, a compound object is created by combining two or more objects. The compound object types covered in this lesson are Boolean, Loft, Scatter, and ShapeMerge.

An Archway can be quickly created using Boolean operations

Objectives

After completing this lesson, you'll be able to:

- Union, subtract, and intersect objects using Boolean operations
- Create complex forms using the Loft tool
- Use the Scatter tool to distribute one object over another
- Use ShapeMerge to refine a mesh.

Booleans

Booleans are compound objects that work with operations based on the volume of the objects being used. In this lesson, you'll explore three types of Boolean operations:

- **Subtraction**: The intersecting volume of one object is removed from the other.

- **Intersection**: The common volume of two objects creates a resultant geometric object.

- **Union**: The whole volume of both objects becomes one object. Edges and faces of the two objects are clearly defined.

- **Merge**: A similar operation to Union. Operands are joined together into one object. However, Merge does not clean up the intersecting edges between the operands.

The Boolean object is found on the Create panel, under **Geometry → Compound Objects**.

There are two tools for the creation of Boolean objects: the Boolean tool and the ProBoolean tool. Throughout this lesson, you'll be using the newer ProBoolean tool. The Boolean tool is mostly left for compatibility purposes for previous releases of 3ds Max and 3ds Max Design.

The ProBoolean Tool found in the Compound Objects Panel

Boolean Object found in Compound Objects

The following is a visual description of Boolean operations:

Subtraction

You use Boolean subtraction to remove one or many objects' volume from another.

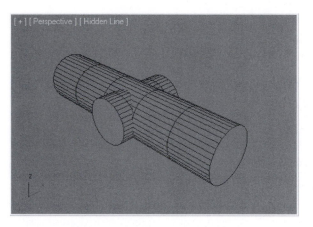

Two initial cylindrical volumes

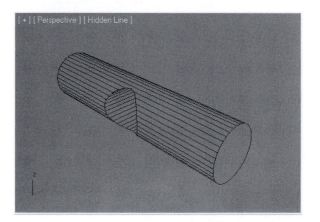

The middle cylinder is subtracted from the longer cylinder

Chapter 02 | Modeling

Intersection

You use Boolean intersection to find the area common to two objects. It can be used to create a new object that is the result of two objects. You can also use it for interference checking.

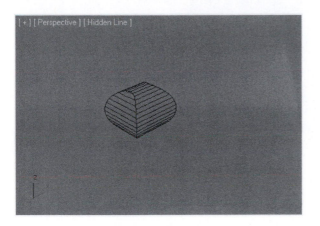

The same cylinders are intersected. Only the common volume is retained

Union

A Boolean union combines two or more separate volumes and removes excess faces. In addition, it creates correct edges where the volumes intersect. Shown below are intersecting volumes before and after a Boolean union operation. Note the intersecting lines and the lack of a line along the intersecting edges.

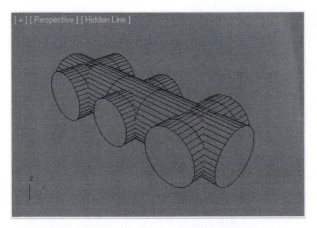

Cylinders that interesct but have not been unioned.

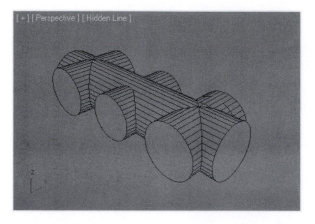

The same cylinders after a union operation

The volumes render much better once they're unioned.

Merge

The Merge method works similarly to Union, in that it also combines objects together to make a single object. The difference is in the treatment of edges and faces. Although objects are combined together, the intersection between them is not cleaned up.

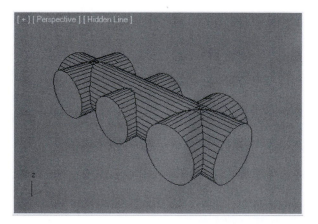

The cylinders after a merge operation

With a union, the edges in the intersecting volume are removed. With a merge, the edges in the intersecting volume remain. These additional edges can be used to further edit the volume with poly or mesh editing tools.

ProBoolean Operations

ProBoolean operations include some interesting modification and editing tools, some of which are highlighted as follows.

Changing the Boolean Operation

By selecting the Boolean Operand in the List of operands, the operand type can be changed. When you want to change the operation, you must select the operand in the history list. You would then change the operation at the top of the parameters panel, and then click the Change Operation button. The panel illustrated will change the operand center (the center cylinder) from a Union to a Subtraction operation.

The cylinders after a subtraction operation

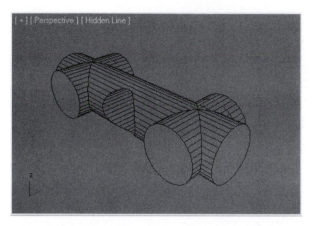

The cylinders after changing the operation of the center cylinder

Multiple Selections

When you click the Start Picking button in the Pick Boolean rollout, you have the ability to press the **H** key and select multiple objects using the Pick Object dialog box.

Reorder Operands

Occasionally, it becomes important to have Boolean operations occur in a particular order. The illustrations show a more complex use of Booleans based on the previous example. Note how the inside of the main cylinder is not completely hollow as is desired. This is due to the incorrect order of operations. The two side parts were unioned after the inside of the main cylinder was subtracted.

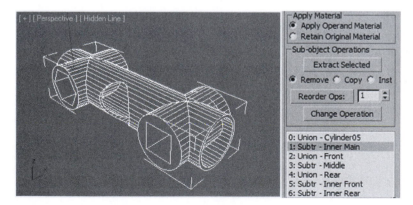

Hollow cylinders Booleaned in an incorrect order

Chapter 02 | **Modeling**

Fortunately, you can reorder the operations and perform the subtraction of the inner cylinder last, where it should have been done initially. Simply select the operand, type the number where it should be placed, and click the Reorder Ops: button.

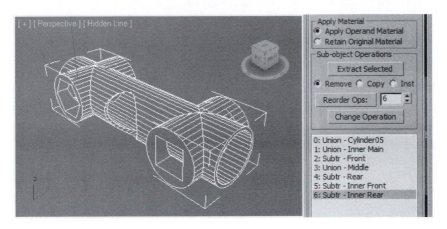

Booleans reordered to produce desired result

Lofts

A Loft object is a compound object that uses existing shapes to generate 3D geometry. A Loft operation requires both a path and a shape. Lofts can produce objects with a high degree of complexity. The power of Loft objects lies in the ability to change shapes in their construction process. In Following illustration, a screwdriver blade is created by transitioning from a circle to a rectangle.

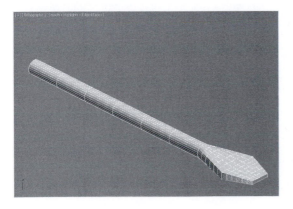

Screwdriver blade created using the Loft tool

The Loft tool is found on the Create panel, under **Geometry** → **Compound Objects**.

Loft tool in the Compound Objects panel

Drawing Paths and Shapes

When you create a loft, you'll need to first create a path and one or more shapes. Following are several considerations when creating these objects:

- Paths and shapes can be open or closed.

- When drawing a straight path set Drag Type to Corner; this avoids accidentally creating a Bezier vertex.

- Your path should generally not have corners with a sharper radius than the radius of your shape. Otherwise a corner with overlapping vertices is created.

- A loft can use multiple shapes along the path.

- Shapes used in a loft can have multiple splines.

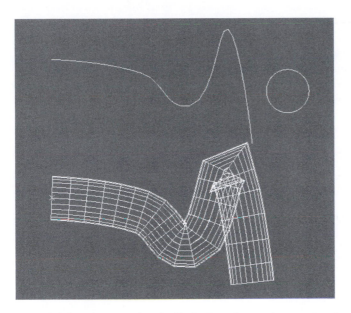

A simple loft with a curved path. The indicated areas show overlapping vertices that would not render well.

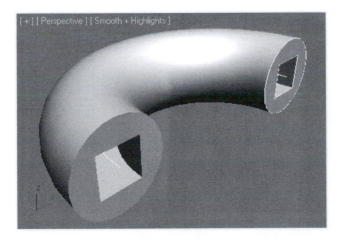

A loft with a multiple spline shape

Alignment and Pivot Points of Shapes

When you create a shape for a loft and use transformation commands and/or spline editing commands, the alignment of the shape and the location of the pivot point may be altered. You may find that you need to rotate or move the shape or its pivot point once it's part of the loft. You do this at the sub-object level of the loft.

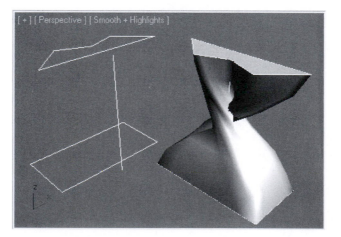

Loft sub-object levels

Multiple Shape Lofts and the First Vertex

When you work with multiple shapes in lofts, you inevitably encounter situations where the shapes on a loft are not properly aligned.

A twisted loft

A twisted loft usually points to a problem where the two shapes in the loft have misaligned first vertices. Once a loft is created you can use the Compare tool at the Shape sub-object level to check the locations of first vertices.

The Compare tool shows the locations of the first vertex for each shape. When the vertices are not aligned, the loft becomes twisted.

The Compare tool

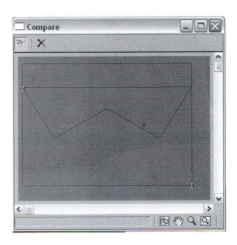

The Compare tool

To rotate the shapes properly, you will need to use the Select and Rotate tool while in the Shapes sub-object level.

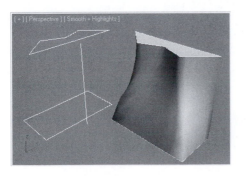

The multi-shape loft with first vertices properly aligned

This example also shows another potential situation when creating lofts. When there are shapes along the path with different vertex counts, there can be some unpredictability with how 3ds Max Design will generate surfaces. Refining the shapes so there is as good a correlation between vertex count and placement will give the best and most predictable results.

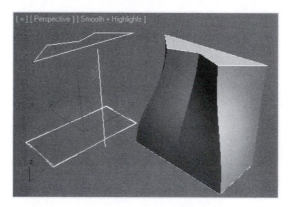

A vertex is added along one side of the base rectangle to match the top shape

Shape Steps and Path Steps

The Skin Parameters rollout allows you to control the number of faces used in the creation of lofts. Other important parameters can also be found in this rollout. Shape Steps controls the number of faces around the loft, while Path Steps controls the number of steps along the path.

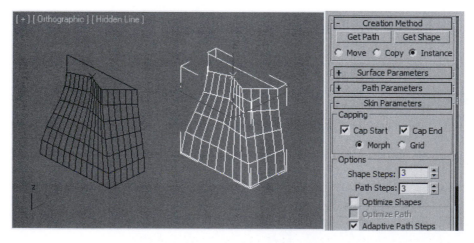

Shape and Path steps were lowered to 3 on the right-hand object from the default of 5 on the left.

Chapter 02 | Modeling

Deformation Grids

You can use deformation grids in lofts to produce interesting 3D geometry. There are five deformation grids: Scale, Twist, Teeter, Bevel, and Fit. The Scale Deformation grid lets you change the shape size along the length of the path.

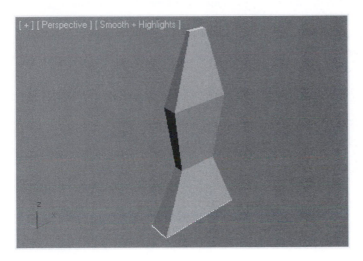

Scale deformation used equally in X and Y

The scale deformation grid becomes even more flexible when you scale differently in the X- and Y-directions.

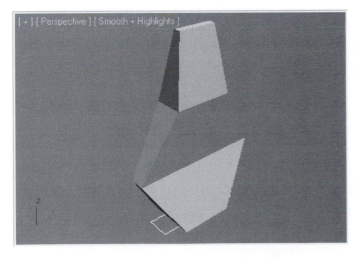

Scale deformation used with different X and Y scale values

Scatter Tool

The Scatter tool lets you distribute one object over another. It is useful whenever a multitude of objects are required over the surface of another object, such as rocks or trees over a landscape.

The Scatter object is found in the **Create panel** → **Geometry** → **Compound Objects**.

The Scatter tool

Distributed rocks over an uneven terrain

ShapeMerge

The ShapeMerge tool uses both a 3D geometry object and a shape. The Shape is used to rapidly refine the geometry of the 3D object so that it can be removed or detached or simply to create a new element or collection of faces. A simple example of ShapeMerge is where you have a landscape form and you wish to draw a walking path through the form that follows the undulations of the 3D geometry. Simply draw a shape of the path, and use the ShapeMerge compound object on the landscape.

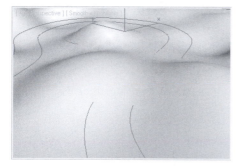

A 3D Landscape and spline

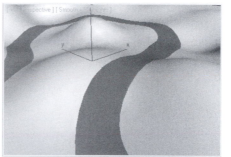

ShapeMerge used to create the path

The ShapeMerge tool is found in the **Create panel** → **Geometry** → **Compound Objects**.

The ShapeMerge tool

Exercise | Using Booleans to Create a Building Shell

In this exercise, you'll be using ProBoolean operations to edit the geometry of the gas station building.

1   Open the file *Gas Station Shell.max*. The scene contains two wall shells extruded from 2D splines.

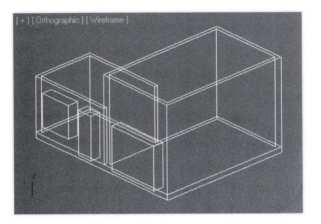

2   Select the **Upper Walls** object on the right side of the **User** viewport.

3   Go to the **Create** panel, and in the **Geometry** category choose **Compound Objects** from the drop-down list.

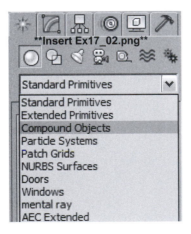

4   On the **Object Type** rollout, click the **ProBoolean** button.

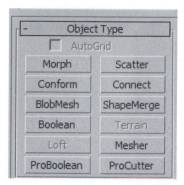

5   Make sure **Operation** is set to **Subtraction**.

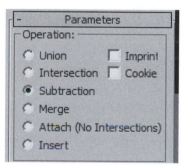

6   Click the **Start Picking** button.

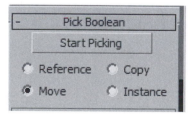

7   Select the *Open1* object that defines the positive volume of the garage door opening. The positive volume of the garage door opening now forms a negative space in the wall: the opening.

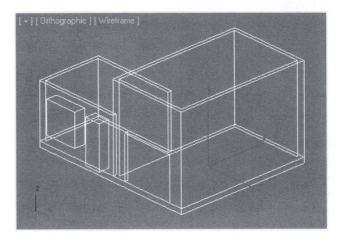

8   Change the **Operation in the Parameters** rollout to **Union**.

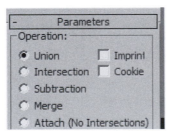

Note: *The Start Picking button is still active.*

9   Click the *Lower Walls* object to the left of the *Upper Walls*.

Note: *The edges between the two volumes are automatically cleaned up.*

10   Change back to **Subtract Mode**, the **Start Picking** button is still active.

11 Select the *Open2* object (box). You now have a door opening in the lower section of the building.

12 Select the *Open3* object that forms the opening for the window.

13 In the **Orthographic** viewport, press **F3** to switch to a shaded view. Below is the completed wall shell of the building.

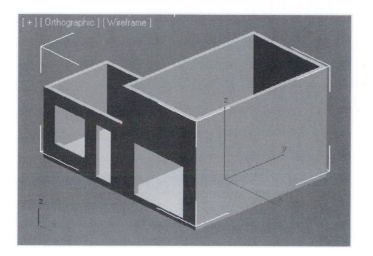

14 Press the **Start Picking** button to exit that mode and then **Esc** to exit the **Boolean** operation.

15 Right-click and choose **Unhide All**.

16   Click **Yes** in the dialog that appears.

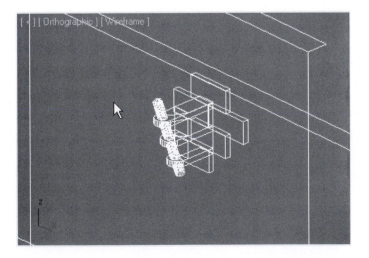

17   Press **F3** to switch the **User** viewport back to wireframe mode.

18   Some new elements appear in the viewport: a series of rectangular objects that will be used to make the concrete block walls more irregular and a flagstaff.

19   Make sure the shell of the building is still selected.

20   Go to the **Modify** panel and set the **Operation** type to **Union**.

21   Click the **Start Picking** button.

22   Zoom in if you need to and Pick the *Flag Staff* object. The flag staff object is added to the volume.

23 Change the **Operation** to **Subtraction**.

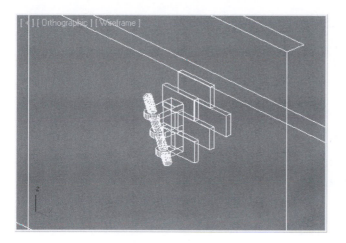

24 Press the **H** key.

25 Select all objects that start with the word *Block*.

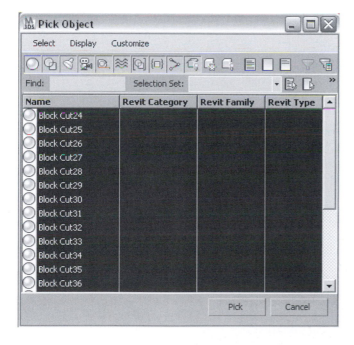

26   Click the **Pick** button in the dialog.

This operation has quickly removed the Block objects. But there are a few things that will need to be corrected. You might notice that two of the rectangular blocks near the middle of the right wall have disappeared. These blocks were named "Block Pushout" and "Block Pushout1." These elements were meant to be added (Union operation) with the walls to add mass. By mistake, they were subtracted in the previous operation. You'll correct this in the next few steps.

27   In the **Modify** panel, at the bottom of the **Parameters** rollout, use the scroll bar to find the two **Block Pushout** objects at the bottom of the list of operands.

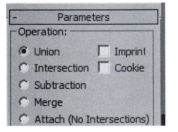

28   Select both objects in the list. You can use the **Ctrl** key to make multiple selections.

29   Select **Union** in the **Operation** area of the **Parameters** rollout.

30   Click the **Change Operation** button. The missing blocks reappear on the concrete block wall.

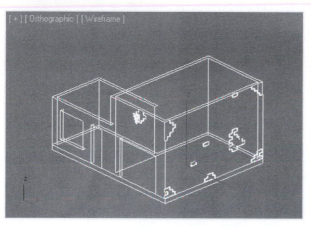

31   Zoom into the flagstaff area in the user viewport and switch into **Smooth + Highlight** mode
(**F3**) with **Edged Faces** on (**F4**).

*Notice the gap between the flagstaff and the wall now that the blocks were subtracted. This
problem would not have occurred if the Union operation was performed last. The flag staff is
detached from the wall due to the subtraction of the block cutout objects.*

32   Click the *Flag Staff* object near the top of the list of operands.

33   In the **Edit** box next to the **Reorder Ops** button, enter **60**. This will ensure that the union
occurs at the very end, after all operations in the list have been calculated.

34   Click the **Reorder Ops** button.

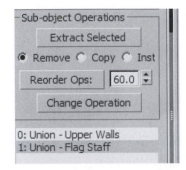

The Union operation is calculated last and no gaps are shown between the wall and the flagstaff.

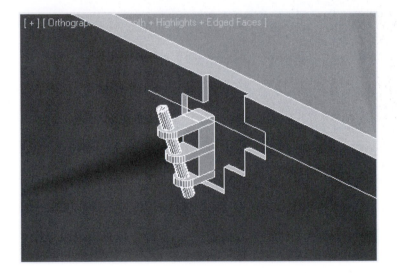

Exercise | Creating a Screwdriver Blade

In this exercise you will create a screwdriver blade using the loft tool

1   Open the file *Loft Start.max*. The scene shows three simple shapes: a line, a circle, and a rectangle.

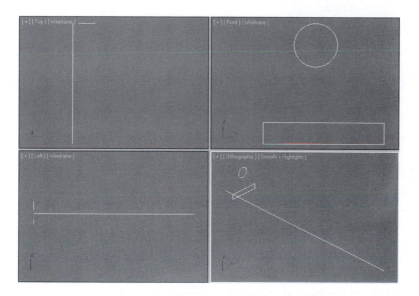

2   Select the *Straight Line* object. You'll use it as a path for the resulting Loft object.

3   In the **Create Command Panel**, under **Geometry**, select **Compound Objects** from the pull-down list.

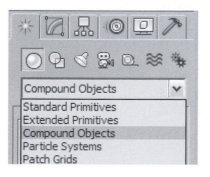

4   Click the **Loft** button in the **Object Type** rollout.

5   In the **Creation Method** rollout, click the **Get Shape** button.

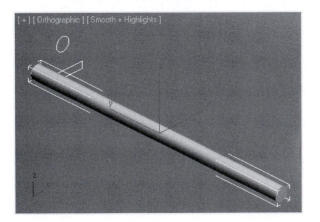

6   Click the circle in any viewport.

Selecting the circle shape extrudes the circle along the linear path. This creates a simple lofted object. Next, you'll make this lofted object a bit more complex by changing the shape at the end of the loft.

7   Go to the **Modify** panel.

8   In the **Path Parameters** rollout, change the **Path Percentage** to **100**.

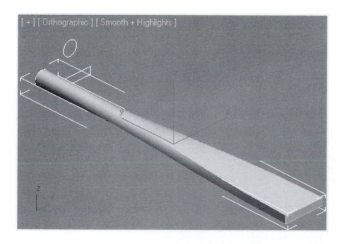

9   Click the **Get Shape** button again but this time, select the rectangle.

The Loft object has a more complex form as the shape transitions from one end to another, going from a circular to a rectangular cross-section.

10   In the **Path Parameters** rollout, change the **Path Percentage** to **75**.

11   Make sure the **Get Shape** button is still selected.

12   Select the circle again.

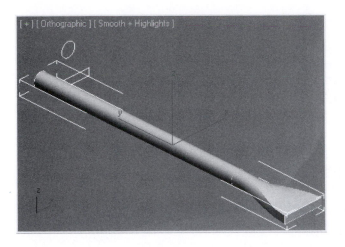

The shape of the loft remains consistent from the start to 75% along the length; then it begins to change into a rectangle.

13   In the **Path Parameters** rollout, change the **Path Percentage** to **85**.

14   Select the rectangle again.

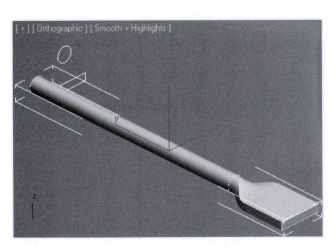

The shape has a faster transition from circle to rectangle.

15   In the **modifier stack**, click the plus sign next to the *Loft* object to open its hierarchy of sub-objects.

Chapter 02 | Modeling

16 Select the **Shape** sub-object level.

17 Click the rectangle next to the circle that creates the circle-to-rectangle transition.

18 Change the **Path Level** to **90**.

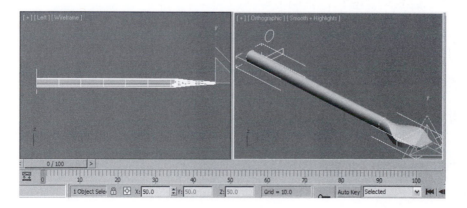

The shape is repositioned along the path, and the loft has a more attractive appearance. Finally, the end of the screwdriver blade should be adjusted to taper down. This could be accomplished in a number of ways, by using another shape, using the more advanced loft deformation tools, or simply scaling the cross-section.

19 Select the rectangular cross-section at the tip of the blade.

20 Using the **Scale** tool, scale down the selected cross-section to about **50%** of its original size.

Although the object appears fine in the shaded orthographic view, the front view reveals a twisting in the lofted object. This can be corrected in the Shape sub-object level. Also, the head of the blade should have straighter angles as opposed to curved edges. You'll be fixing that in the next few steps.

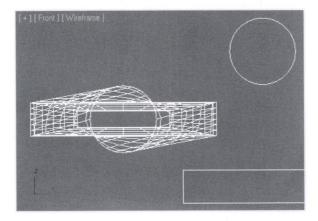

21   In the **modifier stack**, click the **Compare** button in the **Shape Commands** rollout.

22   In the **Compare** window that appears, click the **Pick Shape** button.

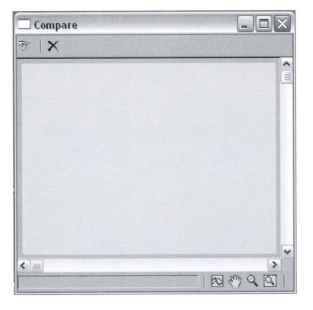

Chapter 02 | Modeling

23 Click the rectangle shape at **90%** along the lofted object. The rectangle shape will be brought into the **Compare** window.

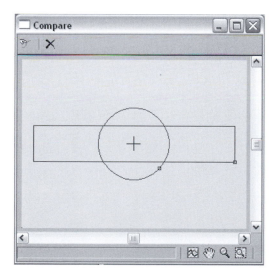

24 Click the **Circle** that is positioned at **75%** along the path.

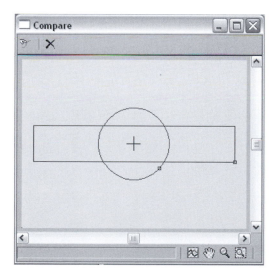

You now see both shapes displayed in the Compare window. The reason you're getting a twisting effect is that the first vertices of the shapes are slightly misaligned. You'll correct this by rotating the shape.

25 Click on the **Pick Shape** button in the **Compare** window to disable it.

26 In the **Orthographic** viewport, select both circular cross-sections positioned at path percent **0** and **75%,** respectively.

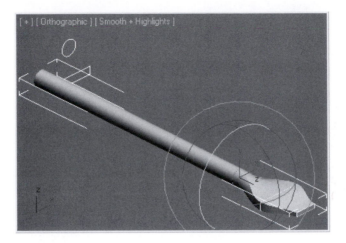

27 On the **main** toolbar, click the **Select and Rotate** button.

28 Still in the **Orthographic** viewport, click and drag on the blue circle of the **Rotate** gizmo (local Z-axis) until you see the twisting in the **Front** viewport disappear. The first vertex on the circle in the **Compare** window should be pointing "South/East", the same as the first vertex on the rectangle.

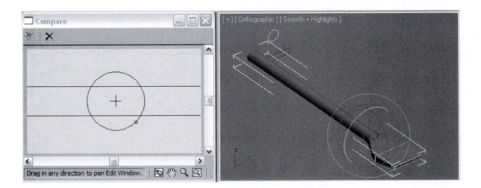

29 Close the **Compare** window.

30 In the **Modify** panel, exit **Shape** sub-object mode.

31 Expand the **Skin Parameters** rollout and enable **Linear Interpolation** to remove the curvy look of the blade head.

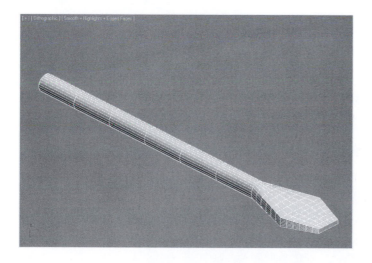

32 Maximize the **Orthographic** view, and switch the **Display** mode to **Smooth** + **Highlights** + **Edged Faces**.

33 Save your file.

Exercise | Enhancing a Building Landscape

In this scene, you'll use ShapeMerge and Scatter to enhance a Building Landscape.

1 Open the file *LakeHouse_Landscape.max*.

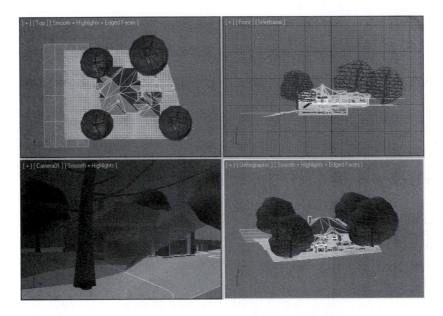

2 In the **Layer** toolbar, turn off all the layers except *Ground_Landscape*.

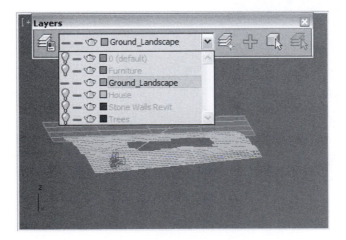

Only a few objects remain in the scene.

3   In the **Orthographic** viewport, zoom in to the area at the front of the undulated plane. There is a spline that indicates where the driveway and walkway should be in front of the house.

4   Select the **Landscape** object.

5   Go to the **Create** tab in the **Command** panel.

6   In **Geometry**, select **Compound Objects** from the pull-down list.

7   Select **ShapeMerge**.

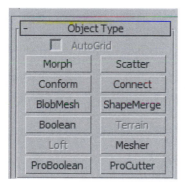

8   Click on the **Pick Shape** button in the **Pick Operand** rollout.

9   Click on the *Line02* object.

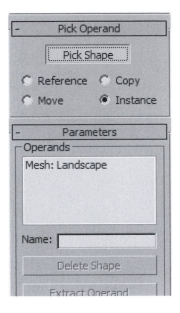

At this point the ground surface has been refined although it is a bit hard to see.

10   Go to the **Modify** tab in the **Command** panel.

11   Select **Edit Poly** from the **Modifier List**.

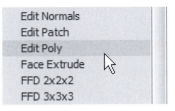

12   Go to the **Element** sub-object level

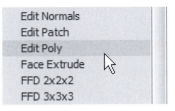

The surface area defining the driveway and walkway is selected.

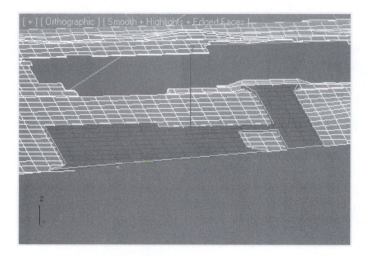

13 In the **Edit Geometry**, click the **Detach** button.

14 In the **modifier stack**, right click and select **Collapse All**.

You now have two separate objects, that define the surface of the landscape.

15 Select the area that defines the driveway and walkway.

16 **Rename** the object *Hard Surfaces*.

17 Change the object color to a dark blue.

18 In the **Orthographic** viewport zoom in to the area just in front of the driveway.

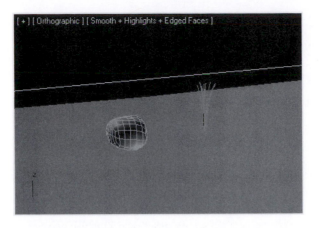

You should see a rock and a small plant. You will use these objects to add some variety to the surface of the landscape outside of the driveway and walkway.

19 Select the *Rock* object.

20 In the **Create** tab, select **Scatter**.

21 Click on the **Pick Distribution Object** button

22 In the **Camera** view, select the **Landscape** object outside of the hard surfaces.

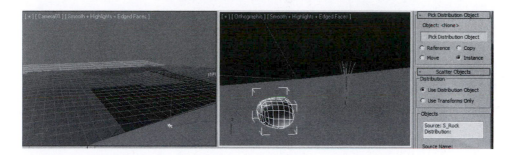

The Landscape object changes color. Scatter creates a duplicate distribution object that can be turned off. You probably will not see the effect of the Scatter either since by default only one object is created in the Scatter.

23 In the **Modify** tab, go to the **Display** rollout of the **Scatter** object.

24 Select **Hide Distribution Object**.

25   In the **Scatter** objects rollout, in the **Source Object Parameters** group, increase the duplicates to **100**.

You should be careful when you use Scatter, since it has the potential to greatly increase the number of polygons used in your scene.

26   In the **Distribution Object Parameter** group, select **Random Faces**.

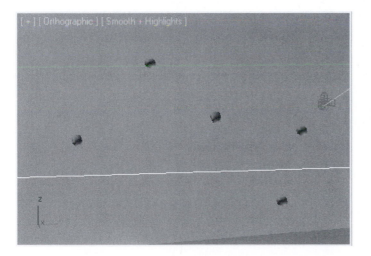

This will make the distribution of the Rock object more random over the landscape surface.

27   In the **Orthographic** viewport, zoom in to an area where you can see several of the *Rock* objects.

28   Turn off **Edge Faces** mode.

The rocks are oriented and sized identically; you will introduce randomness in their pattern in the next few steps.

29   In the **Transform** rollout, enter the following values: **X=20, Y=15, Z=45**.

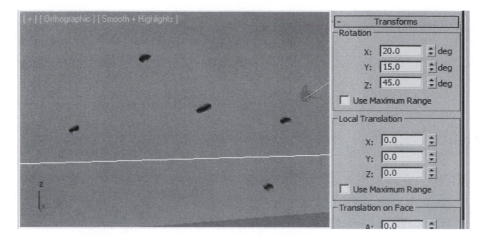

These values introduce randomness in the rotation of the rocks in X, Y, and Z.

30   In the **Scaling** group, type **X=20, Y=10, Z=30**.

This will introduce randomness in the size of the Rock objects.

31   In the **Display** area, click on **Proxy**.

32 Change the **Display** value to **25%**.

These values change the number of objects that Scatter displays in the viewport only. Reducing the number and complexity (through a proxy, which is a simplified object) helps the regeneration of the display of the scene - for example, during zooms and pans.

Note: *If you do not like the distribution of objects, you can change it by using a seed value in the **Uniqueness** group.*

If you wish to continue the exercise, distribute the plant object in a similar fashion over the landscape surface.

Lesson 18 | Light Types

Introduction

Lighting is an essential part of the visual process. Without proper lighting, the best models, materials, and camera placements will not create good images. 3ds Max® and 3ds Max Design offer a variety of ways to achieve proper lighting. In this lesson, you will learn about various light types and some fundamentals of lighting.

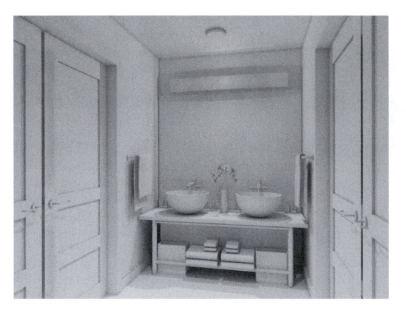

Each lighting situation provides challenges; good lighting is the beginning of an excellent image

Objectives

After completing this lesson, you will be able to:

- Use the standard light types
- Describe how photometric lights work
- Use mental ray area lights
- Use color, intensity and distribution of lights to create lighting setups
- Apply and modify different shadow types to lights in a scene

Go to the Customize menu, select Custom UI and Defaults Switcher. Select Max.mentalray for the initial settings for tool options, at the upper left. Select ame-light if required for the UI schemes to the upper right.

Custom UI and defaults switcher

You will need to restart 3ds Max afterwards for these changes to take effect.

Light Types

Standard Lights

Standard lights are very flexible and easy to use. They can be controlled and adapted to fit the kind of lighting designed by the artist. They are not physically accurate, but their range of controls helps achieve the kind of realism an artist craves for.

Omni Light

The Omni light simulates rays shining out from a single point in space. Rays are emitted uniformly in all directions. This is somewhat similar to a bare light bulb.

Scene lit with an Omni light

Spot Light

The Spot light also simulates rays shining out from a single point but limits the illumination to a specific cone-shaped volume. This kind of control, which allows you to aim a light at a specific target, makes the Spot a popular choice for many lighting artists.

Scene lit with a spotlight

You have total control over the beam of light that defines the illumination cone. In fact, there are two cones that you can control: the hotspot (inner cone) and the falloff (outer cone).

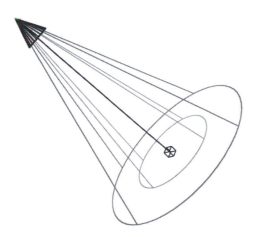

Spotlight cones

When the two values are close, the cone of light becomes very sharp and translates into a crisp pool of light in the scene. However, if you set a Falloff value significantly higher than the Hotspot value, then you get a much softer-edged cone of light as the light intensity spreads from the inner to the outer cone.

Equal-sized Hotspot and Falloff values

Falloff value twice the size of the Hotspot value

A Spot light can be targeted or free.

Target Spot

When you create a Target Spot, you use the target object (in the form of a small square) to orient the spotlight. The spotlight itself will always point to (look at) that target. This makes the Target Spot very easy to position in the scene. In addition, by linking the target to an animated object in the scene, you can ensure the spotlight will always follow the animated object.

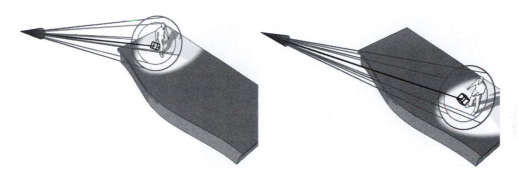

Target Spots make it easy to highlight and follow objects

Free Spot

When you create a Free Spot, you orient that spot using the Rotate tool. A good example of when to use a Free Spot is when simulating the headlights on a car. As you animate the car in the scene, the spotlights' orientation follows that of the car.

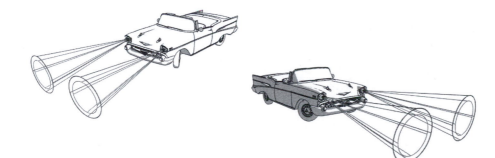

Free Spots are useful when attached to objects

Direct Light

A Direct light has roughly the same workflow as a Spot light but casts rays through a cylinder instead of a cone. The rays are therefore parallel, making the Direct light suitable for simulating distant light sources, such as the sun.

Because the Direct light casts parallel rays, it does not matter how far you place it from the objects in the scene; the only thing that matters is the direction in which it's pointed.

Scene lit with a Direct light

Much like a Spot light, you can control the softness of the Direct light's cylindrical beam with Hotspot and Falloff values. A Direct light can also be targeted or free.

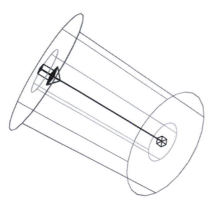

Direct light Hotspot and Falloff cylindrical beams

Chapter 03 | Lighting

Photometric Lights

When you use photometric lights, the software provides physically based simulation of the propagation of light through an environment. The results are not only highly realistic renderings, but also accurate measurements of the distribution of light within the scene. The measurement of light is known as photometry.

Because photometric lights are physically accurate, they require that the scene is set using realistic units. A light that is adequate to illuminate a bedroom will not be sufficient to illuminate a football stadium.

Light Distribution

Photometric lights use different distribution methods: Isotropic/Diffuse, Spot, and Web. These methods determine how light is distributed from a light source. Choosing Web Distribution gives you the ability to attach an IES file for specific manufacturer's lights.

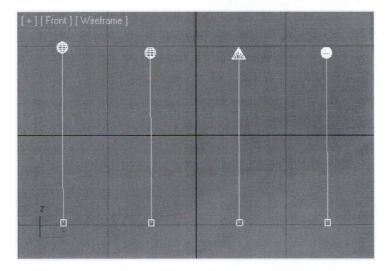

Photometric lights distribution

Isotropic/Diffuse

This distribution type is the default for all new lights. For the point light (Isotropic), the light is the same in all directions. For linear and area light (diffuse), light that leaves the surface at a right angle is at the light's greatest intensity. At increasingly oblique angles, the intensity of the emitted light diminishes. Question this section!!

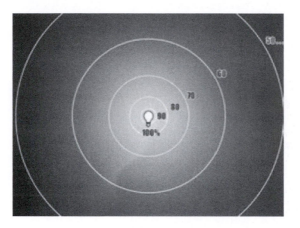

Isotropic/Diffuse distribution

Spot

Only the point light can have this distribution that makes it behave like a focused beam of a flashlight. The Hotspot (Beam) and Falloff (Field) angles can be set as for the standard Spotlight objects.

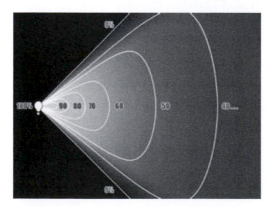

Spot distribution

Web

Web distribution enables you to customize the intensity of the emission. You need a definition file (*.IES) that is usually provided by light manufacturers for each of their light fixtures.

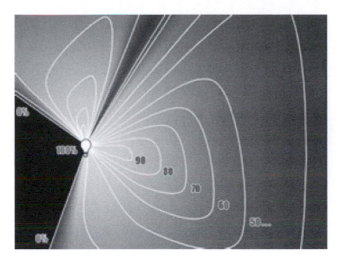

Web distribution

Light Types

A Photometric light, like a standard light, can be either Free or Targeted.

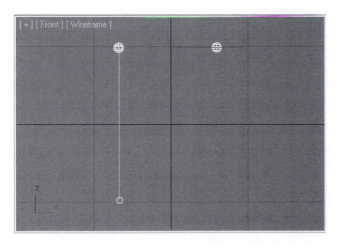

Free or targeted Photometric lights

Area Light

A Photometric Area light emits light from one of six different shapes: point, line, rectangle, disk, sphere, and cylinder.

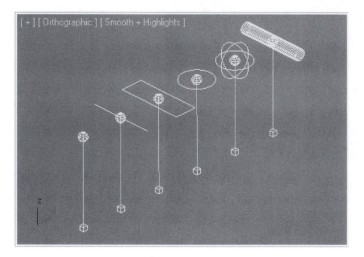

Various shapes of Photometric lights

mr Lights

mr (mental ray) Lights are non physically based lights. They come in two basic forms: mr Area Omni and mr Area Spot. These two lights are mostly useful when you use the mental ray renderer. This is when their special features come into play. mental ray is the default renderer in 3ds Max Design. If you are using 3ds Max, the Scanline renderer is the default. As noted previously you should change the Custom UI and Defaults to Max.mental ray, from the Customize menu.

mr Area Omni Light

When using the mental ray renderer, the mr Area Omni light emits light from a spherical or cylindrical volume, rather than from a point source. This creates a more realistic rendering under mental ray. Keep in mind that area lights take longer to compute.

Shadows from an mr Omni light

mr Area Spot Light

When using the mental ray renderer, the mr Area Spot light emits light from a rectangular or disc shaped area, rather than from a point source. This is different from the mr Area Omni that emits light from a spherical or cylindrical volume. As with all area lights, however, the mr Area Spot lights takes longer to compute. Both the mr Omni and Spot light area properties can be turned off for quick test renders.

Area light parameters rollout

Light Attributes

Color, Intensity, and Distribution

Non-Physically based lights

The subtle use of color is a very powerful tool to reach your audience's emotions. Color can be used in a variety of ways, by applying materials to objects, by using backgrounds, or by affecting the light color, among others.

There's a direct connection between the colors derived from materials on objects and the color of the lights used in the scene. Scenes can become richer and more realistic if there's variety in the colors of the lights illuminating objects. Differences in color temperature, typically ranging from blue (cold) to red (warm), can add realism to your lighting.

The intensity of a light can also be adjusted in many ways, but it's important to remember that lighting a scene is an additive process. This means that if you have multiple lights in the scene, the sum of all light intensities makes up the resulting illumination. Therefore, when you start adding multiple lights, you inevitably want to adjust their multiplier values so that the final scene is not over-exposed.

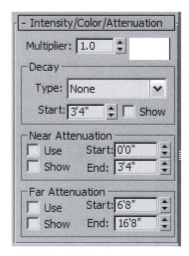

Intensity/Color/Attenuation rollout for non-physically based lights

Attenuation is the process of a light's intensity diminishing with distance. You can control this effect with Standard and mr lights by specifying exact distances where attenuation begins and where it ends, or by using Decay values. You can also choose the (unrealistic) solution of not attenuating a light at all, in which case its distance to an object in the scene becomes irrelevant.

With a Standard or mr light selected, Color, Intensity, and Attenuation can be set in the Modify panel under the appropriately named Color/Intensity/Attenuation rollout.

Physically based lights

Color and Intensity work differently with Photometric lights than they do with Standard or mr lights. Even Attenuation has fewer controls as it always works in an Inverse Square format when dealing with photometric lights.

The light color in a photometric light is typically set using predefined standard values found in a drop-down box. The light intensity is set in Lumens, Candelas, or Lux at a specific distance. These values can be obtained from light manufacturers. A 100-watt bulb is about 1750 lumens, or 139 candelas.

Intensity/Color/Attenuation rollout for physically based lights

Shadows

Importance of Shadows

We see shadows every day but we seldom stop to consider how vital they are in helping to establish the relationships with the spaces that surround us. CG shadows differ greatly from those in the real world, however, and creating believable shadows in a 3D environment requires skill and the ability to analyze shadow form, color, density, and general quality. Arguably, the most important visual cues that shadows provide are perception of depth and positioning between objects in an environment.

The car on the left appears to be floating in space. The car on the right is more grounded because of its shadow.

The Importance of shadows

Various shadow types are available in 3ds Max and 3ds Max Design but all are based on either of two algorithms: shadow maps and ray-traced shadows. There are considerable differences between the two types as the choice will ultimately dictate rendering quality and speed.

Shadow Maps

The shadow map method uses a bitmap that the renderer generates before final rendering. The process is completely transparent and does not store any information on the hard drive. The bitmap is then projected from the direction of the light. Shadow maps can be fast to calculate and can produce soft-edged shadows. On the downside, they are not very accurate and do not take objects' transparency or translucency into account.

Shadow map with soft edges. The shadowing is uniform and does not recognize the transparency of the glass.

Shadow map shadows

Ray-Traced Shadows

Ray-traced shadows are generated by tracing the path of rays from a light source. They are more accurate than shadow maps but generally produce hard-edged shadows. Because ray-traced shadows are calculated without a map, you do not have to adjust resolution as you do for shadow-mapped shadows, making them easier to set up. Ray-traced shadows take transparency and translucency into account, and can even be used to generate shadows for wireframe objects.

Ray-traced shadow with hard edges. The transparency of the glass is taken into account.

More Shadow Types

There are other shadow types that you can use. Advanced ray-traced shadows are similar to ray-traced shadows but provide better anti-aliasing control and can generate soft-edged shadows. Area shadows simulate shadows cast by a light that has a surface or a volume as opposed to a point. Shadows of this type tend to become more blurred with distance. Mental ray shadow maps are to be used with the mental ray renderer.

Advanced ray traced shadow

Area shadow

In addition to these shadow types, the shape and size of the light source will affect the sharpness of the shadows.

Ray traced shadow from a point light source

Ray traced shadow from a spherical light source

Viewport Shading

Viewport Shading is a new method of displaying lighting setups before committing to rendering the scene. You will find controls for viewport shading in the Shading viewport label menu, under Lighting and Shadows.

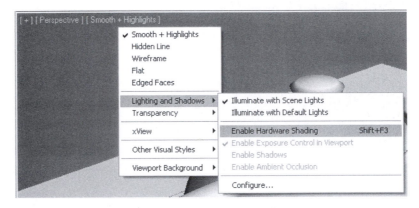

Hardware Shading allows you to Display more precise lighting in the viewport

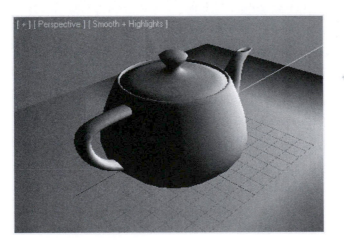

Before Hardware Shading is turned on, the outline of the spotlight is not properly defined.

With Hardware Shading, the cone of the Spot light and the falloff of the light are apparent

Once Hardware Shading is enabled, you can also turn on Shadows display. You can enable Shadows in the Shading viewport label menu, under Lighting and Shadows.

Enabling Shadows in the Shading viewport label menu

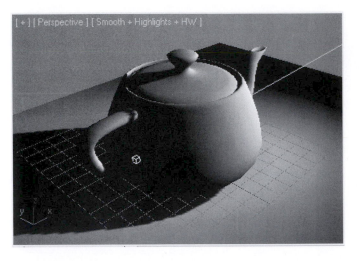

Shadows enabled

When a light that supports soft shadows is being used, such as an mr Area Spot or a photometric light, soft shadows can be turned on in the viewport display. In this case you will need to go to the Viewport Configuration dialog, Lighting and Shadows tab.

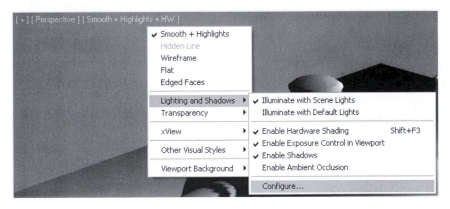

Configure selection

In this dialog you can toggle the display of Hard and Soft shadows.

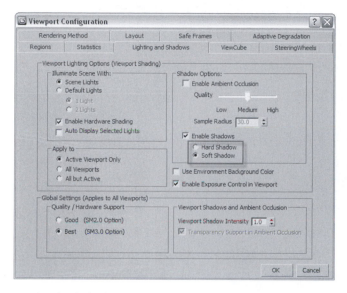

Hard and Soft shadow toggle

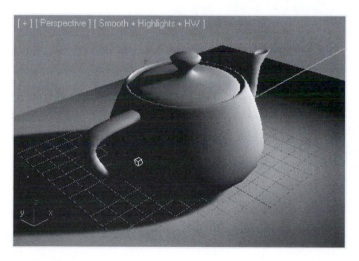

Soft Shadows enabled

Exercise | Creating a Target Spot

1   Reset 3ds Max Design.

2   Open the file *shadows.max*. The scene shows a wine glass on a flat wooden surface.

3   Make sure the **Perspective** viewport is active and then press the **F9** key to render the scene.

The rendered scene looks flat for lack of contrast. The lighting is uninteresting and the absence of shadows makes for a weak connection between the glass and the tabletop.

4   Right-click the **Front** viewport to activate it.

5   On the **Create** panel, click the **Lights** button. Make sure you have the **Standard in the type list** selected.

6   Click **mr Area Spot** on the **Object Type** rollout.

7   In the **Front** viewport, click and drag from the top-right corner onto the wine glass.

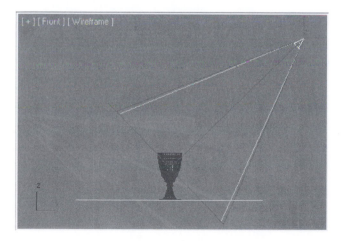

8   Go to the **Modify** tab of the **Command** panel. In the **General Parameters** rollout, make sure that **Shadows** are enabled.

9   Activate the **Perspective** viewport.

10 Click on the **Shading** viewport label menu, and select **Lighting and Shadows** →
       Enable Hardware Shading.

11 Click once again on the **Shading** viewport label menu, and select **Lighting and Shadows** →
Enable Shadows.

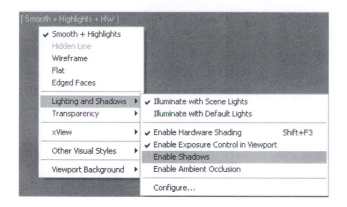

*Hardware Shading gives you a more accurate representation of the lighting directly in the
viewport.*

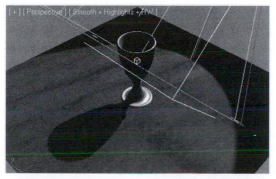

12 Render the scene again.

By default, the Spot light casts shadows. The Hotspot and Falloff values are very close, making a "theatre spotlight" effect as the edge of the pool of light is very crisp.

13 Make sure the light is still selected, go to the **Modify** tab, and expand the **Spotlight Parameters** rollout.

14 Set the **Hotspot/Beam** value to **15.0** to decrease the light cone, where the intensity is at its maximum.

15 Set the **Falloff/Field** value to **100.0** to increase the overall diameter of the light so that the Spot light encompasses more of the 3D environment.

16 Render the **Perspective** viewport again.

17 With the light still selected, open the **Area Light Parameters** rollout at the bottom of the **Modify** panel.

18 Change the type to **Disc**, and the **Radius** value to **100.0**. This value changes the effective size from which light is emanating.

19 Render the **Perspective** viewport.

The shadow is blurred now, which would be consistent with light coming from a large surface rather than a single point.

Lesson 19 | Simple Lighting Setup

Introduction

Lighting setups can be fairly complex, but in many situations a simple lighting setup will suffice. In this lesson, you will learn about a simple lighting setup called the three-point light setup.

Sometimes a simple lighting setup is all you need

Objectives

After completing this lesson, you will be able to:

- Use the three point-lighting system for simple lighting setups

Three Point-Lighting

As its name implies, the technique of three-point lighting uses three lights with very specific functions. It is a technique that is firmly established in cinematography and is one of the foundations in CG lighting as well. This technique emphasizes three-dimensional forms in a scene.

Rendered scene with default lighting

Rendered scene with three-point lighting

The Key Light

The key light is the main or dominant light in the scene. It is often the only one that casts shadows and is used as the primary light source in the scene.

The key light

The Fill Light

The primary purpose of the fill light is to control shadow density. It is often not enough to control the density of the main light's shadows. The fill light helps to remedy that problem by softening the effect of shadows in the scene. At the same time, it acts as a bounce light, simulating or enhancing global illumination. Typically, the fill light is less intense than the key light.

The fill light

The Backlight (or Rim light)

The backlight's sole purpose is to separate the subject from the background, giving the scene greater depth. It works by illuminating the back of an object or character so that the silhouette is easier to see.

The backlight

Exercise | Working with Three-Point Lighting

In this exercise, you will use a simple lighting technique called three-point lighting. This technique provides you with good lighting without the need for indirect illumination, thereby speeding up render times.

1   Reset 3ds Max Design.

2   Open the file *3-point_start.max*.

3   With the **Camera** viewport active, press the **F9** key to render the scene.

The scene shows the rendering of a statue based on 3ds Max's default lighting. The general mood is far from interesting, so you'll use the three-point lighting technique to make the scene more appealing. This technique does not require indirect illumination, so for the purposes of this exercise you will turn it off.

4 In the lower part of the **Render Window**, move the **Final Gather Precision** slider to the left to turn off Final Gather.

Final Gather Precision:

Final Gather Disabled

5 Dismiss the **Render Frame** window.

6 On the **Create** tab of the **Command** panel, click the **Lights** button.

7 Make sure the **Light Type** list is set to **Standard**.

8 Choose **mr Area Spot** from the **Object Type** panel.

9 In the **Front** viewport, click and drag from the top-left corner to the statue.

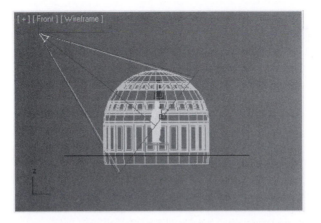

10 On the **main** toolbar, click the **Select and Move** button. In the **Top** viewport, move the spotlight and position it in the bottom-left corner of the viewport.

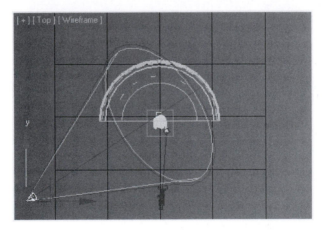

11 On the **Modify** tab, rename the spotlight *Main_Light*.

Chapter 03 | Lighting

12 In the **Camera** viewport, click on the **Shading** viewport label menu. Select **Lighting and Shadows** → **Enable Hardware Shading**.

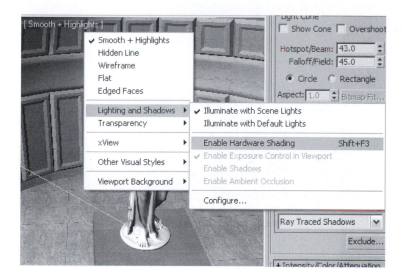

13 Click on the **Shading** viewport label menu again. Select **Lighting and Shadows** → **Enable Shadows**.

Hardware Shading gives you a better idea of the effect of the lights.

Before you make adjustments to the main light, you'll create the fill light and backlight.

14   On the **Create** panel, under **Lights**, choose the **mr Area Spot** again.

15   In the **Front** viewport, create a second light by dragging it from the center-right of the viewport to the statue.

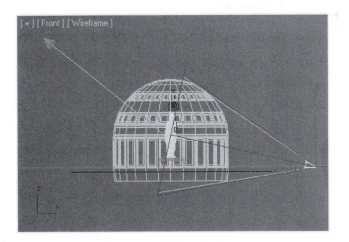

16 Using the **Move** tool, adjust the position of the new spotlight in the **Top** viewport so that it's directed at the statue from roughly the opposite direction of the main light, using the camera vector as a mirror plane.

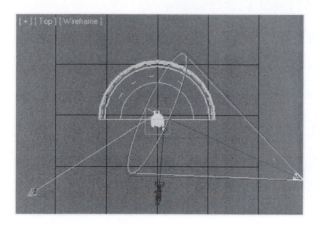

17 Rename the second light *Fill_Light*.

18 Create one more spotlight in the **Front** viewport, dragging from the top-center of the viewport to the statue.

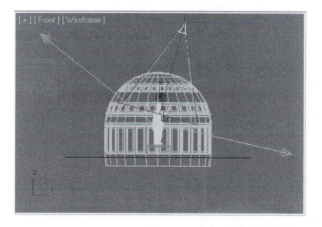

19 In the **Top** viewport, move the new spotlight so that it's directed at the statue from the northeast direction.

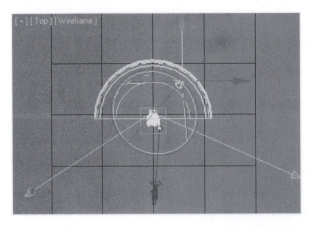

20 Rename the light *Back_Light*.

With the three lights inserted, the lighting is too bright. In the next several steps you will make adjustments to balance the lighting.

21 Select the *Main_Light* and go to the **Modify** panel.

Chapter 03 | Lighting

22 On the **General Parameters** rollout, verify that **Shadows** are on and that the type is set to **Ray Traced Shadows**.

23 On the **Spotlight Parameters** rollout, set **Hotspot** to **30.0** and **Falloff** to **100.0**.

24 Select the *Fill_Light*.

25 In the **General Parameters** rollout, turn off shadows.

26 On the **Intensity/Color/Attenuation** rollout, set the **Multiplier** value to **0.4**. This makes the fill light less intense than the main light.

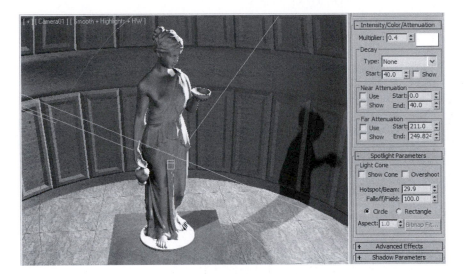

27 In the **Far Attenuation** group, turn on **Use**. This causes the light intensity to fall off with distance, based on Start/End distances you specify.

28 Adjust the **Start/End Attenuation** values so that the light attenuates from the front of the statue to the vault wall. Keep an eye on the **Top** viewport for reference.

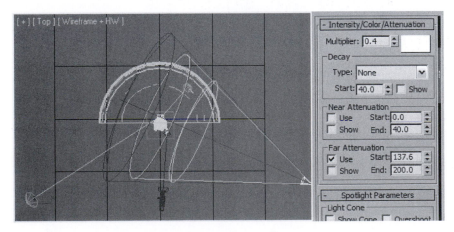

29 Select the *Back_Light*.

30 In the **General Parameters** rollout, turn off shadows.

31 On the **Intensity/Color/Attenuation** rollout, set the **Multiplier** value to **0.6**.

32 In the **Far Attenuation** group, turn on **Use**.

33 Adjust the **Start/End Attenuation** values so that the light attenuates from the statue's head to its knees. Keep an eye on the **Front** viewport for reference.

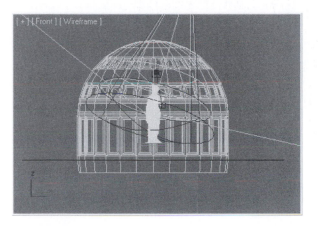

Notice how much better the lighting in the viewport appears.

34 Select the *Main_Light*. and go to the **Modify** tab of the **Command** panel.

35 In the **Area Light Parameters** rollout change the **Type** to **Disc**, and the **Radius** Value to **5.0**.

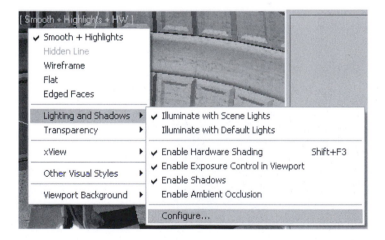

This creates a light that is projected from a larger surface that will produce a soft-edged shadow.

36 In the **Camera** viewport, click on the **Shading** viewport label menu. Select **Lighting and Shadows** → **Configure**.

37   In the **Viewport Configuration** dialog, **Lighting and Shadows** tab, change the **Shadow Options** to **Soft Shadow**.

38   Render the **Camera** viewport.

39   Compare the rendering to the first test render you created early in this exercise.

Lesson 20 | Lighting Tools

Introduction

In this lesson, you will learn about some lighting tools and techniques. These tools will help you manage lighting in your scenes better.

Alternative lighting setups can be quickly created with lighting tools

Objectives

After completing this lesson, you will be able to:

- Use the Light Lister to manage multiple lights
- Use the Manage Scene States dialog to save lighting setups

Light Lister

The Light Lister is a dialog that lets you control a number of features for each light. It is a very useful tool for managing multiple lights in your scene. You can easily turn lights off and on, turn shadows off and on, and change various other light parameters, such as multiplier values and shadow types, etc.

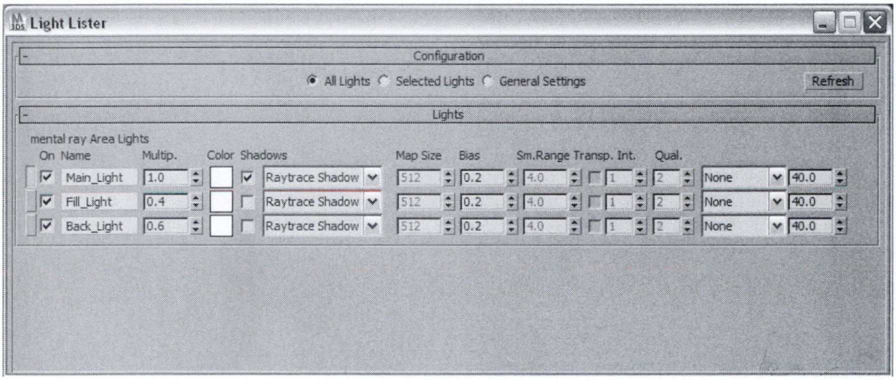

The Light Lister dialog

The Light Lister is accessed through the Tools menu.

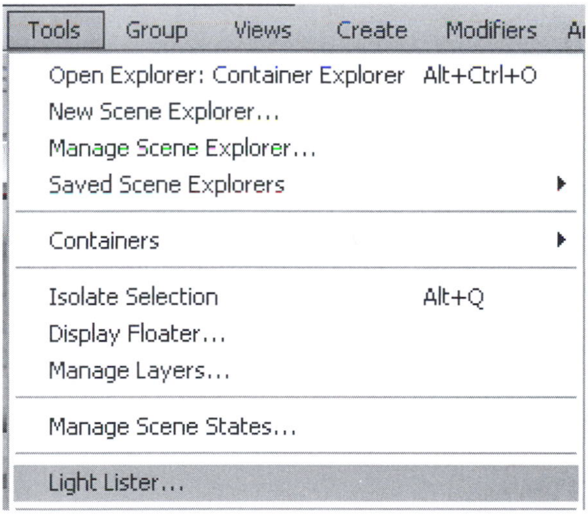

Tools menu

Manage Scene States

Although not exclusively about lighting, the Manage Scene State dialog bears some mention at this point. In the dialog you can save two parameters that are related to lighting: Lighting Properties and Lighting Transforms.

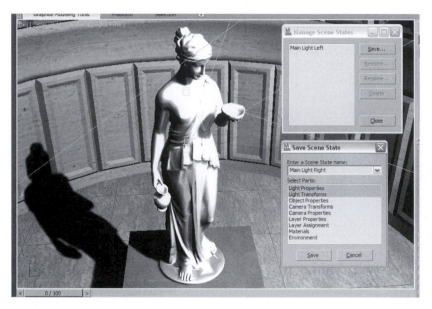

Manage Scene States dialog

The Manage Scene States dialog is accessed through the Tools menu.

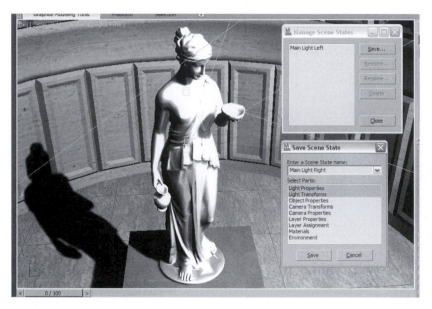

Tools menu

Exercise | Using Lighting Tools

1 Open the file *Light_Tools.max*.

2 From the **Tools** menu, choose **Manage Scene States**.

3 In the **Manage Scene States** dialog, click **Save**.

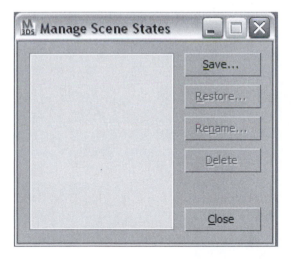

4　In the **Save Scene State** dialog, select **Light Properties** and **Light Transforms**, as the parts to save. Enter a **Scene State Name** such as *Main Light Left Default*. Click **Save**.

5　Close the **Manage Scene States** dialog.

6　From the **Tools** menu, choose **Light Lister**.

7   Make the following changes to the lights in the Dialog:

- Change the **Main Light Multiplier** to **0.4**.
- Turn off the *Back_Light*.
- Turn on shadows for the *Fill_Light*.
- Change the color of both lights to an orange color (**R:255**, **G:150**, **B:50**).

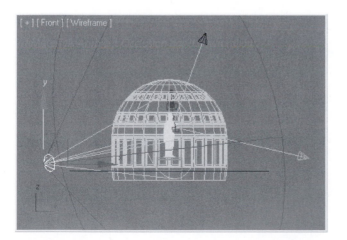

8   Exit the **Light Lister** dialog.

9   Click on **Select and Move** and **Move** the *Main_Light* in the **Front** viewport to a position resembling the **Fill Light**.

10   Select the **Fill Light** on the right side of the **Front** viewport.

11   Go to the **Modify** tab In the **Command** panel.

12   In the **Intensity/Color/Attenuation** rollout turn off **Far Attenuation** by removing the check in the **Use** value.

13   From the **Tools** menu, choose **Manage Scene States**.

14   Click **Save** in the **Manage Scene States** dialog.

15   In the **Save Scene State** dialog, enter a new name, **Emergency Lighting**, and click **Save**.

You now have two scene states saved, which in this case will allow you to switch from one lighting setup to another quickly and easily.

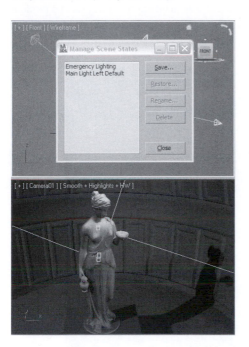

16 In the **Manage Scene States** dialog select the **Main Light Left Default** scene state, and click **Restore**.

17 When the **Restore Scene State** dialog appears, click the **Restore** button.

The scene is restored back to its original lighting.

18 In the same fashion restore the **Emergency Lighting** scene state.

Lesson 21 | Indirect Illumination and Exposure Control

In this lesson, you will work with two controls to adjust the quality and brightness of a rendered image. Final Gather will be the main tool used in adjusting indirect illumination. Exposure Control will be used to adjust brightness and contrast.

Images can be greatly enhanced through Indirect Illumination and exposure controls

Objectives

After completing this lesson, you will be able to:

- Use Final Gather and adjust values to refine indirect illumination.

- Describe Global Illumination.

- Adjust exposure controls to control brightness in the rendered image.

Final Gather

Final Gather is a setting used to control indirect illumination when using the mental ray renderer. There are several controls that are accessible in the Render Frame window and the Render Setup dialog.

Bottom of the Render Window dialog

The bottom of the Render window dialog contains the most important controls for Final Gather. The Final Gather Precision slider allows you to control the settings of Final Gather in an easy to use slider. Moving the slider to the extreme left will disable Final Gather entirely. Placing the slider in between the extreme left or right will select a series of Final Gather values that will improve the results of the Indirect Illumination calculation.

Final Gather disabled

Final Gather medium preset

In the Render Setup dialog, Indirect Illumination tab, the same controls appear as in the Render window dialog with an additional number of controls that can be used to further refine your Final Gather setup.

Render Setup dialog, Indirect Illumination tab

The Render Setup dialog can be accessed either on the main toolbar or from the top of the Render window.

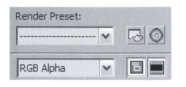

Render Setup button in the Render window   Render Setup button on the main toolbar

A few points about Final Gather:

- When Final Gather is off, your render will proceed more quickly, but your shadows will generally be very dark. If at all possible when doing test renders, turn off Final Gather.

- Turning on Final Gather will lighten shadows and produce indirect illumination automatically. The precision of the calculation is generally set to draft until you are ready to do a final render. Settings of low to medium are common even at final render stages.

- The more Final Gather bounces you use, the better the effect, although more than three bounces and the increased effect is barely noticeable.

Global Illumination

Global Illumination is a general term used in CG use to describe indirect illumination. In mental ray, Global Illumination is used to describe an alternative method of calculating indirect illumination called photon tracing. Controls for Global Illumination are found in the Render Setup dialog, Indirect Illumination tab.

Caustics and Global Illumination rollout

You can use Global Illumination independently, or in combination with Final Gather. In general, for most scenes the use of Final Gather should suffice to produce proper indirect illumination.

Exposure Controls

Exposure control is, as its name would suggest to photographers, a method of controlling the exposure in a rendering. mr Photographic Control is the preferred method to use with mental ray.

Exposure Control in the Environment and Effects dialog

There are two basic methods of controlling the exposure control using this tool: Exposure Value (EV) and Photographic Exposure.

Exposure Value is a simple numeric value; the default of 15.0 represents a good value for exterior sunlight. Selecting a preset value for an interior rendering will change this to 2.0. Higher values will create darker images.

Photographic values might be preferable for individuals who are more familiar with photographic settings. Here Shutter Speed, Aperture, and Film Speed can be adjusted as you would if you were taking a picture with a camera. Using photographic values will be more appropriate when you are using photometric lights with scenes built in real-world units.

Exposure will adjust in the viewport if you have Hardware Shading and Exposure Control enabled in the viewport. This can be turned on through the Shading viewport label menu.

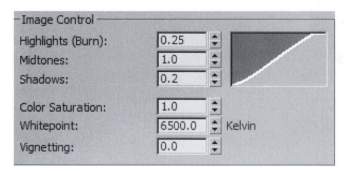

Shading viewport label menu

In addition to the controls available for adjusting the overall brightness of the image, there are individual controls that allow you to control the brightness of the Highlights, Midtones, and Shadows of the image.

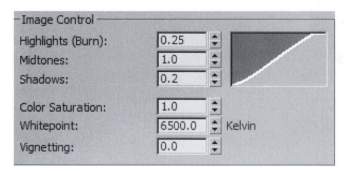

Image Control values

Chapter 03 | Lighting

- Higher values for Highlights brighten the brightest areas of the image. This value is restricted between 0 and 1.0.

- High values for Midtones will brighten the overall image, but will lead to loss in contrast. This value is restricted between 0 and 4.0.

- High values for Shadows will darken shadows and provide more contrast to the image. This value is restricted between 0 and 1.0.

- Color and Whitepoint are values that control the saturation and color of the image.

- Vignetting values produce an image with darkened corners.

Image with a maximum vignetting value of 25.

Exercise | Indirect Illumination and Exposure Control

In this exercise, you will use Final Gather and Exposure Control to adjust the shadows in an image, and then the overall image brightness and contrast.

1 Start or reset 3ds Max Design.

2 Open the file *Indirect Illumination.max*.

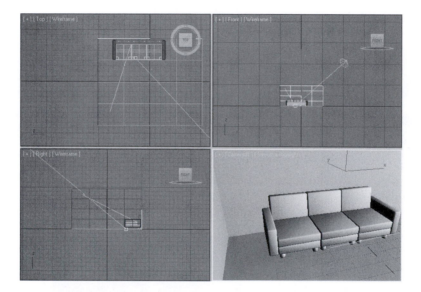

3 Press **F9** to render the **Camera** view.

Final Gather has been disabled in this render so that it can render quickly. A single light source in the scene produces a stark image with a dark shadow.

4 In the lower area of the **Render** window, move the **Final Gather Precision** slider one position to the right. It should now read **Draft**.

Final Gather Precision:

Draft

5 Click on the **Render** button in the **Render** window.

The image has brightened and the shadows are lighter, revealing some details in the shadows.

6 In the **Trace/Bounces Limits** area of the **Render** window, change the **FG Bounces** value to **2**.

Final Gather Precision:

Draft

Trace/Bounces Limits
Max. Reflections: 4
Max. Refractions: 6
FG Bounces: 2

7   Render the image again.

The image is considerably brighter now and slightly overexposed. We will correct this by applying photographic exposure controls.

8   In the upper left of the **Render** dialog, click on the **Environment and Effects** button.

9   In the **Exposure Control** rollout, select **mr Photographic Exposure Control**.

10 In the mr **Photographic Exposure Control** select **Non Physically Based Lighting** from
    the **Preset** List.

11 Select **Exposure Value (EV)** and set the value to **1.0**.

12   In the **Render** window click **Render**.

The image renders better but the image has lost some of its contrast. In the next few steps you will make adjustments to the image. Render if you like after each change to see the effect it has on the image.

13   In the **Image Control** change the **Highlights** value to **0.5**.

14   Change the **Midtones** value to **0.65**.

15   Change the **Shadows** value to **0.75**.

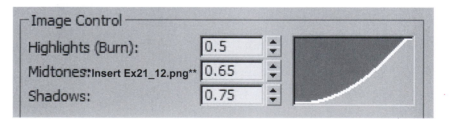

16 Go back and change the **Overall Exposure Value** to **0.5**.

17 Render the image one final time.

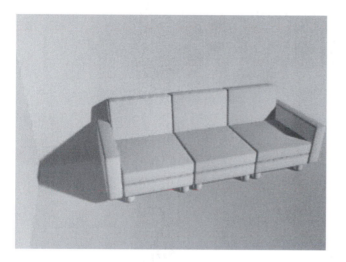

Lesson 22 | Simulating Sunlight

Introduction

Sunlight, whether it is simply used to illuminate an exterior scene or when it enters an interior space, provides for interesting and potentially dramatic lighting effects. 3ds Max Desig, has specific tools to simulate its effects.

Light is a very interesting phenomenon. We see it every day, it surrounds us, interacts with us, and yet we understand very little about it, as its physical properties rely on complex formulas. As an artist, you need to understand the subtleties of light without delving too deeply into its complex nature. The key to that effect is to study light around you, understand how it is affecting its surroundings, and try to emulate that in different 3D environments.

An interior space lit from daylight

Objectives

After completing this lesson, you will be able to:

- Apply how light works in the real world to a CG scene
- Simulate the sun and sky in a 3D scene
- Describe the use of a Sky Portal

Light in the Real World

Light Sources

When lighting a scene, it is important to define how many light sources affect the environment. This is easier said than done. In any scene, there may be light sources that you may not have noticed that are a crucial part of the overall lighting. Therefore, you may need to place more lights than anticipated, based on your study of the scene. Bear in mind that all scenes are different and that a lighting scenario in one may not work in another.

Consider the scene below: assuming there's no artificial lighting inside the room, it's easy to assume that we are dealing with a single light source (the sun) coming from outside where, in fact, there can easily be three to four lights illuminating the scene.

Scene without any lights (default lighting)

Scene lit with three light sources. The final render is a sum of the effects discussed below.

Sunlight

The first light and most prominent is sunlight itself. This is created using a direct light or a direct-based light system such as sunlight or daylight.

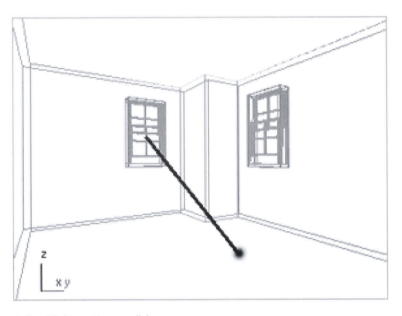

A direct light casting parallel rays

When Raytraced shadows are turned on and final gather is turned off, light entering into a room will produce a bright area in an overall dark space

Bounced or diffuse light

Another light source to consider, is the the main light bouncing off surfaces. Light reflects in the real world. Some of its energy is absorbed, but the rest is reflected onto other surfaces, taking with it some of the properties of the bouncing surface. With the mental ray render, this bouncing of light is handled through indirect illumination (final gather).

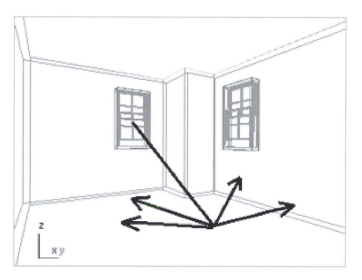

Light rays coming from the sun bounce off the floor and illuminate the walls and ceiling

Turning on final gather in the mental ray render will generally give you excellent results for bounced light

Scattered light

The third and last light needed for this scene is the sky light (ambient lighting coming from outside). That's an important piece in addition to the sunlight itself. The light coming from the windows is an important contributor to the scene. The window panes become effectively light sources, portals if you will, to the ambient lighting outside.

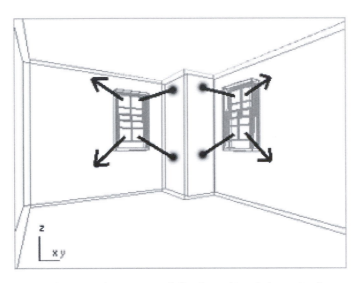

The window panes become portals for the ambient light coming from outside

A Sky Portal object allows you to simulate ambient light entering a space through an opening

When you combine the effects of all three lights, the interior space is properly illuminated.

Final render with the effects of all lights

Simulating the Sun and Sky

Because of the distance of the sun to the earth, the sun is modeled as a parallel light source, which makes the incident direction of sunlight constant over all surfaces in the scene. Even though the sun can be viewed as a point light far, far away, it is not convenient to use an Omni light or even a Spot light to simulate the sun (imagine placing either of these lights at 150 million kilometers from your scene). For that reason, the sun in most 3D applications is based on a direct light that casts parallel rays.

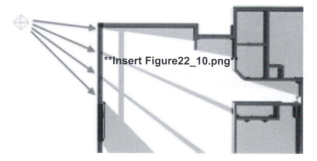

Effect of an Omni or Spot light through windows

An Omni or a Spot light placed near the scene produces diverging shadows, which is not accurate for a sun representation.

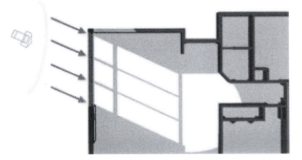

Effect of a direct light through windows

Using a direct light or a direct-based lighting system, the rays and the shadows run parallel, simulating the sun's behavior based on its great distance from the earth.

The Sunlight System

The Sunlight system uses light in a system that follows the geographically correct angle and movement of the sun over the earth at a given location. You can choose location, date, time, and compass orientation. You can also animate the date and time. This system is suitable for shadow studies of proposed and existing structures. In addition, you can animate Latitude, Longitude, North Direction, and Orbital Scale. At its core, the Sunlight system is based on a standard direct light.

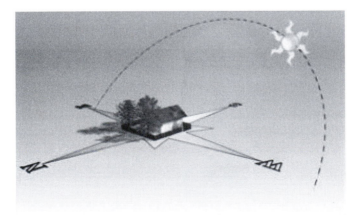

Sunlight system

The Sunlight system is found in the Create tab of the Command panel by clicking on the Systems icon.

Sunlight tool

A Sunlight system is typically created in the top view, first with a click and drag to define a rose compass (North direction) and then an additional drag to define the orbital scale (position of the "sun" in the form of a direct light). Once created, these parameters can then be edited in the Motion panel.

The Daylight System

A Daylight system has many similarities to the Sunlight system, in that it is created exactly the same way in the viewport and the properties such as geographic location, date, and time of day are identical in the Motion panel. However, the Daylight system has many advantages over the Sunlight system, since it actually combines the Sunlight system with ambient light (Skylight) and a background map for the sky and ground.

In addition, the Daylight system uses mental ray-specific lights, and it can also use photometric light data to feed the sunlight and skylight channels.

As with the Skylight system you will find the Daylight system in the Create tab of the Command panel by clicking on the Systems icon.

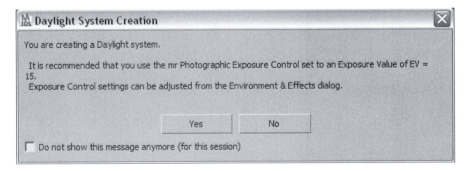

Daylight tool

The process of creating a Daylight system is similar to a Sunlight system except you will be prompted along the way for specific responses. First you will be prompted to use mr Photographic Exposure Control.

Enable Exposure Control with the Daylight system

Next you will be prompted to use the mr Physical Sky as a background map.

Creating an mr Physical Sky with the Daylight system

It's generally a good idea to accept these defaults.

Editing a Daylight System

When you wish to edit a Daylight system, there are a few places where you will need to look. The first thing to know is that a Daylight system has many components, two of which are immediately displayed when you look for the object in the Select From Scene dialog.

The Daylight system in the Select From Scene dialog

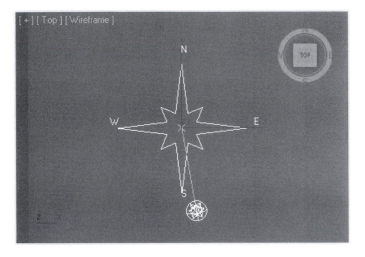

The Daylight system in the scene

The Compass object is a helper that controls the position and rotation of the entire system. When the Daylight system is created, north points directly up along the positive Y-axis.
Rotating the Compass will allow you to position north to be consistent with the scene.

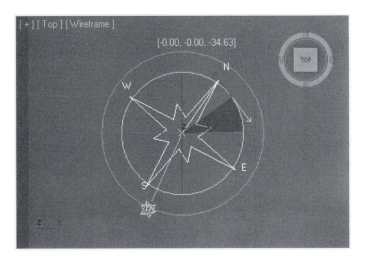

Rotating the Compass

The Daylight object is a special type of group called an assembly. When you select the Daylight system and go to the Motion panel you have access to geographic data to set the sunlight position.

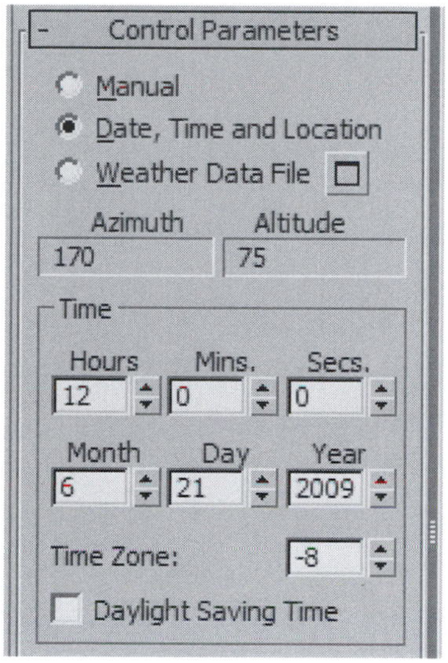

The Motion panel

The Modify tab provides you access to the light information.

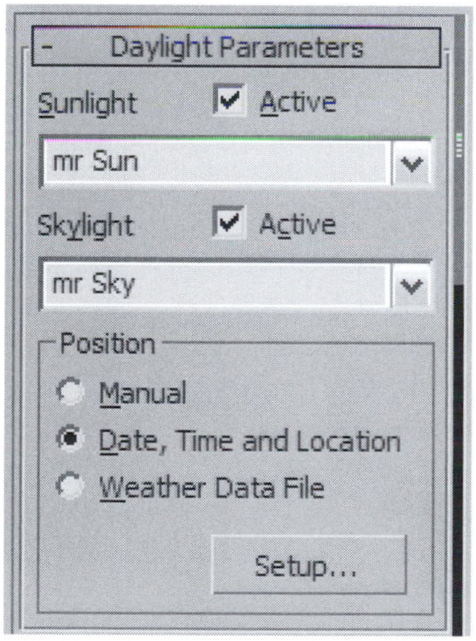

The Modify panel

In the Light Lister the lights associated with a Daylight system are listed separately.

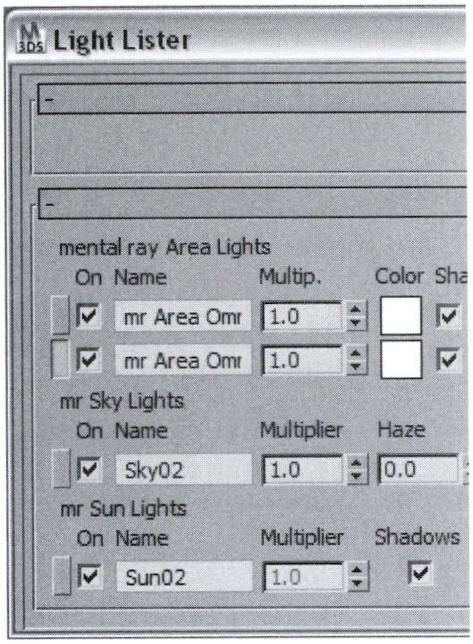

The Light Lister

mr Physical Sky

As soon as you place a Daylight system in your scene when mental ray is active, a warning appears suggesting you use the mr Physical Sky as a background. When you accept this default, the mr Physical Sky will be placed in your Environment dialog.

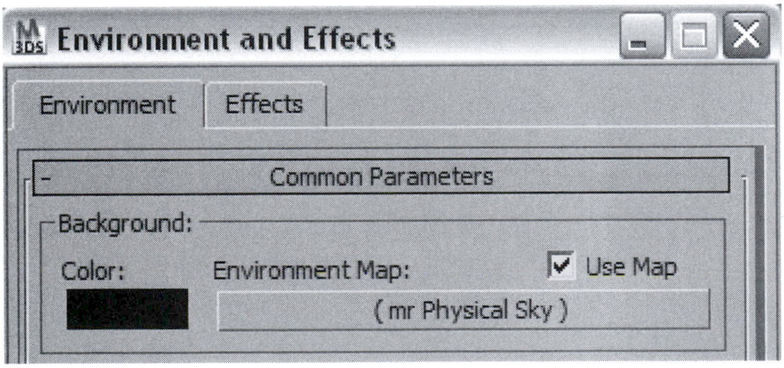

Scene rendered at 2 pm

This special map type creates a sky gradient that changes based on the time of day. It has a direct influence on the reflections calculated in the scene, and you are encouraged to use it in conjunction with the Daylight system.

Scene rendered at 2 pm

Same scene rendered at 7 pm

Note that the mr Physical Sky will also render an image of the sun if it appears in the view of the camera.

mr Sky Portal

mr Sky Portal is a tool used like a light (it is found in the Photometric Lights panel) and its purpose is to concentrate Final Gather rays in an area that you define, usually a window or a door opening.

Mr Sky Portal tool

You create the Sky Portal object with a click and drag. Its shape is rectangular. It also has a direction defined by a small arrow. Although you can create it in any view and then reorient and resize it, it is best to use it in conjunction with the Autogrid feature, so you can automatically align to any face in your scene.

Positioning an mr Sky Portal

You will notice an increase in quality using the Sky Portal, even without increasing the number of final gather rays. The following picture shows a solution without the Sky Portal (background image) and one with the Sky Portal used on the curtain wall (foreground). Notice the obvious differences on the side of the sofa and near the entrance door.

The Sky Portal brings more light into the interior space

Exercise | Lighting the Courtyard

1   Start or reset 3ds Max Design.

2   Open the file *Courtyard_Light_Start.max*.

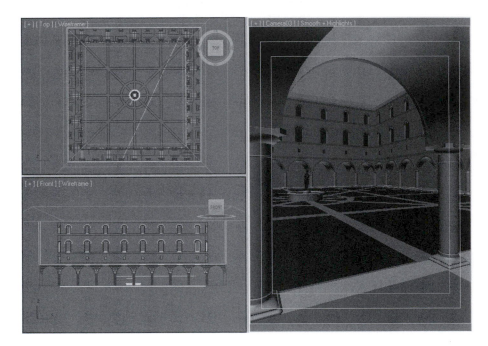

3   Make the **Top** viewport active.

4   From the **Create** menu, select **Lights Daylight System**.

5   In the **Daylight Object Creation** dialog, select **Yes** to turn on **mr Photographic Exposure Control**.

6   Click and drag a point in the approximate center of the courtyard to create the compass **Rosetta** portion of the **Daylight System**. The **mental ray Sky** dialog appears.

7 Click **Yes** in the dialog to add a **mr Physical Sky environment map**. A Daylight system is created.

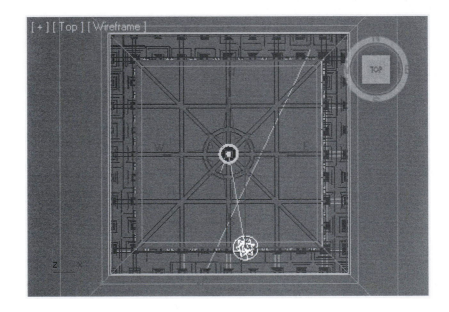

8 Move the mouse and click to finish positioning the Daylight system.

9   In the **Motion** tab of the **Command** panel, set the **Hours** to **11**.

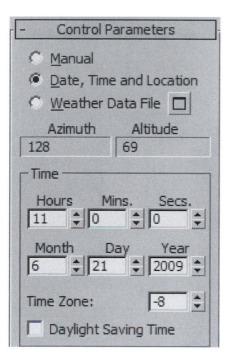

10   Click on the **Render Frame Window** icon on the **main** toolbar.

11   At the top of the **Render Frame Window** select the **Camera03** viewport from the list.

12   Click on the **Lock** button to the right of the list.

13   Click on the **Render** button at the bottom of the **Render Frame Window**.

The image is quite dark even in the area lit by the sun. An adjustment to the exposure control is in order.

14   In the **Render Window** click on the **Environment and Effects** dialog button.

15   In the **Environment and Effects** dialog, change the **Exposure Value (EV)** to **12**.

16   Click the **Render Preview** button. A small rendered image appears. There is an improvement in the brightness of the sunny areas of the courtyard.

17   Click the **Render** button in the **Render Frame Window** to Render the **Camera03** view again.

The scene is considerably brighter now, but the shadow areas are still extremely dark. You will change this using Final Gather.

18   At the bottom right of the **Render Frame Window,** move the **Final Gather Precision** slider one notch to the right to activate **Draft** mode.

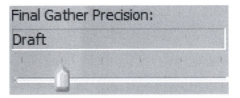

19   Render the **Camera03** view again.

The image has a good quality, but the dark areas are still a bit too dark.

20   In the **Rendering** menu, select the **RAM Player**.

Rendering	Lighting Analysis	Customize
Render	Shift+Q	
Render Setup...	F10	
Rendered Frame Window...		
Indirect Illumination...		
Exposure Control...		
Environment...	8	
Effects...		
Render To Texture...	0	
Render Surface Map...		
Material Editor...	M	
Material/Map Browser...		
Material Explorer...		
Video Post...		
View Image File...		
Panorama Exporter...		
Batch Render...		
Print Size Assistant...		
Gamma/LUT Setup...		
mental ray Message Window...		
RAM Player...		

21 In the **RAM Player**, select the **Open Last Rendered Image in Channel A** button and click **OK** to accept the default in the **RAM Player Configuration** dialog.

22 In the lower left of the **Render Frame Window,** change the **FG Bounces** to **2**. This will make each individual light ray bounce a few more times before dying away, and help illuminate the areas in the shadows.

23 Render the **Camera03** view.

24 In the **RAM Player** dialog, select the **Open Last Rendered Image in Channel B** button.

In the RAM Player you can now compare the before (Bounces = 0) and after (Bounces = 2) images by sliding the arrow along the top of the image.

25   In the **Environment and Effects** dialog, **Image Control** area, change the **Shadows** value to **0.1**.

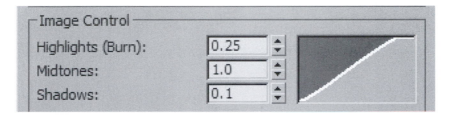

The shadows are further lightened by the reduction in the Shadows value.

26   Save your file.

Lesson 23 | Lighting Effects

Introduction

In this lesson, you will learn about several lighting effects. These effects will help you add realism to your rendered scenes.

Objectives

After completing this lesson, you will be able to:

- Place a highlight on an object
- Use Color Bleed to enhance color effects
- Describe how Ambient Occlusion works
- Project an image with a light
- Use Volume lights to simulate light passing through mediums like liquid or smoke-filled air.

Place Highlight

Place Highlight is a tool that is used to place a light in such a way that it will create a highlight on the selected face of an object. The tool is found in the Align flyout on the main toolbar.

Once you create a light in the scene, you can select the light and use your cursor to place a highlight on an object in the scene. Simply drag the cursor over the surface of the object to be highlighted.

Align flyout on the main toolbar

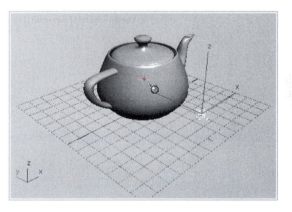

Placing the highlight on an object

Before placing the highlight

After the highlight is placed

Color Bleed

Color Bleed is an important part of CG lighting as it emulates real-world situations. When light bounces off a surface, it collects some of the properties of that surface, including color information. Therefore, the bounce light is tinted with the color of the bounce surface.

The effect can be simulated and adjusted in a number of ways, by changing the color of a fill light or by using some of the advanced lighting features found in Light Tracing, Radiosity, and mental ray.

Scene illuminated without the effect of color bleed

Bouncing light (fill Omni light) carrying the effect of the green color from the tabletop.

Ambient Occlusion

Ambient Occlusion is a technique developed by ILM (Industrial Light & Magic) to simulate the effect of Global Lighting without the cost of full global illumination. The technique, in fact, relies on a shader (material component) to simulate a light effect. Ambient Occlusion (often referred to as a dirt map) works by determining the proximity of objects to calculate dark areas between them. An Ambient Occlusion map is often a black and white map that can be calculated directly at render time or as a separate pass to be composited over the diffuse render at a later time.

Diffuse

Ambient Occlusion

End result

The effect of Ambient Occlusion on a scene can have a great effect on objects in close proximity. Notice how the details of the crates came alive.

How Ambient Occlusion Works

Ambient Occlusion works by calculating how much ambient light a surface point is likely to receive. In an office space, for example, a surface point under the desk would end up much darker than a surface point on the desktop, although other objects on the desk may affect that surface point too.

Ambient Occlusion starts from your position looking at the scene. Every single point visible to your eye gets calculated in the following way: A number of rays are cast from that point in a randomized, hemispherical way, out to do "hit-tests" on the rest of the scene.

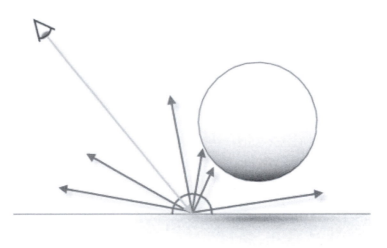

Ambient Occlusion

Some rays collide with other objects; some don't. The surface point is then shaded by a ratio of hit-rays. If only a few rays hit obstacles, the shading is light. If most rays hit obstacles, the shading of that point is dark.

The Ambient Occlusion Shader

The Ambient Occlusion shader is typically something you can easily activate in the Arch & Design or ProMaterials.

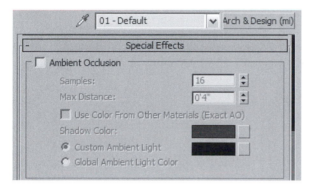

Ambient Occlusion is included in the Special Effects rollout in the Arch & Design material.

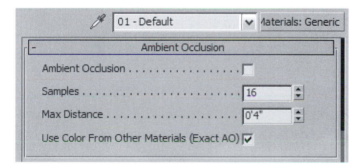

In ProMaterials Ambient Occlusion has its own rollout.

The most important values that you will need to adjust are Samples and Max Distance.

- The Samples value determines the number of rays cast from any given surface point. The default is 16 and may yield a grainy look to the rendering. A value between 32 and 64 is usually preferred. Higher values yield better results but can increase render time.

- The Max distance value determines how far the rays travel before they die away. A value of 0 means the rays travel indefinitely. A value other than zero would restrict the distance traveled to that amount. If an obstacle is reached within that distance, then the surface point is occluded. If not, then that ray is considered "non-occluding."

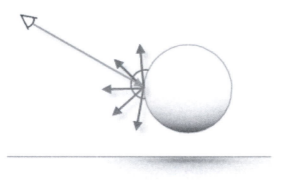

Rays are limited to travel a specific distance. In this case the distance is short and the rays do not collide with any obstacles, therefore, the surface point is not shaded.

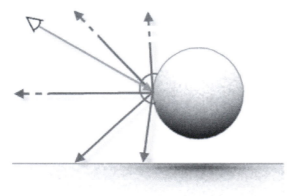

Rays are not limited (max distance = 0) and they keep traveling indefinitely. In this case, two out five rays collide with an obstacle and the surface point is moderately shaded.

The Effects of Ambient Occlusion

As mentioned, Ambient Occlusion is used as an "add-on" effect, to pump up the illumination of a scene by taking into account cracks and contact shadow, all this without the cost of a full global illumination calculation.

Scene lit with default lighting. The result is very unappealing

Scene with no lights and using Ambient Occlusion. Already, the effect is far more realistic. The various surfaces of the car and between the car and the ground occlude one another to create a realistic render.

Same scene (with default lighting) as above but using textures instead of a white material. The effect is just as unappealing without proper lighting.

Ambient Occlusion makes this rendering far more appealing.

Projecting an Image in a Light

A light generally projects uniform light, which is controlled by the parameters that you set for that particular light object. There are special circumstances where you may wish to project an image through a light. You may wish to simulate light that is entering an underwater environment or simply entering through a window opening that is not actually modeled.

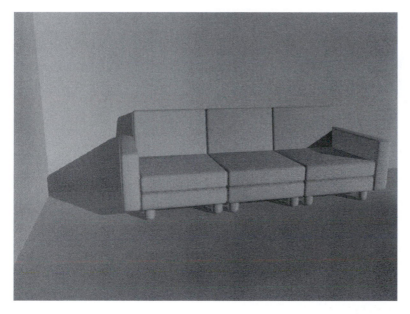

Space modeled with a fill light only

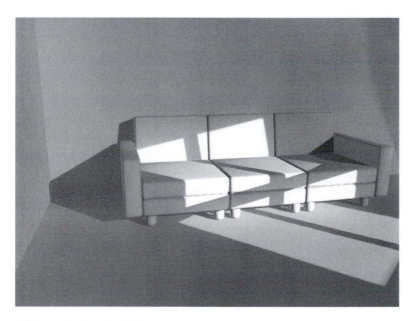

Addition of a Projector light

Projector lights are set up in the Light object's Advanced Effects rollout.

Projector Map setup

When setting up a Projector Light you may find it useful to set one of your viewports to display the Projector Light's view. This way you will see exactly where the light will project the image.

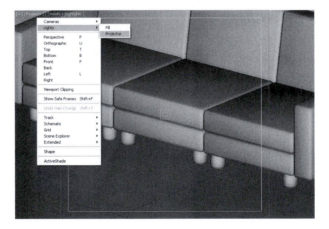

Projector Light view displayed in the viewport

Volume Light Effects

A Volume Light is an effect where you simulate the effect of light passing through a medium other than perfectly clear air. This could be to simulate light penetrating the depths of the ocean or through the air of a smoke-filled room.

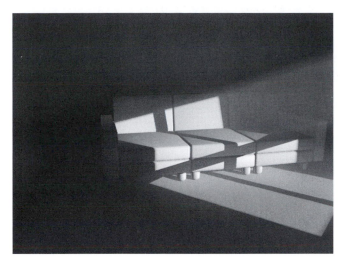

Volume Light effect applied to a Projector Light

The Volume Light effect is created in the Atmosphere rollout of the Environment tab of the Environment and Effects dialog.

Atmosphere rollout

When you click on Add, the Add Atmospheric Effect dialog appears. Here you would select the Volume Light effect.

Add Atmospheric effect dialog

Once selected, the Atmosphere rollout changes to include the parameters of the Volume Light. You then need to select the light or lights that you want the effect applied to. Then adjust parameters.

Volume Light parameters rollout

The Parameters of Density and Noise will probably have the most dramatic effects on the appearance of your volume light.

- The Density value defaults to 5.0 and increasing the value will make the volume effect more apparent, but if the values are too high, the effect will wash out the scene.

- Noise produces a more irregular Volume Light effect. When you turn on noise and set an amount from 0 to 1, you will note that the volume effect will be reduced somewhat. You would need to go back to the Density value and increase the level to get the same effect.

The illustration has a Volume Light with a density of 5.0, Noise = 0.75, Size = 2.0.

Volume Light with Noise

Exercise | Lighting Effects

1   Start or reset 3ds Max or 3ds Max Design.

2   Open the file *Lighting_Effects.max*.

3   Render the **Camera** view.

The image's lighting is dull and interesting. There is a single light and final gather has not been turned on.

4   At the bottom of the **Render Window** dialog, move the **Final Gather Precision** slider to **Draft**.

5   Render the **Camera** view again.

The Image is considerably brighter, and there is a noticeable color bleed from the bright colors of the sofa to the adjacent white walls.

6   Click on the Render Setup button at the top of the Render Window dialog.

7   In the Indirect Illumination tab, change the final gather multiplier to 0.75.

Final Gather
Basic

☑ Enable Final Gather   Multiplier: 0.75

FG Precision Presets:

Draft

This will reduce the effect of the Indirect Illumination and the color bleed effect.

8 Render the **Camera** view.

The Color Bleed effect has been reduced somewhat as well as the brightness of the image.

9 Click on the **Material Editor** button on the **main** toolbar.

10 Click on the first material sample sphere at the upper left of the sample areas.

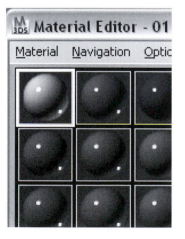

11 In the **Special Effects** rollout, turn on **Ambient Occlusion**, and change the **Max** distance to **20**.

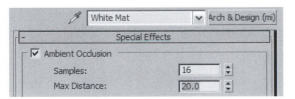

12 Repeat this process for each of the **3** other materials.

13 Render the **Camera** view.

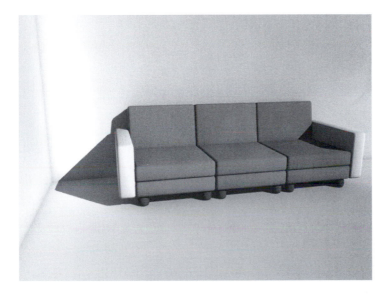

You can see an obvious occlusion effect at the corners of the walls and floors

14   Go to the **Select From Scene** dialog, and select the light called *Projector*.

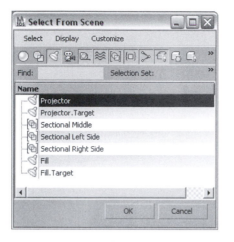

15   In the upper left viewport, select the **Point-Of-View (POV)** viewport label menu, and Select **Lights → Projector**.

The viewport switches to a view of what would be seen if the POV was positionned at the light's location.

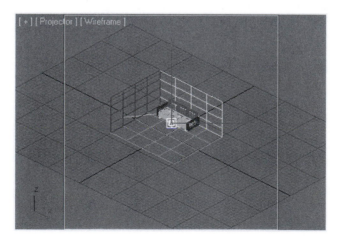

16 In the **Modify** panel of the **Projector light**, change the **Hotspot/Beam** value to **50** and the **Falloff/Field** to **52**.

Directional Parameters
Light Cone
☐ Show Cone ☐ Overshoot
Hotspot/Beam: 50.0
Falloff/Field: 52.0
○ Circle ● Rectangle
Aspect: 1.0 Bitmap Fit...

17 Render the **Camera** view.

The light beam is focused into a rectangular area. In order to simulate some diffuse light, you will turn on a fill light.

18 In the **Tools** menu, select **Light Lister**.

19 In the **Light Lister** dialog, place a check in the box next to the **Fill** light.

20 Render the **Camera** view.

The bright areas of the scene are a bit too bright right now, but this will change when we use a Projector light to simulate light coming in through a window.

21 With the **Projector** light still selected, go to the **Advanced Effects** rollout. Click on the button labeled **None** in the **Projector Map** area.

22   In the **Material/Map Browser**, select **Bitmap** and click **OK**.

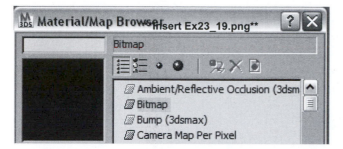

23   Navigate to your project folder and select the file *Window Project.jpg*. Click **OK**.

24   Render the **Camera** view.

The next step will be to add a volume light effect to simulate the light passing through the air of the interior space.

25   From the **Render Frame Window** select the **Environment and Effects** button.

26   In the **Atmosphere** rollout click on the **Add** button.

27 In the **Add Atmospheric Effect** dialog, select **Volume Light**.

The Environment and Effects dialog changes to now include Volume Light parameters.

28 In the **Volume Light Parameters**, click on the **Pick Light** button.

29 Press the **H** key on the keyboard, and from the **Pick Object** dialog select the **Projector** light.

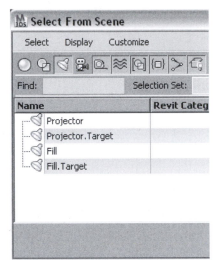

30 Render the **Camera** view.

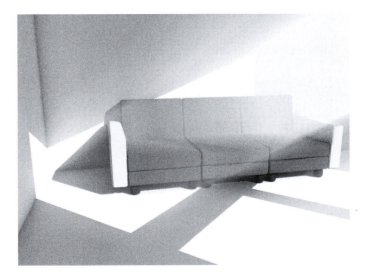

There is a definite beam of light now, but it is much too prominent and washes out much of the image behind it.

Chapter 03 | Lighting

31 In the **Volume** area of the **Volume Light,** change the **Density** to **2.5**.

32 Render the **Camera** view.

The effect of the Volume Light is much less prominent but at this point it is very uniform. You will add some noise to the effect to make it more random.

33 In the **Noise** area of the **Volume Light Parameters**, select the checkbox to turn **Noise On**.

34 Set the **Amount** to **0.75**.

35 Set the **Size** to **10.0**.

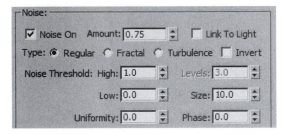

36 Render the **Camera** view.

Although the image is looking pretty good now, you have lost a bit of the Volume Light effect by adding the random noise.

37 Increase the **Density** value to **4.0**.

38   Render the **Camera** view one last time.

Chapter 04
Materials

Introduction

Once you have created and positioned models in a scene, you need to learn about creating materials and working with the Material Editor in 3ds Max® Design. In this section, you will learn about materials and their uses, as well as why a good material is important. You'll also learn how to create materials and work with several of the tools available.

After completing this section, you will be able to:

- Work with the Material Editor
- Describe the differences between different Material types
- Use Predefined ProMaterials from Preset Material libraries
- Use different Map types
- Create a ProMaterial
- Apply and adjust mapping co-ordinates
- Create Arch & Design materials
- Create and adjust Multi Sub-Object materials

Material Overview

When you look around, what do you see? Maybe a desk and a carpet? Perhaps you're outside. You might see grass and a stone wall. Materials are everywhere, from the floor to the sky and everything in between. A material is the combination of all the elements that make up the look and feel of a surface. Some materials can be simple, like a colored plastic ball, or more complex, like an old wooden chest. Some materials are not even photorealistic. Whatever your need, you can find a material to fill it. Real or imagined, materials make up the visible world we live in.

The Purpose of Materials

Materials serve many purposes and can be used to portray different types of surfaces. For example, a steel urn has a very different look from the same shape made of clay. Materials also help impart an object's age, such as the difference between freshly cut, polished wood and a board that had been sitting on the beach for years. Even though the two objects are made of wood, there are visible differences that provide hints as to the age of the item.

Substance

Substance defines the look and feel of the material when it's applied to an object. An object made from red clay does not have the same substance as one made from metal.

Identifying the substance of a object

Using materials, you can make objects, such as these urns, look unique.

Age

Materials can be used to show the relative age of an object.

Identifying the age of an object

Note the differences between the new, shiny, highly-polished urn on the left and the aged, tarnished urn on the right.

Style

You can also create materials that fit whatever style you're looking to create in your images and animations.

Image and animation style can be defined in the materials

The urn on the left uses an Ink 'n Paint material, while the urn on the right uses a Standard material.

Material Importance

A well-made material can make a difference in telling the story of an object or scene element. A scratch on the surface of a desk can tell a tale of what happened to the desk, who owns it, and what it's used for. While a simple scratch can tell a tale, the importance of a well-made material is visible to all who see the final image. Whether you're creating a photorealistic environment or taking a flight through a world of fantasy, the materials you use will make the difference between a good image and an image that sells your idea.

Materials and Lighting

Computer-generated materials and those found in the real world have one thing in common without light, they do not exist. When creating a material, you must think about how it will look under various lighting conditions, as well as how the light will interact with the material. Is the material shiny or dull? Is it reflective or transparent? The answers to these questions all depend on lighting.

Materials and light

The lighting is the same, but the materials react very differently to the light. The urn on the left is shiny, showing the highlight where the light hits the object, while the urn on the right is dull and flat.

Lesson 24 | Working with the Material Editor

Introduction

The Material Editor is an essential tool in 3ds Max Design. With the Material Editor, you can simulate an endless number of real-life materials and present them at whatever level of photorealism desired.

Materials applied to a 3D product design

Objectives

After completing this lesson, you will be able to:

- Manipulate the UI of the Material Editor
- Assign materials to objects in a 3D scene
- Use the Material Explorer

The User Interface

You'll be spending a good deal of time working in the Material Editor when creating your scenes. It's important that you become comfortable with the interface and how to navigate it. There are three ways to access the Material Editor:

• On the main toolbar, click the Material Editor button .

• From the main menu, choose **Rendering** → **Material Editor**.

• Press the m key.

The Material Editor dialog comprises five sections:

• The menu bar

• The sample slots

• The toolbars

• The material type and name

• The material parameters

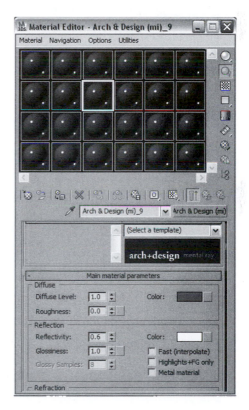

The Material Editor

Material Editor Menu Bar

The Material Editor menu bar provides access to many Material Editor functions also available on the toolbars and the right-click menu, plus many options that are not. You can use the menu commands to apply materials, navigate through materials, and access options and utilities.

Material	Navigation	Options	Utilities	
		Propagate Materials to Instances	
		Manual Update Toggle	
		Copy/Rotate Drag Mode Toggle	
		Background	B
		Custom Background Toggle	
		Backlight	L
		Cycle 3X2, 5X3, 6X4 Sample Slots	X
		Options...	O

The Material Editor Menu bar

Material Sample Slots

The sample slots let you visualize your material as you create it and edit it before you apply it to an object. By default, you can see the entire 24 available slots. In 3ds Max Design the sample area will be populated with a small variety of sample materials.

The Sample slots in 3ds Max Design

You can change the number of sample slots visible by using the right-click menu in the sample area. Select 3 x 2 or 5 x 3 sample areas.

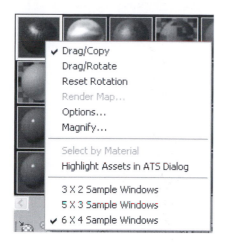

The Sample slot right-click menu

Although you will see fewer sample areas, the samples will be larger.

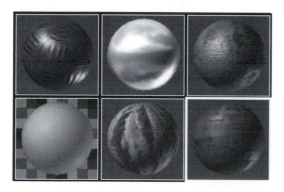

3 x 2 Sample slots

In addition, you can double-click on a sample area and a new window will appear with the sample enlarged in the resizable window.

Enlarged floating sample window

Note: *While the Material Editor shows a maximum of 24 materials at a time, the number of materials present in the scene is limited only by the computer memory.*

Sample Window Indicators

The material sample window provides more than just a method of visualizing the current material; it also provides the status of each material. As your scenes grow, these indicators become more and more important, telling you the status of your material in relationship to the scene. When you assign a material to an object in a scene, the material sample slot appears with small triangles in each corner. These triangles indicate whether a material is assigned to an object in the scene and if it's assigned to the currently selected object.

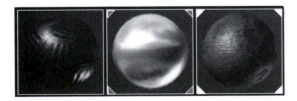

Sample slots status

The Sample slot on the left is not assigned in the scene. The Sample slot in the middle is assigned in the scene. The Sample slot on the right is assigned to the selected object in the scene.

Assigning Materials

There are a few common ways to assign materials. Which method you choose will depend on individual situations and your personal preference. You can use the software's drag and drop ability to drag a material from the sample area onto an object in the scene.

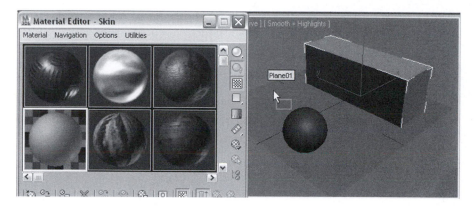

Assigning materials through drag and drop

A drag and drop operation can be done when an object is selected or not. If you drop a material onto a several selected objects, you will be prompted to choose whether the material will be assigned to the selection or to the object you dropped the material on.

Assigning Materials dialog

You can also assign materials with the Assign Material to Selection button, on the toolbar of the Material Editor. This method is useful in scenes that are particularly crowded with objects.

Assign Material to Selection button

Here are some of the commonly used options as shown on the vertical toolbar to the right of the sample slots:

Sample Type flyout: Lets you change the shape of the object in the active sample slot.

Background: Toggles the display of the background image in the active sample slot. This is especially useful when you work with reflective or refractive materials.

Options: Opens the Material Editor Options dialog.

Material/Map Navigator: Opens the Material/Map Navigator dialog, providing a hierarchical view of your materials.

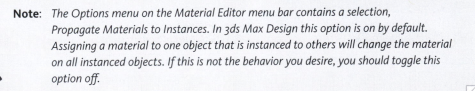

Note: *The Options menu on the Material Editor menu bar contains a selection, Propagate Materials to Instances. In 3ds Max Design this option is on by default. Assigning a material to one object that is instanced to others will change the material on all instanced objects. If this is not the behavior you desire, you should toggle this option off.*

Material Explorer

An alternate method to viewing the structure of a Material is though the Material Explorer. When you select Material Explorer from the Rendering menu a dialog appears listing all of the materials in the scene. Selecting one of the materials will allow you to see the structure of the material in the lower window.

Material Explorer

Exercise | The Material Indicators

In this exercise, you familiarize yourself with how the material indicators work in the Material Editor.

1   Open the file *Clock_radio.max*.

2   Press the **M** key to open the **Material Editor**.

3   In the **Material Editor**, click the third sample area on the second row. The border around the sample slot is white, indicating that it's the active slot. The rollouts in the **Material Editor** will affect the active sample slot.

> **Note**:   *The other sample slots in the Material are Editor adjacent to the active slot. Some of the corners contain gray triangles, indicating that the slot is assigned to an object in the scene.*

4   Click on the **Select by Name** button, to open the **Select From Scene** dialog.

5   In the **Select From Scene** dialog, double-click on the **Back Panel Trim** object to select it in the scene.

Note: *The triangles in the second sample area along the first row turn white. This indicates that this material is assigned to the object you selected.*

Exercise | Applying a Material to an Object

In this exercise, you will assign materials to objects in the scene. In addition, you will pick a material from objects in the scene so they can be further manipulated.

1   Open the file *Clock_radio_01.max*.

2   Open the **Material Editor**.

3   In the **Material Editor**, click the **Neutral Grey** material contained in the first slot on the first row.

4   Click and drag the Material from the Sample area onto the horizontal surface (*Plane01*) around the clock radio. The surface will turn grey to match the material appearance.

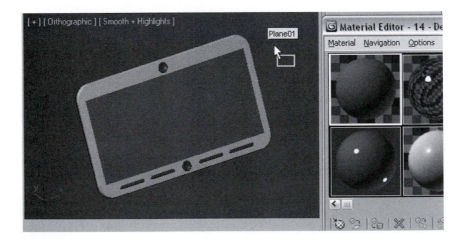

5   Click on the **Select by Name** button to open the **Select From Scene** dialog.

6   Select the following objects from the Select From Scene dialog:

- Back Panel
- Front Panel
- Back Stand

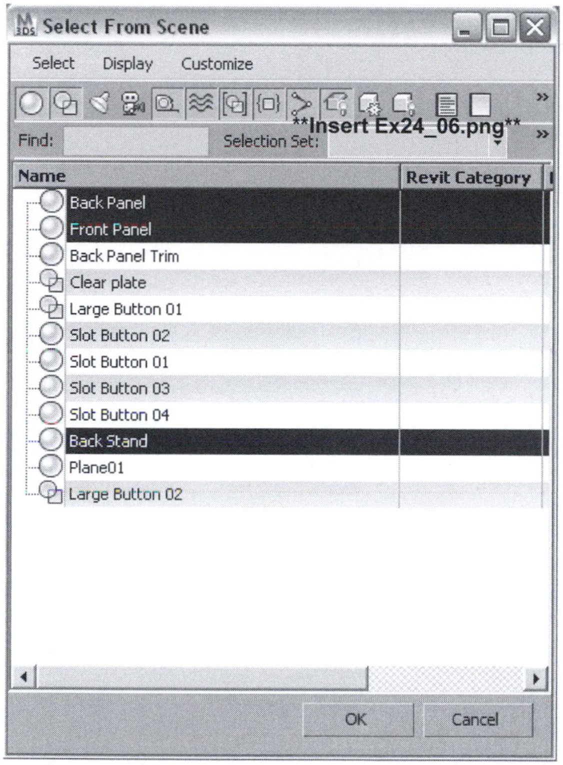

7   Click **OK** to select the objects in the scene and exit the dialog.

8   Select the **Black Plastic** material in the **Material Editor** (3rd sample area, first row).

9   Drag and drop the material on the **Front Panel** object in the scene.

10   In the **Assign Material** dialog, make sure **Assign to Selection** is picked, and click **OK**.

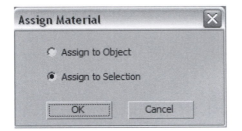

11   Select the **Chrome** material (2nd sample, 1st row).

12   Select the object, **Back Panel Trim**, from the **Select From Scene** dialog.

13   Click on the **Assign Material to Selection** button on the horizontal toolbar of the **Material Editor**.

The material is now assigned to the object in the scene. The material for the buttons of the clock radio have already been assigned to the objects in the scene, but the material does not appear in a sample area in the Material Editor.

14   Click on the 1st sample area in the 2nd row. It is currently assigned a default **Arch & Design** material.

15   Click on the **Pick Material from Object** button.

16 Bring your cursor to one of the buttons on the front of the clock radio and click on the object.

The material assigned to the object will now be assigned to the active sample slot. You can now edit the material parameters if desired.

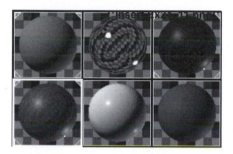

17 To complete the assignment of materials, assign the **White Plastic** material to the **Clear Plate** object.

Lesson 25 | Material Types

Introduction

Materials are all around you. Some are simple materials like a red ball, while others are much more complex, like the waves on the ocean. 3ds Max Design offers several different types of materials that can be used for multiple purposes.

Materials fall into two major categories: single materials and multiple materials. A single material is a material that works on its own, such as the ProMaterial. Multiple materials, like Blend, are not meant to be used by themselves but in conjunction with single materials.

Different material types are appropriate for individual situations

Objectives

After completing this lesson, you will be able to:

- Identify the differences between the different material types.
- Decide when one material type would be more appropriate than another.

Choosing Material Types

There are two ways to choose a material type: You can click the Get Material button in the lower toolbar of the Material Editor or click the Material Type button to the right of the material name. Either option brings up the Material/Map Browser; however, they perform getting a material in two different ways:

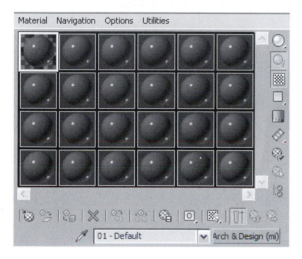

Material Editor

- The Get Material button replaces the material currently in the active slot with the new material. If the replaced material is assigned to an object in the scene, the object is not affected. The material definition in the editor is replaced so you can create a new material for another object.

Arch & Design (mi)

- On the other hand, if you have a material assigned to an object in your scene and you click the Material Type button, you replace the old material with the new one. This will affect all scene objects that are assigned that material.

Regardless of the method you use to select a material, you next step will be to decide which material to choose in the Material Map browser.

Material/Map browser

The materials that are identified with a yellow sphere are those that are optimized for use with the mental ray renderer. These materials cannot be used with the Scanline renderer. In fact, if the Scanline renderer was active, these materials would not be available for selection in the Material/ Map browser. In this lesson, you will see more about the ProMaterials and the Arch & Design materials.

The materials that are identified with a blue sphere are those that can be used with the Scanline renderer. In addition, they can be used with the mental ray renderer, but will not use all the features of that rendering engine. If you have any doubt which rendering engine you will eventually use, these materials will allow you to switch from one renderer to another.

ProMaterials

ProMaterials are one of the material types that are used extensively in 3ds Max Design in combination with the mental ray renderer. ProMaterials are essentially a version of the Arch & Design material, with interfaces in the Material Editor optimized for a particular material application. ProMaterials can produce photorealistic representations of materials.

When you browse for a new material, you will see a whole section of the Material/Map Browser dedicated to these materials.

ProMaterials: Ceramic
ProMaterials: Concrete
ProMaterials: Generic
ProMaterials: Glazing
ProMaterials: Hardwood
ProMaterials: Masonry/CMU
ProMaterials: Metal
ProMaterials: Metallic Paint
ProMaterials: Mirror
ProMaterials: Plastic/Vinyl
ProMaterials: Solid Glass
ProMaterials: Stone
ProMaterials: Wall Paint
ProMaterials: Water

ProMaterials

Selecting one of the material types reveals a simple rollout for the ProMaterial parameters.

The Water ProMaterials rollout

Arch & Design Material

The Arch & Design material is the backbone of materials that are created for use with the mental ray renderer. It contains a number of easy-to-apply templates, along with an extensive list of material parameters that can be adjusted to give your materials the look you require for your scene. The Arch & Design material can produce photorealistic representations of materials.

When selecting the Arch & Design material from the Material/Map browser, the Material Editor will change to look as shown below.

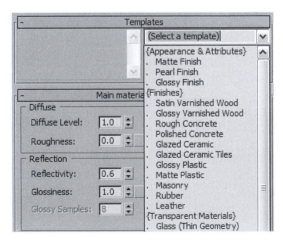

The Arch & Design material

The Arch & Design material contains a template area at the top of its material parameters.

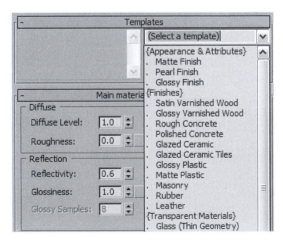

The Arch & Design material templates

Selecting a template redefines the material parameters, allowing you to adjust the material for your given situation. Note as well that each template contains a description on the left side of the Templates rollout.

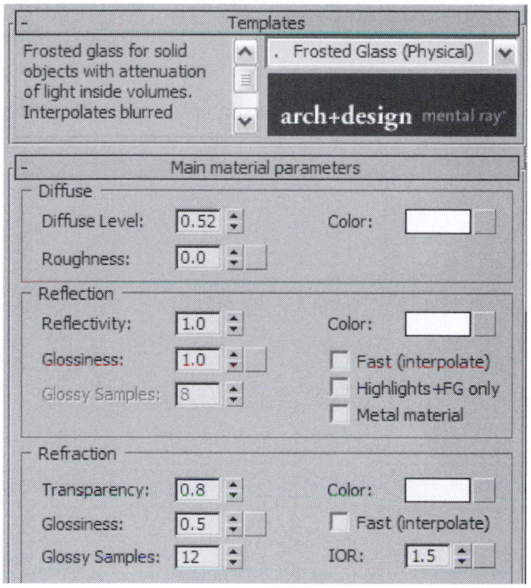

Arch & Design template

The Arch & Design material contains numerous rollouts that contain parameters that can be adjusted to modify the appearance of this material.

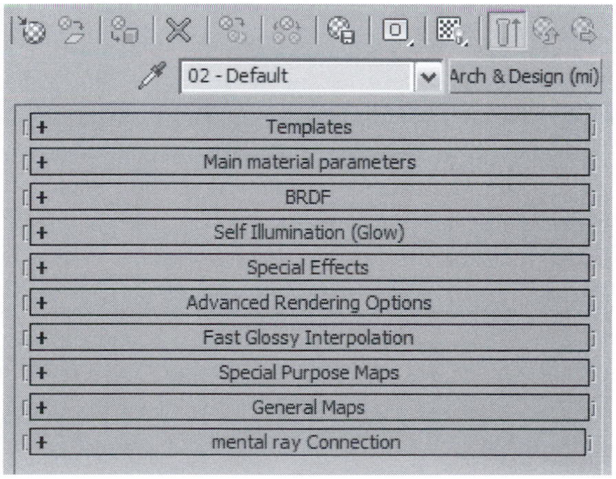

Arch & Design rollouts

The Architectural Material

The Architectural material differs from ProMaterials and Arch & Design materials in that it can be used with the Scanline renderer. The settings for this material are actual physical properties. This material can be used in conjunction with Advanced Lighting (Radiosity) to produce highly realistic renderings and accurate lighting calculations.

In most scenes, if you are using mental ray, you will continue to use the ProMaterials and Arch & Design materials.

Architectural material also has a Templates rollout that includes a drop-down list of preset materials. The templates give you a set of material values to get your material started, which you can then adjust to improve the material's appearance.

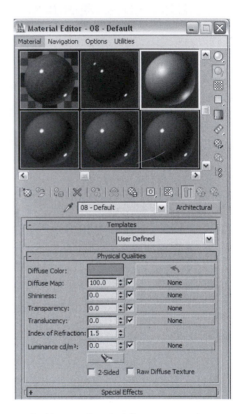

Architectural material templates   Architectural material

The Standard Material

The Standard material is one of the base materials that has existed in the software since its inception. The Standard material type is extremely flexible; you can use it to create an unlimited variety of materials.

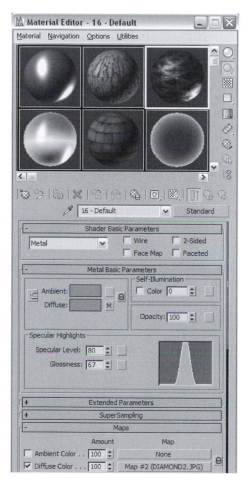

Standard material

The Standard material provides an assortment of Shaders for controlling how the surface looks. A Shader is a mathematical formula that defines how a surface is affected by light hitting it. There are eight Shaders available on the Shader Basic Parameters rollout. Although the Standard material has several common parameters, each Shader has parameters that are specific to that Shader. When you choose a Shader, the Basic Parameters rollout controls change accordingly.

Multi/Sub-Object Material

The Multi/Sub-Object material type is a multiple material, and therefore requires the use of other materials. It is a material that is useful when a single object requires a number of materials assigned to different surfaces.

Foliage object with a Multi/Sub-Object material applied

The Multi/Sub-Object material is used on some standard objects like this foliage object. The Multi/Sub-Object material allows you to have flexibility with material assignments while retaining the integrity of a parametric object.

Multi/Sub-Object material

The Material Editor shows all of the materials contained in the Multi/Sub-Object material at the top of the material's hierarchy tree. Selecting one of the materials on the interface brings you to the materials of that individual material. Materials such as Arch & Design, ProMaterials, and Architectural materials can be used as well as the Standard materials shown here.

Blend Material

The Blend material type is a multiple material and therefore requires the use of other materials. With Blend, you can combine two materials either by mixing them or by using a mask. The mask is a map, such as a bitmap image or a procedural map like Noise. Blend uses the mask's grayscale values to control the blending. You can use Blend to create a variety of surface types, such as peeling paint, wet floors, and rusted metal.

Lesson 26 | Using Predefined ProMaterials

Introduction

3ds Max Design contains a series of predefined ProMaterials that can be used in your scenes. It is a good idea to identify where these materials can be found and what is contained in the different material libraries. There are hundreds of predefined ProMaterials that you can use, sometimes without modification in your scenes.

Water surface over Riverstone Blue

Objectives

After completing this lesson, you will be able to:

- Locate the predefined ProMaterial libraries
- Access materials in the predefined Material libraries
- Sample some of the materials in the ProMaterial libraries
- Use the predefined ProMaterials on a sample scene

Locating the Material Libraries

When you install 3ds Max Design, the installation of the software will include a subdirectory under the main software folder called *materiallibraries*. When you navigate to this folder, you will notice a number of files contained in the folder.

Address C:\Program Files\Autodesk\3ds Max 2010\materiallibraries

File and Folder Tasks

Other Places

Details

Name ▲

- 3dsmax.mat
- AecTemplates.mat
- architectural.materials.concrete.mat
- architectural.materials.doors & windows....
- architectural.materials.finishes.mat
- architectural.materials.furnishings.mat
- architectural.materials.masonry.mat
- architectural.materials.metals.mat
- architectural.materials.sitework.mat
- architectural.materials.thermal & moistur...
- architectural.materials.woods & plastics....
- Autodesk.Max.ProMaterials.Ceramic.mat
- Autodesk.Max.ProMaterials.Concrete.mat
- Autodesk.Max.ProMaterials.Generic.mat
- Autodesk.Max.ProMaterials.Glazing.mat
- Autodesk.Max.ProMaterials.Hardwood.mat
- Autodesk.Max.ProMaterials.MasonryCMU...
- Autodesk.Max.ProMaterials.Metal.mat
- Autodesk.Max.ProMaterials.MetallicPaint....
- Autodesk.Max.ProMaterials.Mirror.mat
- Autodesk.Max.ProMaterials.PlasticVinyl.mat
- Autodesk.Max.ProMaterials.SolidGlass.mat
- Autodesk.Max.ProMaterials.Stone.mat
- Autodesk.Max.ProMaterials.WallPaint.mat
- Autodesk.Max.ProMaterials.Water.mat
- mrArch_DesignTemplates.mat
- Nature.mat

The Material libraries folder

Accessing Materials in the Predefined Material Libraries

When you are working in 3ds Max Design, and are in the Material Editor, you have seen how to get new materials using the Get Material button. When you click on the Get Material button, you are brought to the Material/Map Browser. By default, the Material/Map Browser is set to Browse From New, which means 3ds Max browses from new material definitions.

The Material/Map Browser

In order to access the predefined Material libraries, you need to set the Browse From setting to Mtl Library. Then select the Open button in the File section of the dialog.

Material/Map Browser set to browse for a material library

By default the Open file button brings you to the *materiallibries* folder of the current project folder.

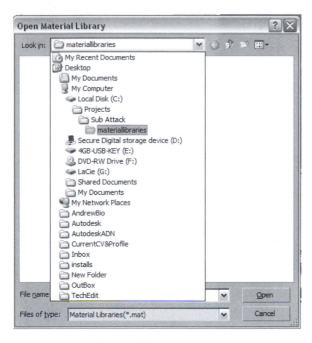

Default material libraries folder

Navigate to the *materiallibraries* folder under the software folder and select one of the .mat files that contain ProMaterials.

3ds Max predefined Material library folder

ProMaterials Material library file

Once you select the ProMaterial library your Material/Map Browser will contain numerous material definitions. You can double-click, select and click OK, or drag and drop your materials into your Material Editor.

Predefined ProMaterials in the Material/Map browser

Note: *ProMaterials are defined to work with real-world mapping coordinates. The unit of measure used is inches; therefore, if you change your system units to metric units you will need to make adjustments to the map sizes.*

Sample Materials in the Predefined Material Libraries

It's a good idea to experiment with the various materials already predefined in the material libraries. Here are a few samples of materials in the various ProMaterial libraries.

Autodesk.Max.ProMaterials.Ceramic.mat

This Material library contains 40 plus materials for ceramic surfaces, including ceramic tiled surfaces. Some samples include:

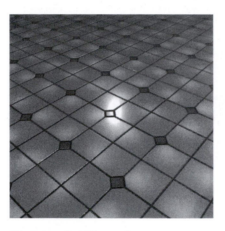

Tile Square Red Diamond

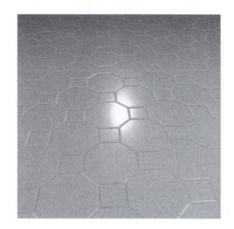

Ceramic Tile Blue Iceberg

Ceramic Tile Green Lime Brick

Autodesk.Max.ProMaterials.Concrete.mat

This Material library contains almost 30 materials for a concrete and stucco surfaces. Some samples include:

Concrete Exposed Aggregate Warm Gray

Concrete Blocks

Concrete with Stone 2

Autodesk.Max.ProMaterials.Generic.mat

This Material library contains almost 90 materials for a variety of surfaces, including fabrics, glass, wallpaper, and exterior landscape materials. Some samples include:

Glass Luminous Orange

LED Materials Red, Yellow, Green

Grass Light Rye

Autodesk.Max.ProMaterials.Glazing.mat

This Material library contains almost 20 materials for flat glass surfaces (glazing).
Some samples include:

Glazing Blue Reflective

Glazing Light Bronze Reflective

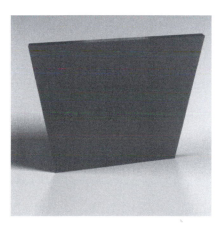

Glazing Dark Blue Reflective

Autodesk.Max.ProMaterials.Hardwood.mat

This Material library contains more than 150 materials for hardwood floors and wood surfaces. Some samples include:

Hardwood Flooring Red Oak Natural - Classic

Wood Particle Board

Wood Elm Burl Stained Light No Gloss

Autodesk.Max.ProMaterials. MasonryCMU.mat

This material library contains more than 50 materials for masonry, CMU and stone landscaping. Some samples include:

Stone Fieldstone Weathered

Brick Red Non-Uniform Running

CMU Light Gray Running

Autodesk.Max.ProMaterials.Metal.mat

This Material library contains almost 60 materials for metal surfaces. Some samples include:

Steel Checker Plate

Brass Satin Screen

Brass Satin Brushed Heavy

Autodesk.Max.ProMaterials.MetallicPaint.mat

This Material library contains over 30 materials for metallic paint surfaces.

Autodesk.Max.ProMaterials.Mirror.mat

This Material library contains and materials for mirror surfaces.

Autodesk.Max.ProMaterials.PlasticVinyl.mat

This Material library contains over 60 materials for plastic surfaces and vinyl flooring.
Some samples include:

Vinyl Flooring Dots Pattern

Vinyl Flooring Mosaic Pattern

Vinyl Flooring Slate Pattern

Autodesk.Max.ProMaterials.SolidGlass.mat

This Material library contains over 20 materials for solid glass. Some samples include:

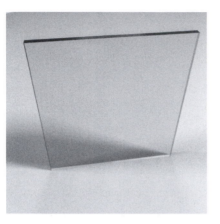

Glass Amber

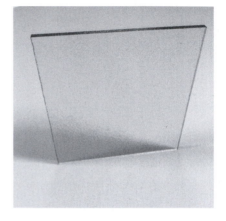

Glass White Rippled

Glass White Frosted

Autodesk.Max.ProMaterials.Stone.mat

This Material library contains 27 stone surfaces. Some samples include:

Marble Rose

Riverstone Blue

Cobblestone Interlocking

Autodesk.Max.ProMaterials.WallPaint.mat

This Material library contains over 80 materials that represent various colors and finishes of wall paint.

Autodesk.Max.ProMaterials.Water.mat

This material library contains and materials for water surfaces. For the most part these materials will be either clear or somewhat opaque and not look terribly interesting until you adjust some of their parameters.

In the example, the Water Reflecting Pool material was applied to a surface above the riverstone material found in the stone section of this lesson. The only adjustment to the preset material was changing the wave height to 10.0 from 0. This creates distortions in refractions and highlights in the reflections on the surface..

Water surface over Riverstone Blue

Exercise | Using Predefined ProMaterials

In this exercise you will use some predefined ProMaterials to add realism to some surfaces in a mechanical scene.

1   Open the file *Mechanical Scene.max*.

2   Click on the **Render Production** button on the **main** toolbar.

The scene has a few materials already applied, but you will add a few more materials to it.

3   Open the **Material Editor**.

4   Select the 1st Sample slot along the top row.

5 Click the **Get Material** button.

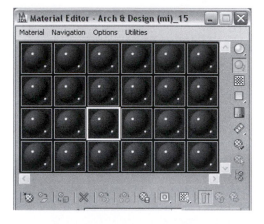

6 In the **Material/Map Browser** click on the **Mtl Library** button in the **Browse From** button.

7 Click on the **Open** button in the **File** area.

8   Navigate to the folder that contains the Material libraries. This will be under the folder where you installed the software, typically *\Program Files\Autodesk\3ds Max 2010\materiallibraries*.

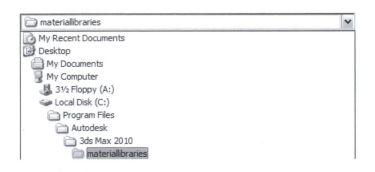

Note: *When you click on the File button 3ds Max defaults to the **\materiallibraries** folder of your current project. By default this will be **\My Documents\3dsmax\ materiallibraries**. This folder is also empty by default. Therefore, you will need to navigate to the above mentioned folder.*

9   Select the file *Autodesk.Max.ProMaterials.Concrete.mat*.

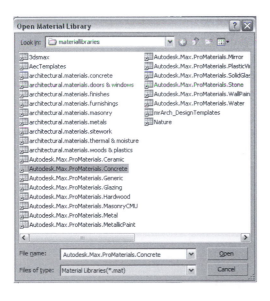

The Material/Map Browser becomes populated with materials.

10 Double-click the material called *Concrete Non-Uniform Warm Gray*; it will now occupy the selected Sample slot.

11 Close the **Material/Map Browser**.

12 In the scene, select the object named *Floor*.

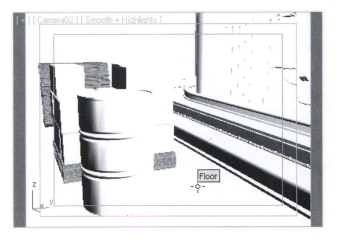

13 In the **Material Editor** click on the **Assign Material to Selection** button.

14 Click on the **Render Production** button on the **main** toolbar.

There is now a material on the Floor object but the pattern looks unrealistically large.

15 Make sure the Floor object is still selected, and go to the **Modify** tab of the **Command** panel.

16 In the **Parameters** rollout, of the **Extrude** modifier, click to enable **Real-World Map Size**.

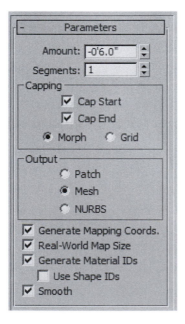

17   Render the **Camera** view again.

The texture on the floor looks much better now.

18   Back in the **Material Editor**, select the 2nd Sample slot along the top row.

19   Click on the **Get Material** button.

20   Navigate to the folder that contains the material libraries.

21   Select the file *Autodesk.Max.ProMaterials.MasonryCMU.mat*.

22   Double-click the *CMU Light Gray Running* material.

23 Select the object named *Walls*. This will be easiest from the **Select From Scene** dialog.

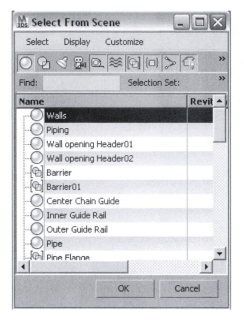

24 Assign the *CMU Light Gray Running* material to the walls.

25 Render the **Camera** view again.

The pattern appears on the walls but it is very faint. For the purposes of this render, you will exaggerate the strength of the pattern by adjusting the height of the pattern.

26 Back in the **Material Editor**, in the **Masonry/CMU Parameters** rollout, change the **Height** value to **5.0**.

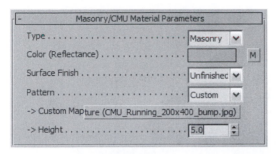

27 Render the **Camera** view again.

The texture on the walls is much more apparent now.

Lesson 27 | Using Maps

Introduction

When looking at two objects side by side, one with a burl oak finish and the other with a brushed aluminum finish, it's easy to see the difference in the texture of the objects. It is important to understand how to translate that information into a 3D environment. In this lesson, you will learn what maps are used for and how to apply them to objects.

A rendered Image of a scene using maps

Objectives

After completing this lesson, you will be able to:

- Tell the difference between a material and a texture
- Use map channels in different material types
- Build a material with different map channels
- Create realistic real-world textures and understand the difference between 2D and 3D maps

Chapter 04 | Materials

Maps in Material Definitions

When you look at an old wooden desk or a newly polished wooden floor, you are looking at the texture of the surface. For example, the difference between burl oak and knotty pine is the texture of the wood itself. In 3ds Max Design, you can use image maps and procedural maps in a material to create textures for an object. These can create an infinite variety of textures and looks for the rendered object. A texture, however, is not just a map; textures can be simple, like the glass used in a bottle, or they can be very complex, like an old weathered pine fence.

Textures and Maps

By definition, a texture is the distinctive physical composition of an element with respect to the appearance and feel of its surface. Essentially, it's what you see when you look at something.

A real-world example of old peeling paint on a concrete barricade post

A close-up photo of weathered boards at the beach

In 3D software, the texture is the end result of a material; whether the material uses maps or not does not matter. 3ds Max Design provides you a variety of maps that let you create textures that can be applied to objects for any purpose. Materials are able to define categories of textures. For example, you can create a wood material with properties that are common to various types of woods; however, wood is not a texture. If you were to ask someone to create "wood", he or she might not know what type of wood to create. That's where the texture of a surface comes in. If you tell someone to create highly polished burl oak, he or she will be able to deliver what you want.

Material: Steel Drum. The drum is rendered with a generic material.

Texture: Aged 55-gallon gray painted radioactive waste drum. The drum is rendered with a material that results in a defined texture.

Maps

Textures can be simulated without maps; however, if you want to add any detail or other texture definition to the surface, a map is the way to do it. Two types of maps that can be used in a material definition: a bitmap and a procedural map. Although the results can be similar, they function very differently.

Bitmaps

A bitmap is a 2D image made up of individual picture elements (pixels) in a rectangular grid. The more pixels in an image, the higher its resolution (size) and the closer you can look at it without noticing the pixels. The size of the bitmap is important as you create images where the camera moves close to a material containing a bitmap. A small- or medium-size bitmap works for objects that are not too close to the camera. A larger bitmap might be needed if the camera zooms in on part of an object. The following example shows what happens when the camera zooms in on an object with a medium-size bitmap. This phenomenon is known as pixelation.

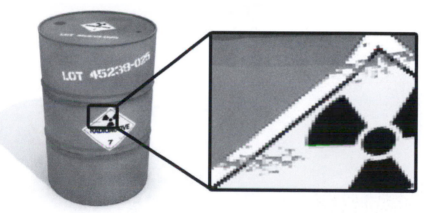

The bitmap image applied to the drum reveals its resolution when the camera zooms in.

In the above example, using a higher-resolution bitmap would reduce the amount of pixelation. Be careful, because higher-resolution bitmaps require more memory and take longer to render.

Procedural Maps

Unlike bitmaps, procedural maps are derived from simple or complex mathematical equations. One advantage to using procedural maps is that they do not degrade when you zoom in on them. You can set up procedural maps so that when you zoom in, more detail is apparent.

This pallet of pink granite blocks is created using a series of procedural Noise maps.

The magnification reveals more details about the granite texture.

The flexibility of procedural maps provides a variety of looks. 3ds Max Design includes a myriad of procedural maps, such as Noise, Tiles, Checker, Marble, and Gradient.

Maps and Materials in the Material Editor

In the Material Editor, maps and materials will display and behave differently. Generally, maps are incorporated as a sub element of a material into one of the map channels. In some situations you will bring a map directly into a Sample slot to edit and adjust its parameters so it can be used for such objects like a projector light or background.

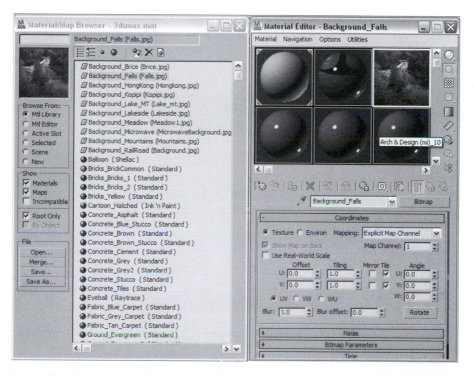

Materials and Maps dragged from the Material/Map Browser into Material Editor from the 3dsmat.mat Material library.

In the Material/Map Browser, when you search for materials, you should note the icons that appear in the list. The Parallelogram icon denotes a map that is not incorporated as part of a material, and Sphere denotes material definitions, many of which have maps incorporated into them. You can assign a material definition to an object in the scene, but a map must be assigned into a map slot. The map slot can be part of a background, or a material definition.

Map Types

When creating simple or complex mapped materials, you use one or more of the map types available in the Material Editor. You can use a bitmap or procedural map as the diffuse color, bump, specular, or any other available component of a material. You can use maps individually or in combination to get the look you want. Available map types vary among different Shaders and materials, but several map types are relatively common. You can typically access a map type in any of several different ways. Map types can be used together to obtain a final result.

Material Explorer view of a complex mapped material

Definition of Map Types

While many map channels are available for use, we will focus on the commonly used types.

- **Diffuse Color (Reflectance)**: One of the most frequently used map types, it determines the visible surface color of an object.

- **Reflection Color**: Determines the overall reflectivity color, also known as the specular highlight color.

- **Reflection Glossiness or Surface Glossiness**: Determines how polished the material appears, can create chrome (highly polished) to brushed metals (diffusely reflective). Also known as the specular highlight.

- **Anisotropy**: Affects the size and shape of the specular highlight.

- **Cutout or Opacity**: Determines the opacity or transparency of a material based on the grayscale values of the map. White is opaque and black is transparent.

- **Bump or Surface Imperfections**: The effect of bump-mapping on an object can be dramatic. Bump maps create the illusion of sunken and raised portions of a surface by setting a positive or negative value in the amount area. This effect allows you to fake geometry such as a rocky surface or dents.

Map Types in ProMaterials

ProMaterials work exclusively with mental ray. Rather than having one ProMaterial, there are several. Each ProMaterial is optimized for a particular purpose. The ProMaterials: Generic is as its name implies—being the most versatile. In general, if you can use a ProMaterial to suit your purpose, it is better since the ProMaterials interface is cleaner and easier to understand.

The Generic Material Parameters rollout provides access to the most important map channels. Selecting a map is either through one of the small square buttons at the end of a particular value for example, Diffuse Color, or by selecting one of the rectangular buttons that display the word "None" when there is no map applied.

Generic Material Parameters

The Maps rollout provides access to all of the maps in the ProMaterials: Generic. Access to these maps is duplicated in other rollouts in the interface. For example, there are four maps listed under Transparency. You will also find access to these maps in the Transparency rollout.

Maps rollout

Map Types in the Arch & Design Material

To choose a map in the Arch & Design material, click one of the small, square buttons on the Main Material Parameters rollout for the Shader or material. These map boxes appear next to the color swatches and numeric fields. However, not all map buttons are available in the Main Material Parameters rollout. To access all map buttons, use the General Maps or the Special Maps rollout. The Main Material Parameters rollout provides access to some of the more important map channels.

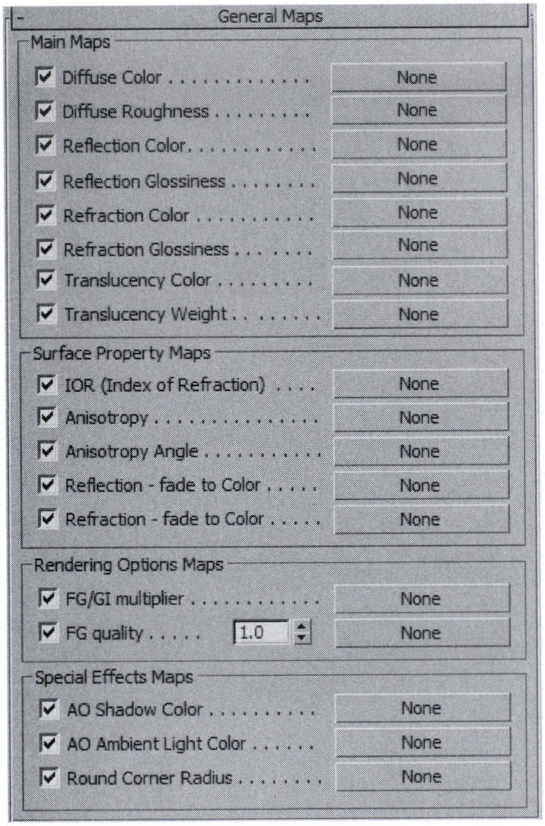

Main Material Parameters

The General Maps rollout provides access to Main, Surface Property, Rendering Options, and Special Effects map channels.

General Maps rollout

The Special Purpose Maps rollout provides access to all Bump, Cutout, and Self Illumination channels.

Special Purpose Maps

Displaying Maps in the Viewports

In order to adjust the appearance of your maps, you need to have them displayed in the viewport, if only temporarily.

Displayed maps give you the advantage of previewing the scene before final render. This feature enables you to work on the maps and adjust their parameters individually, before you render your final scene. Keep in mind that if all of your maps are active, your viewport performance may be affected based on your hardware setup. A good graphics card can make a big difference in the number of maps displayed in the viewport at any given time.

Show Map in Viewport

To display a map in the viewport, you usually use the Show Map in Viewport function found in the Material Editor.

Show Map in Viewport icon

This tool helps you get a better idea of what your scene looks like before you commit to a render. It also helps you if you need to adjust the bitmap on the object you applied it to. You typically turn this option on or off one map at a time. However, you may elect to use this tool globally, affecting all maps in the scene simultaneously. Keep in mind that enabling all maps simultaneously may affect the performance of your system based on the quality of the graphics card.

The Show Map in Viewport control also has an additional option to use the hardware display. It is found in a flyout of the Show Map in Viewport icon in the material editor.

Show Map in Viewport flyout

Activate and Deactivate Maps

To globally activate or deactivate all maps simultaneously, you can find such options in the Views pull-down menu.

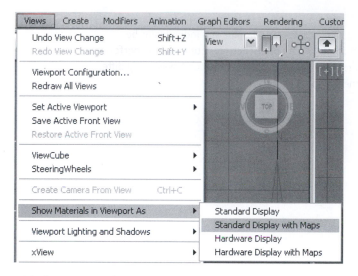

Globally activate or deactivate all maps

All maps are activated. Notice the concrete and wood maps on the walls and floor.

All maps are deactivated. No maps are visible in the viewport.

Mixing Maps

While simple materials will sometimes suffice, most materials in the real world are fairly complex. Look around you; examine the texture of objects and surfaces in the real world. As you can see, virtually no surface has a simple texture. Some surfaces contain multiple layers and others are intricately designed. These aspects of material creation are important to keep in mind while working in the Material Editor.

Several available map types allow you to use several maps together. With the Mix and Composite maps you can combine multiple maps to generate a new map image. In addition, procedural 2D and 3D maps can use multiple maps in order to create textures that mimic real-world textures. Some of those maps include Checker, Gradient Ramp, Noise, and Tiles.

2D vs. 3D

Earlier, we showed how a 3D procedural map can simulate Pink Granite, and used a 2D bitmap to make the texture for the steel drum. The difference between the two types of maps is easily demonstrated on the steel drum and granite blocks. Procedural maps offer an advantage: They can be 3D. That means they fill 3D space, so a granite texture made from several Noise maps goes through an object as if it were solid.

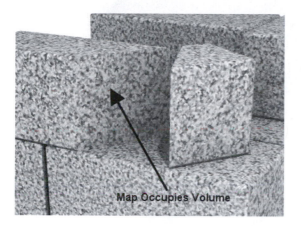

With Procedural Maps the texture continues even though the block has been cut in two.

Bitmaps offer the flexibility of creating any texture you require, but they don't occupy 3D space. Bitmaps require specific mapping coordinates in order to be rendered correctly. Because of this, if you separate an object, it will not show the same way as the 3D procedural map.

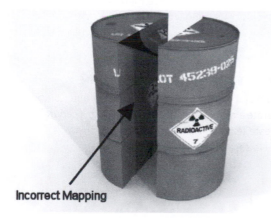

The material doesn't fill the drum properly because the mapping coordinates are not set up for the sliced polygons.

Exercise | Mapping the Drum

This exercise shows you how to apply bitmap images to various material components to get a realistic result. The map types you'll use in this exercise are Diffuse, Specular Level, and Bump.

1   Open the file *Mechanical Scene01.max*.

2   Open the **Material Editor**.

3   In the **Camera02** viewport, select the **55 Gallon Drum Texture** object.

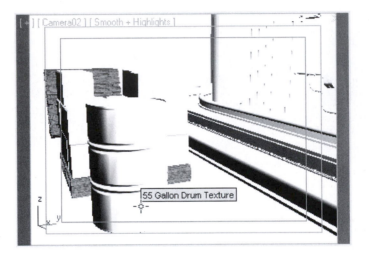

4   In the **Material Editor**, click the 3rd sample slot along the first row.

5   Click the **Get Material** button.

6   In the **Material/Map Browser** make sure the **Browse from Area** is set to **New**.

7 Double-click the **ProMaterials: Generic** material type to get the new material and close the dialog.

8 Set the material name to *Steel Drum*.

9 On the **Generic Material Parameters** rollout, click the **Diffuse Color (Reflectance)** button.

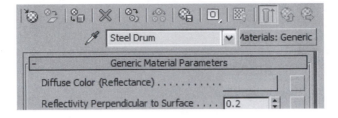

10 Choose **Bitmap** from the **Material/Map Browser**.

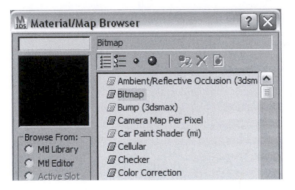

11 Use the **Select Bitmap Image File** dialog to find and open the *Drum Map.png* file.

Chapter 04 | Materials

12   In the **Coordinates** rollout, make sure there is no check in the **Use Real-World Scale** box.

13   In the **Material Editor**, click the **Assign Material To Selection** button.

14   In the **Material Editor**, click the **Show Map in Viewport** button.

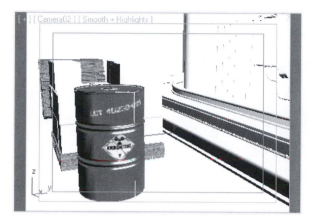

This allows you to see the bitmap in the viewport.

15   Click the **Go to Parent** button.

16   In the **Generic Material Parameters** rollout, click the **Surface Glossiness map** button.

Generic Material Parameters		
Diffuse Color (Reflectance)		M
Reflectivity Perpendicular to Surface	0.2	
Reflectivity Parrallel to Surface	1.0	
Surface Glossiness	1.0	
Surf. Imperf...	None	
Surf. Imperfections (Bump) Amount	0.3	

17   In the **Material/Map Browser**, choose **Bitmap**.

18   Use the **Select Bitmap Image File** dialog to find and open the *Drum Map spec.png* file.

19   In the **Coordinates** rollout, make sure there is no check in the **Use Real-World Scale** box.

20   Click the **Go to Parent** button.

21   In the **Generic Material Parameters** rollout, set the **Reflectivity Perpendicular to Surface** to **0.1**.

Generic Material Parameters		
Diffuse Color (Reflectance)		M
Reflectivity Perpendicular to Surface	0.1	
Reflectivity Parrallel to Surface	1.0	M
Surface Glossiness	1.0	
Surf. Imperf...	None	
Surf. Imperfections (Bump) Amount	0.3	

22 Click on the **Surface Imperfection Map** button.

23 In the **Material/Map Browser**, choose **Normal Bump**.

> mr Physical Sky
> Multi/Sub-Map
> Noise
> Normal Bump
> Object Color
> Ocean (lume)
> Opacity (base)

24 On the **Parameters** dialog, click the **Normal map** button.

Parameters			
Normal:	None	☑ 1.0 ⬍	
Additional Bump:	None	☑ 1.0 ⬍	

Channel Direction
☐ Flip Red (X)

Method
◉ Tangent

25 In the **Material/Map Browser**, choose **Bitmap** and click **OK**.

26 Use the dialog to open the *Drum Map normal.png* file.

27 In the **Coordinates** rollout, make sure there is no check in the **Use Real-World Scale** box.

28 Click the **Material/Map Navigator** button.

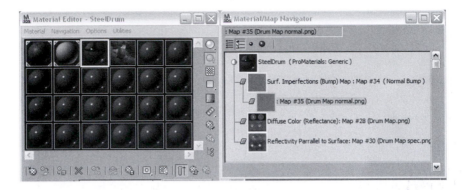

The Navigator dialog provides an interactive method of working with your material, and provides a valuable tool for visualizing the hierarchy of your material.

29 On the **Material/Map Navigator** dialog, click the **View List+Icons** button.

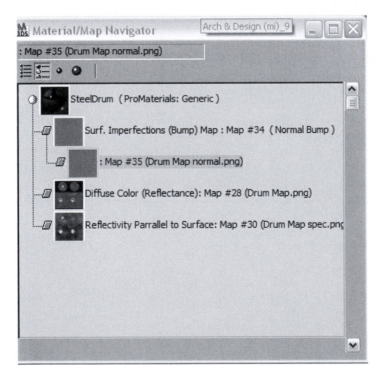

30 In the **Material/Map Navigator** list, click the **Steel Drum (ProMaterials: Generic)** at the top of the hierarchy. This will navigate the parameters of the **Material Editor** to the top of the material.

31 Click the **Render Production** button to render the scene.

Exercise | Creating a Multi-Map Procedural Texture

In this exercise, you'll use multiple Noise maps to create a procedural pink granite texture. Noise is a 3D procedural map that provides a great deal of flexibility for creating textures.

1   Open the file *Mechanical Scene02.max* or continue from the previous exercise.

2   In the **Camera02** viewport, click the *Pink Granite Blocks* group.

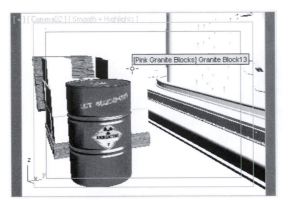

3   Open the **Material Editor**.

4   In the **Material Editor**, click the 1st sample slot along the second row.

5   Click the **Get Material** button.

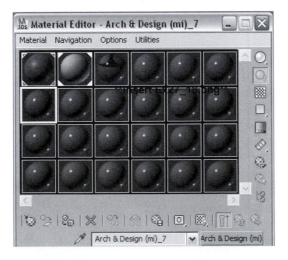

6 In the **Material/Map Browser** list, double-click the **ProMaterials: Stone**. Close the **Material/Map Browser**.

7 Name the material *Pink Granite*.

8   Click the **Assign Material to Selection** button.

9   In the **Stone Material Parameters,** set the **Surface Finish** value to **Matte**.

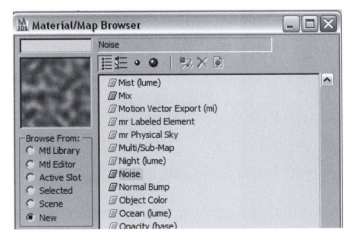

10   Click the **Color (Reflectance) map** button.

11   From the **Material/Map Browser** choose **Noise**, and then click **OK** to use the map.

12   On the **Noise Parameters** rollout set **Noise type** to **Fractal**.

13   Set **Size** to **0.5**. This specifies the size of the noise pattern.

14   Set **High** to **0.69** and **Low** to **0.305**. This setting allows you to adjust the contrast between Color #1 and Color #2.

15   Set **Levels** to **5.4**. This value increases the apparent detail in the noise map.

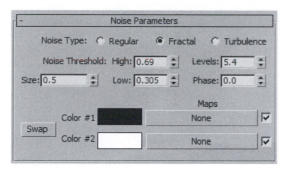

16   In the **Utility** tab of the **Command** panel, click **Color Clipboard** and then click the **New Floater** button.

17 On the **Color Clipboard** dialog, click the **Open** button.

18 Use the **Load Color Clipboard File** dialog to find and open the *Pink Granite.ccb* file.

19 Drag the top-left color from the **Color Clipboard** dialog to the Color #2 swatch on the **Noise Parameters** rollout.

20 In the **Copy Or Swap Colors** dialog, click the **Copy** button.

21 On the **Noise Parameters** rollout, click the **Color #1 map** button.

Access to map types within other maps makes it easier to layer maps for many different purposes.

22 On the **Material/Map Browser** double-click the **Noise** entry.

23 On the **Noise Parameters** rollout set **Noise Type** to **Fractal**.

24 Set **Size** to **0.3**.

25 Set **Noise Threshold** → **High** to **0.63** and **Low** to **0.45**.

26 Set **Levels** to **8.1**.

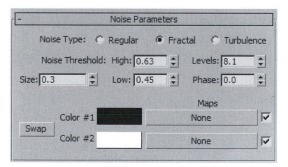

27 From the **Color Clipboard** dialog, drag the top row second swatch to the **Noise Parameters** →
    Color #1 swatch. Use **Copy** when prompted.

28 From the **Color Clipboard** dialog, drag the top row third swatch to the **Noise Parameters** →
    Color #2 swatch. Use **Copy** when prompted.

29 Close the **Color Picker** dialog.

30 Click the **Material/Map Navigator** button.

31 On the **Material/Map Navigator** dialog, click the **Pink Granite** material if it's not already selected.

This will bring you up to the top level of the Pink Granite material.

32 In the **Stone Material Parameters** rollout, set the **Pattern** to **Custom**.

33 Click and drag the **Color (Reflectance) map** button and drop it into the **Pattern Custom Map** button.

34 Click **Instance** in the dialog that appears, and click **OK**.

35 Click the **Render Production** button to render the scene.

36 If you have extra time, see if you can improve the image through the use of ambient occlusion and rounded edges.

Index

Additional Resources

A variety of resources are available to help you get the most from your Autodesk® software. Whether you prefer instructor-led, self-paced, or online training, Autodesk has you covered.

For additional information please refer to the disc that accompanies this training guide.

- Learning Tools from Autodesk
- Autodesk Certification
- Autodesk Authorized Training Centers (ATC®)
- Autodesk Subscription
- Autodesk Communities

Learning Tools from Autodesk

Use your Autodesk® software to its full potential. Whether you are a novice or advanced user, Autodesk offers a robust portfolio of learning tools to help you perform ahead of the curve.

- Get hands-on experience with job-related exercises based on industry scenarios from Autodesk® Official Training Guides, e-books, self-paced learning, and training videos.
- All materials are developed by Autodesk subject-matter experts.
- Get exactly the training you need with learning tools designed to fit a wide range of skill levels and subject matter—from basic essentials to specialized, in-depth training on the capabilities of the latest Autodesk products.
- Access the most comprehensive set of Autodesk learning tools available anywhere: from your authorized partner, online, or at your local bookstore.
- To find out more, visit *www.autodesk.com/learningtools*.

Autodesk Certification

Demonstrate your experience with Autodesk software. Autodesk certifications are a reliable validation of your skills and knowledge. Demonstrate your software skills to prospective employers, accelerate your professional development, and enhance your reputation in your field.

Certification Benefits

- Rapid diagnostic feedback to assess your strengths, and identify areas for improvement.

- An electronic certificate with a unique serial number.

- The right to use an official Autodesk Certification logo.

- The option to display your certification status in the Autodesk Certified Professionals database.

For more information:

Visit *www.autodesk.com/certification* to learn more and to take the next steps to get certified.

Autodesk Authorized Training Centers

Enhance your productivity and learn how to realize your ideas faster with Autodesk software. Get trained at an Autodesk Authorized Training Center (ATC) with hands-on, instructor-led classes to help you get the most from your Autodesk products. Autodesk has a global network of Authorized Training Centers which are carefully selected and monitored to ensure you receive high-quality, results-oriented learning. ATCs provide the best way for beginners and experts alike to get up to speed. The training helps you get the greatest return on your investment, faster; by building your knowledge in the areas you need the most. Many organizations provide training on our software, but only the educational institutions and private training providers recognized as ATC sites have met Autodesk's rigorous standards of excellence.

Find an Authorized Training Center

With over 2000 ATCs in more than 90 countries around the world, there is probably one close to you. Visit the ATC locator at www.autodesk.com/atc to find an Autodesk Authorized Training Center near you. Look for ATC courses offered at *www.autodesk.com/atcevents*.

Many ATCs also offer end-user Certification testing. Locate a testing center near you at *autodesk.starttest.com*.

Autodesk Subscription

Autodesk® Subscription is a maintenance and support program that helps you minimize costs, increase productivity and make the most of your Autodesk software investment. For an attractive annual fee, you receive any upgrades released during your Subscription term, as well as early access to product enhancements. Subscription also gives you flexible license terms, so you can run both current and previous versions (under certain conditions) and use the software on both home and office computers. In addition, Subscription gives you access to a variety of tools and information that save time and increase productivity, including web support direct from Autodesk, self-paced learning and online license management.

- Autodesk Subscription offers a way to make software costs predictable. Whether a customer opts for a one-year subscription or a multiyear contract, the costs are known for the entire term of the contract.

- A complete library of interactive learning tools and high-quality, self-paced lessons help users increase their productivity and master new skills. These short lessons are available on-demand and complement more in-depth training provided through Autodesk Authorized Training Centers.

- Autodesk Subscription makes managing software licenses easier. Customers have added flexibility to allow their employees to use their Subscription software—in the office or at home. Better yet, designers are entitled to run previous versions of the software concurrently with the latest release under certain conditions.

- Get what you need to stay productive. With web support Autodesk support technicians provide answers to your installation, configuration, and troubleshooting questions. Web and email communications deliver support straight to your desktop.

- For more information visit *www.autodesk.com/subscription*.

Autodesk User Communities

Autodesk customers can take advantage of free Autodesk software, self-paced tutorials, worldwide discussion groups and forums, job postings, and more. Become a member of an Autodesk Community today!

 Note: *Free products are subject to the terms and conditions of the end-user license agreement that accompanies download of the software.*

Feedback

Autodesk understands the importance of offering you the best learning experience possible. If you have comments, suggestions or general inquiries about Autodesk Learning, please contact us at *learningtools@autodesk.com*.

As a result of the feedback we receive from you, we hope to validate and append to our current research on how to create a better learning experience for our customers

Useful Links

Learning Tools:
autodesk.com/learningtools

Communities:
autodesk.com/community

Certification:
www.autodesk.com/certification

Student Community:
students.autodesk.com

Find an Authorized Training Center:
www.autodesk.com/atc

Blogs:
autodesk.com/blogs

Find an Authorized Training Center Course:
autodesk.com/atcevents

Autodesk Store
Store.autodesk.com

Discussion Groups:
discussion.autodesk.com

Notes

Notes

 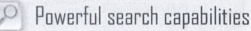

The ACI Workshop was probably the most intense evaluation I've ever had in my life! One of those 'didn't kill me, just made me stronger' type of moments that I'm sure I'll be lecturing my kids about when they get older. It was good to get out of my comfort level and have my weak points exposed. I am using the things I learned from the Workshop in my teaching right now. I feel much more confident in the classroom, and I am now starting to seek out peer evaluation more regularly.

–Geoff Beatty
Philadelphia University

Autodesk Certification Evaluators (ACE)

The ACE Program assembles industry-recognized "Master Trainers" from around the world with the goal of advancing APEX programs and expanding their availability. The primary responsibility of the ACE is to coach, mentor, and evaluate candidates that pursue the Autodesk Certified Instructor (ACI) Program. Membership to the ACE Program is through invitation only. Typical qualifications of an ACE include:

• Autodesk Certified Instructor
• High-level understanding of current production environments and workflow
• Experience in a variety of instructional environments
• Solid leadership capabilities
• Production experience in one or more industry markets (i.e. Film, Games, Television/Broadcast, Design Visualization)
• A background in CG or VFX curriculum development and/or instructional design
• Active contributor (i.e. Speaker/Instructor/Judge) at prominent industry events
• Interpersonal career development experience (i.e. mentoring, tutoring)
• Foreign language skills

Other requirements may apply. To learn more, contact: **me.certification@autodesk.com.**

Autodesk Professional Instructor Community (PIC)

The PIC is a portal on the Autodesk AREA online community where instructors can network, exchange knowledge, and share best practices for instructing with Autodesk Media & Entertainment products. This resource is exclusive to Autodesk Certified Instructors and invited guests. The site includes:

• Discussion forums
• Interviews with industry professionals
• Job boards
• Member galleries showcasing instructor and student work

To learn more, visit **http://area.autodesk.com** or contact: **pic@autodesk.com.**

Realize your potential with APEX

The Autodesk Professional Excellence Program helps professional educators succeed by staying ahead of the curve. To learn more about how you can benefit from APEX, visit **www.autodesk.com/apex.**

Your world. Your ideas.

Student: Emilie Courcelles Petiteau Concept: The Oracle Designed with: Autodesk® 3ds Max® Software

When you're studying to be an animator, game developer, or filmmaker, the Autodesk Student Engineering & Design Community gives you the technology to transform your ideas into compelling 3D designs, the expertise to launch your career, and the power to build things that make an impact on the world.

Build Something
See what students like you are building and download free* Autodesk® software.
autodesk.com/buildsomething

SIX WAYS TO OPTIMIZE YOUR AUTODESK SOFTWARE INVESTMENT

Autodesk® Subscription is a maintenance and support program that helps you minimize costs, increase productivity, and make the most of your investment in Autodesk® software.

With Autodesk Subscription, you can:

1. Save on periodic upgrade costs: The annual fee includes any upgrades or product enhancements released during the Subscription term.

2. Extend your usage rights: **Flexible licensing terms mean you can use your software on both home and office computers.** *

3. Run previous versions: **Use the current release and certain previous versions of your Autodesk licensed software (up to 3 versions back for most products).**

4. Leverage exclusive educational materials: Get interactive training tools, self-paced e-Learning lessons, AU course material, video podcasts, and more.

5. Tap into the Autodesk® Knowledge Base: Access this unified search capability to more than 2 million content sources.

6. Receive web support direct from Autodesk: Get help with installation, configuration, and troubleshooting 24/7. Track your support queries so your entire team can benefit from the answers you receive.

Visit www.autodesk.com/subscription for a complete overview and online tour or contact your local Autodesk Authorized Reseller at www.autodesk.com/reselle